FAMILY DRUG COURTS

An Innovation of Transformation

Including Inspiring True Life
Stories Written by Alumni and
Their Families from the Drug
Courts in Santa Clara County

Created by
Katherine Lucero

Forward by
Judge Leonard Edwards (Retired)

BALBOA.
PRESS
A DIVISION OF HAY HOUSE

ISBN: 978-1-4525-4893-7 (sc)
ISBN: 978-1-4525-4892-0 (e)
ISBN: 978-1-4525-4894-4 (hc)

Library of Congress Control Number: 2012905809

Balboa Press books may be ordered through booksellers or by contacting:

Balboa Press
A Division of Hay House
1663 Liberty Drive
Bloomington, IN 47403
www.balboapress.com
1-(877) 407-4847

Printed in the United States of America

Balboa Press rev. date:5/18/2012

This book is dedicated to all of the
professionals in Santa Clara County
who love our families back to health every day.

TABLE OF CONTENTS

Acknowledgments

No informative work can be put together without the help and support of many. I would like to thank my Drug Court Team for supporting the concept of this book and urging me to manifest the vision of telling everyone about the magic that occurs in our courtrooms.

I would like to thank all of the judges in Santa Clara County for allowing us to create and maintain court departments that are trauma-informed and specialized for the children and families in our county. Santa Clara County Superior Court clearly understands priorities and our Juvenile and Family Courts are proof of that.

I want to thank our Court Executive, David Yamasaki, for helping us build the dream with our court-partnered non-profit, the Chris Shaheen Charitable Foundation - led by Chris Shaheen and Gisela Bushey - who saw an opportunity to support vulnerable families in need and worked to make this partnership a reality, and for creating a way to sustain the Family Wellness and Dependency Drug Court Coordinator after the grant funding has run out, even in these difficult financial times.

I also want to thank Deborah Dohse and Sneha Burnside our specialty court coordinators, Victoria Cervantes our facilities manager and Jean Pennypacker, the court administrator, who all help to smooth the way for the court business to get done even when bureaucracy and the need to be flexible to support humanity seemed incompatible.

I want to express deep gratitude to our stakeholder partners Will Lightbourne, Lori Medina, Jaime Lopez, Gina Sessions, Nancy Pena, Bob Garner, Cheryl Berman, Jenny Lee, Vickie Grove, AnnaLisa Chung, Jennifer Kelleher, Andrew Cain, Hilary Kushins,

John Nieman, Preeti Mishra, Carol Robinson, Teri Robinson, Steve Ashley, Rosalio Chavoya, Kimberly Sanchez, Nancy Marshall, Nancy Fomenko, Dave Cortese, Ken Yeager, Jeff Smith, Dana Bunnett, Melanie Daraio, San Jose State University and the Chris Shaheen Children's Fund. I also want to thank Jenny Lee and Cynthia Ambar who went above and beyond and all of the court staff in both Departments 67 and 70 who were flexible and willing to make these courts a success.

I want to give a special thanks to the Executive Director of FIRST 5, Jolene Smith, for believing so much in the community's responsibility to take care of our children in Santa Clara County. Without her support and motivation our county would be telling another story. She helps all of us to rise to the occasion.

And finally a million thanks to Judge Erica Yew who made the vision of healing families in Santa Clara County a reality.

Forward

By Judge Leonard Edwards (ret.)

The Santa Clara County Juvenile Dependency Court has a long history of collaboration, developing best practices, and court improvement. With innovations such as dependency mediation, one judge-one family, Family Group Conferencing, collaborative meetings, wraparound services,[1] and monthly cross-trainings, as well as being a Greenbook[2] site and becoming a Model Court[3], we have continually examined our practices and procedures in order to improve operations and create a more effective court system, one that will benefit the children and families who come before the court.

It was the commitment to improving court practice that led us to travel to Washoe County in 1997 to visit one of the nation's first family drug treatment courts. Eleven professionals from all parts of our community visited Judge Charles McGee's treatment court

---

1   For a description of wraparound services, see Edwards, L., & Sagatun-Edwards, I., "The Transition to Group Decision Making in Child Protection Cases: Obtaining Better Results for Children and Families," Juvenile and Family Court Journal, Vol. 58, No. 1, 2007, pp. 1-16 and pp. 7-8.

2   The Greenbook is a short-hand term for the publication, "Effective Intervention in Domestic Violence and & Child Maltreatment Cases: Guidelines for Policy and Practice," NCJFCJ, Reno, 1999. The Greenbook created policies and procedures for dealing with domestic violence issues in the juvenile dependency court. Santa Clara County was one of six national implementation sites.

3   A Model Court is a juvenile dependency court that has agreed to work with the Model Courts Project of the National Council of Juvenile and Family Court Judges. The goals of model courts include improving court practice. See "Model Courts," NCJFCJ, January, 2006.

in Reno to learn whether this innovation would be valuable for our court system. We concluded it would. Approximately a year later, we launched our family drug treatment court to become, along with San Diego County, the first drug treatment court in California.[4]

We started slowly the first year with very few cases. Clients and attorneys were wary of this new court where there was no court reporter, where the judge talked with the client in a fashion similar to that of a counselor, where multiple professionals worked closely with each client, and where the court team developed an individualized service plan requiring the client to work harder and to come to court more frequently. Little by little, the clientele increased. In particular, the attorneys for parents encouraged their clients to participate. They realized that their clients had the best chance to rehabilitate and regain custody of their children by participating in this new court.

The court team included social workers, substance abuse experts, a mental health expert, housing experts, attorneys, service providers, and the judge, but many more interested professionals and community members attended the crowded drug court courtroom every Wednesday afternoon. The pre-court and court sessions were long, with extensive discussions between team members and clients. The results were outstanding with high family reunification rates and clients sustaining their recovery.

The drug treatment court has always been a work in progress. Improvements occur almost monthly. Creating the Mentor Moms program (a nationally recognized model) led to the Mentor Parent program which now includes male and female mentors who are graduates from the treatment court. Attempts to sustain recovery include events such as an annual Thanksgiving dinner that brings everyone together for a meal including graduates. Then we added a summer picnic. Working with a variety of agencies, we were able to identify over 100 beds for recovering addicts and, if appropriate, their children. We implemented Celebrating Families, an outstanding parenting class for recovering

---

4   For a short history of the growth of family drug treatment courts in the United States see Edwards, L., "Sanctions in Family Drug Treatment Courts," Juvenile and Family Court Journal, Vo. 61, No. 1, Winter, 2010, pp. 55-62, 56.

addicts and their children. Attorneys for parents volunteered to work with the parents in other court settings in order to address issues such as old criminal and traffic warrants and thus enable them to become eligible for their driver's licenses again. The treatment court team has always had a problem-solving attitude. Our success has persuaded everyone that there were no problems we could not solve.

In March of 2008 the innovations continued when the dependency court created a second treatment court, the Family Wellness Court. Focusing on dependent children from zero to five, this innovative court raised collaboration with the community to new heights. Doctors, nurses and other professionals who work with infants and their mothers joined the Family Treatment Court team as did First Five, the county-based organization dedicated to improving outcomes for children from zero to five. The Treatment Court continues to thrive with stunning reunification rates of 70%.

The results have been gratifying. From over 3,800 children in care in 1985 to well under 1,400 children today in 2011 (in spite of an increase in county population), our court system has learned how to dismiss cases safely and in a timely fashion, how to reach timely permanency for children who cannot be returned home[5], and how to increase the family reunification rate so that families can be reunited. Our family drug courts have set an outstanding national example. The five year federal study of four family drug treatment courts (Santa Clara County, San Diego County, Washoe County - Reno, and Suffolk County, New York) demonstrated conclusively that family drug treatment courts work and that Santa Clara County had created the most effective and successful family drug court in the evaluation.[6] The study showed that Santa Clara's treatment

---

5   In 2003 the Santa Clara Juvenile Dependency Court was awarded the Adoption Excellence Award by the Children's Bureau of the federal Department of Health and Human Services for its outstanding achievements in adoptions. See generally, Edwards, L., "Protecting Children and Reuniting Families: The History of Juvenile Dependency Court," Bench & Bar Historical Society of Santa Clara County and the Santa Clara Superior Court Historical Committee, San Jose, 2008, p. 25.

6   Worcel, S., Green, B., Furrer, C., Burrus, S. & Finigan, M., Family Drug Treatment Court Evaluation, Final Report, NPC Research, Portland, OR, 2007.

court provided more treatment, faster reunification, less time in foster care, fewer babies born with positive toxicology screens for drugs, and higher rates of family reunification than the other three jurisdictions.[7]

It is difficult to explain just what enables people to recover from long-standing problems such as addiction. The list of differences between a family drug court and a traditional dependency court offers a start, but frankly one has to see the court in action to begin to appreciate the atmosphere created when everyone, including the judge, supports a client-perhaps for the first time in that person's life. Coming to court must be a wonderful experience, one that reaches the hearts and souls of people who have been living miserable lives. I know that I found the afternoons talking with clients about their addiction, their lives, their children, and their hopes were the most rewarding experiences of my judicial career. It persuaded me that miracles can occur and that the family drug treatment court can make them happen.

This book will give you numerous perspectives on what makes our family drug treatment court work. It includes perspectives from judges, substance abuse experts, social workers, service providers, and, most importantly, parents, children and family members who participated in the court process. You will learn about the chaotic and tragic lives these parents lived, how they lost their children, and then, through their participation in the family drug treatment court combined with their hard work, regained their lives and their children. You will learn about the power of collaborative engagement. It is an important story that must be told. Our community must realize that people can change – that the most neglectful and abusive parents can turn their lives around and safely rear their children. That is the final message of the family drug treatment court.

---

7   Ibid, pp. 65-67.

Introduction

It was a normal day in court in Santa Clara County. Sandra Parker[8] came into my courtroom pregnant with her seventh child to a hearing designed to assist her in getting back her 6th child, a little boy, age 1. She was frazzled and had just tested positive for methamphetamine use, despite being in her eighth month of pregnancy. I gave her the same lecture I always gave at this point: that she was endangering her unborn child and that she would not get her baby boy back unless she stopped using drugs. She looked at me as though I were asking her to go to the moon. I recognized that look of hopelessness and helplessness because I had seen it so many times before in this court. I knew in my heart of hearts that she would not be able to change her behavior on her own and I was not really sure that we could help. I told her that I would see her for a review in a couple of months.

Not surprisingly, a Protective Custody Warrant[9] came across my desk for a "Baby Boy Parker." Sandra Parker was about to go into labor and the Department of Family and Children's Services (DFCS) was preparing to take her 7th child due to ongoing drug use. I signed it.

A few weeks after I signed the warrant to pick up the newborn, Ms. Parker came to court for her 6th child's case as was expected and planned. She did not look pregnant any longer. Before the case was called, all the attorneys had a discussion with me about the fact that the police and the social workers could not locate the newborn. Ms. Parker had the baby somewhere, but it was not at a local or

---

8   Not her true name.

9   This is a legal document that lists the reasons a judge should allow the removal of a child from their parent or guardian.

neighboring hospital. They had also searched her apartment and could not locate the new baby. My heart sunk. What were we doing here? The best we could do is to plan to take baby after baby from this woman?

I called the case and asked Ms. Parker where her newborn baby was located. She refused to answer me. She was belligerent and probably high at the time. She said that she would never let us have her newborn. I was asked by DFCS to hold her in contempt and put her in jail until she revealed the location of her baby. The Protective Custody Warrant that had been issued gave the court the authority to take such emergency jurisdiction. It was all bad as far as I was concerned: jail a mother for hiding her baby until she tells the whereabouts of it, or let her go and endanger the baby with her chronic illegal drug use and dangerous drug-centered lifestyle which had been well documented. At the time I believed that those were my two choices. So I incarcerated her. At that moment I did not know if I was going to bring more harm to the baby or not. I would spend many sleepless nights wondering where the baby was and whether I had taken the right action.

I told her that she held the key to her own jail cell in that if she told me the location of the baby, I would have the baby taken into protective custody and then I would release her to freedom. I brought her back to my courtroom day after day. I would ask her to reveal the location of the baby, she would refuse and I would have her taken back to her cell. She was using the jail phone to make collect calls to people all over the United States. At one point, she made several calls to Illinois so a police team went to Illinois to see it they could find the baby. They couldn't. All of her calls from jail were pulled and transcribed. Many law enforcement members were working on the case around the clock. The expenditure of public dollars on this situation astounded me.

I thought of all the other women I was seeing each day that were losing their children to their addiction and how it was one child and then the next, and then the next. I wondered what we were doing to the soul of that person who could not stop using drugs in the face of such dire consequences.

So, I kept bringing her back to court. I told her that over the weekend, if she decided to reveal the location of the baby that I would be available to have her released from jail. What I noticed about Ms. Parker is that over time she became softer, less belligerent and even began to have a twinkle in her eye. Her skin cleared up and she gained a little bit of weight from eating three meals a day. Her hair looked shiny and her demeanor became lighter. She got clean by being in jail. After 6 weeks, she agreed to tell my deputy (who was quite familiar with her now from all the trips back and forth from the holding cell) where the baby was located so long as the people caring for the baby would not get into any trouble. My deputy relayed that message to me in open court. I agreed.

That day the baby was brought in by a number of family and friends. He was fat and happy. He was a beautiful baby boy. I let Ms. Parker go free, but the baby was taken into protective custody and she was never to act as his mother in the future. She went back to using drugs as soon as she could. She lost the 6th baby as well. Altogether, she lost 7 children to her addiction.

Ms. Parker was only one case of a multitude of cases that were all too similar. We have the addict mother who cannot stop using drugs. We then take the baby and she cannot stop her drug use because of the pain, trauma and shame of being an addict mother and losing her child in the first place. The long waiting lists for drug assessments and treatment only add insult to injury. I did not feel sorry for these women; but I felt that true justice required a different approach. The law mandates that we return these babies to their parents if they can complete services to rehabilitate themselves. I was not sure if the services were truly in place.

We had a specialized drug treatment court at the time, but it was voluntary and space was very limited. Only those who were "ready" to stop being an active addict applied. I knew that I had to make a change because research showed that forced treatment is as effective as voluntary treatment[10]. This book talks about that change and the expansion of the drug treatment model that we know is working for families all over the country. Ms. Parker's case was the tipping point for Santa Clara County.

10   Research shows that treatment need not be voluntary to be effective. <http://www.urban.org/UploadedPDF/410618_NIDA1_KnowledgeRpt.pdf>

Reunited Against the Odds

By Mario Montemayor

After about 10 years of doing life my way, I found myself deep in my drug and alcohol addiction. Lonely and cold, sitting on a bench at the bus depot was where I could be found on any given day. Each night, as the skies grew dark, the cold air blanketed my body. I would go into survival mode and seek shelter to hopefully get through the long cold nights. Sometimes an abandoned building would do the trick, and other times an unlocked car would become my refuge. And yet, there were also times where the cold concrete floor of the bus depot would be my saving grace. I would find a blanket in the donation drop off at a nearby thrift store. After finding a blanket, I would head to the bus depot, find a good spot to lie down on and sleep the night away. At one point I even lived in an abandoned laundry room outside of my friend's apartment complex. I boarded up the windows and covered every crack to assure that no light could be seen from the outside in. As I would lay there, resting my head, I would think about my daughters and how much I missed them. My biggest fear was that I would never see my girls again.

My daughters were in the process of being adopted. I would beat myself up about this, and I carried the guilt and shame of losing my daughters every day of my life. I would suppress those feelings with drugs and alcohol. I would constantly ask myself, "How did my life get to this point"? I could not believe that my children were now suffering too because of my drug addiction. My daughter Brianna, who is now 6 years old, was my pride and joy. I remember that from the time she was in her mother's womb I would talk to her every day and sing to her the song "You Are My Sunshine." When she was born I was there to receive her into this world. She was the most beautiful thing I had ever seen in my life. She was perfect.

I remember feeling so proud that I was this little girl's father. I pictured a perfect life for my little family. However, when she was born, her toxicology report came back positive for methamphetamine. We were told by hospital staff that my daughter would not be discharged from the hospital and that someone would be there to speak to us at some point. That day, I was overwhelmed with fears. I didn't know what was going to happen with my daughter. As we waited, every minute seemed like hours. Time could not pass quickly enough.

When we met with the lady from Child Protective Services When we met the lady from Child Protective Services (CPS), she told us, she told us that the toxicology report indicated that my daughter had been born with high levels of methamphetamine in her system. Because of this, we could not take our daughter home. Instead, we would have to report to the Gilroy Family Resource Center to meet with a social worker and a team of people to decide on a way in which to address our current drug problem. The reason for this was so we could raise our daughter in a clean and sober household. We were given a family maintenance case plan that we completed successfully.

My oldest daughter and I had an awesome father-daughter relationship during her first two years of life. I would sing her to sleep with the Sunshine song every night, and when she would wake up crying, I would run to her rescue and cuddle with her until she fell back to sleep. However, our addiction progressed drastically and soon, my partner was pregnant again. At just 24 weeks gestation, we had an emergency and on the way to the hospital, my partner gave birth to another baby girl in the ambulance. We named her Danielle Hope. Danielle was also born with a positive toxicology for methamphetamine. My new daughter weighed 2 pounds and 1 ounce at birth and was placed in the hospital's Neonatal Intensive Care Unit. It was there that I held my daughter in my arms for the first time. I watched as her little chest went up and down as she struggled to breathe. I felt helpless and angry with myself. I knew there was nothing I could do for her but pray. But I had hope (hence her middle name) that God was going to take care of her and she would pull through and be okay.

My partner and I were now involved with CPS again and we were given another case plan. During this process, we still continued to use, and failed to comply with court orders. As badly as I wanted to be there for my daughters, my addiction had a stronger grip on me. My addiction made my life unmanageable.

One day, while getting ready to leave to see my daughter at the hospital, I was making my oldest daughter her lunch, when I saw two police officers walking up the driveway of our house. I heard the knock at the door. I hesitated to open it because I was high, so I went to my room and laid down with my oldest daughter. Our roommates opened the door and about five police officers rushed into the house. From the room, I could hear heavy footsteps walking down the hallway and then heavy knocking on my bedroom door. I could hear my heart pounding in my chest. I feared the worst. I kissed my daughter on her forehead and when I opened the door I was pulled out of the room, handcuffed and arrested.

As I was escorted out of my house, I remember seeing a woman who was not dressed in a police uniform. She approached my partner as she walked out of the bedroom with our daughter in her arms. Once she was near enough, the women grabbed my daughter out of her mother's arms and said she was taking our daughter from us. At that moment, I felt the ground fall out from under my feet. I was powerless over the situation. As I was taken into custody, I asked the police officers where they were taking my daughter, and why. An officer responded by saying that we were not good parents and because of that, my daughter was going to be taken somewhere safe.

When I was released from jail, I went to the hospital to see my youngest daughter, who was still in intensive care. I was turned away by the hospital social worker. I learned that my oldest daughter was placed with my parents immediately after her removal. It was at this moment in my life that I developed a huge resentment towards social services. I knew I was going to have to do another case plan and, even then, I would only be allowed supervised visitations with my own daughter.

During this time, both of my daughters were placed with my parents. Knowing this was a big relief for me. I figured that as long as they were with my parents, they'd be fine. I thought that as long as I didn't lose them *permanently*, everything would be okay. Unfortunately, I later learned that my oldest daughter did not handle the transition well. In fact, she cried for the next year, and whenever she would hear the Sunshine song, her little lips would pout. Whenever she was in a car and she would see a man that resembled me riding a bike, she would cry. I still get choked up when I think about this. We wanted our children back. This time, we engaged in our case plan and showed up at almost every visit.

But then, due to life circumstances, my partner and I became homeless because we wouldn't leave each other. Both our families were willing to help us out, but individually. My family would help me out, but only if I left her. Her family would help her out, but only if she was without me. Because of this, we ended up couch surfing for a while, but eventually we ended up living in a park. At night, we slept on the top of the playground platform and in the mornings, we would wake to the sound of children playing in the park from the nearby daycare and YMCA. We would fold our blanket and hide it up in a tree. We did this repeatedly day after day. I would panhandle money to buy booze and dope. When my girlfriend would get hungry I would panhandle more money for food and, of course, more booze. If I did not make enough money for food, I would steal the food to have enough money for booze or dope. This went on month after month.

When my girlfriend found out that she was pregnant again, I told her that she would have to go live with her dad to take care of herself and our unborn child. She did. I went to stay with my aunt and got a part time job at a car wash. During this time, both my partner and I were clean and off of the meth. Things were starting to look up for us when our third daughter, Emily, was born. She was born healthy and clean, and went home to live with her mom right after her birth. On her second day at home, Child Protective Services arrived at the house and removed her from her mother's care because of a "sibling protocol." My daughter was placed in foster care. This devastated us because we were really trying to get our kids back, but the system continued to remove them from our care.

My partner and I relapsed. We stopped complying with the case plan and as a result, we were soon faced with our parental rights being terminated. On the day we lost our parental rights, I remember I was physically in court, but mentally and emotionally, I was not present. I was too far gone in my addiction to comprehend what was really happening. When I came to, I was overwhelmed with emotions of guilt and shame. I felt that there was no way I'm ever getting my kids back. My partner and I ran amok, living carelessly in the world. Eventually my partner became pregnant again. She was in jail and I was on my own. At this point, I had lost my family, my children, my partner, and had nearly lost my mind. With no responsibilities for anyone but myself, I ended up living on the streets and sleeping on sidewalks. Pushing around a shopping cart collecting aluminum cans to recycle and being a small time crook was my only means of survival. I lived in a world of despair. Day after day, I walked the streets from one end of town to the other, stop for a minute, only to realize that there was nowhere to go. The loneliness was tearing me apart. And I was missing my family.

By the time my partner was released from jail, she was almost due. She entered a residential program and while she was there, she went into labor and gave birth to our fourth baby girl, Hailey. When I went to see them at the hospital, my heart was filled with joy. Hailey was so beautiful. As I held my little girl I couldn't help but fear that CPS would come and take her away too. My partner told me that we would be going back to court soon, and that this time, we had a chance at a fresh start, and we might be able to keep our baby girl this time. She told me that if I wanted anything to do with her or our baby, that I would have to get off the dope and get straight. As I held my daughter that day in the hospital, something happened inside of me. Having a glimpse of hope that I could be a father again filled me with excitement. I was determined to get off the streets and get clean.

And that's exactly what I did. I entered a residential treatment program and my spiritual journey began. I was introduced to a 12 step program while in this facility and when I left the program, I found local meetings in my area and quickly hit the ground running. In these meetings, I would hear that if I had the desire to stay clean I would never have to use or go back to those ugly places ever again. I also heard people talking about getting their children back after having lost them to the system as I had. They warned me that it wouldn't be easy; it would require working the 12 steps and being honest with others and with myself.

At seven months of sobriety, as I continued working the steps I started noticing positive changes in my life. I was introduced to a loving and caring team in the Family Wellness Court. I was assigned a parent mentor by the name of Steve. My mentor stood by my side every step of the way. He was there through the court process and he would share his life stories with me while we waited in court. I remember one particular time while waiting at court, Steve showed me his 31 years of sobriety chip and told me I could have that amount of time one day, if I kept working on my recovery.

The Family Wellness Team was really encouraging and believed in me. They would tell me encouraging things; they would really lift my spirit up. It was nothing like any other family court that I'd experienced before (to say the least). For the first time, I would leave a courtroom feeling good about myself; like I actually had a fighting chance, and everybody wasn't against me. They made me feel like they really wanted to help me be a better father. And when I would walk out of the courtroom, I knew that things were going to be OK. I had never met a judge like Judge Yew. She was genuine and transparent, one of the most loving people in the world. I was given a case plan and I did whatever I had to do to complete it successfully. I was the first father to graduate from Family Wellness Court; and I say that proudly.

The courts weren't the only ones who noticed the positive changes in me. My parents also did and after three years, they began to let me see my daughters, whom they had adopted. I hugged my girls tightly. When I saw my oldest daughter she was so excited to see me and the look on her face was like saying "Yes, he's back!" I knew she had missed me a lot. We hugged each other for a long time and right then, at that very moment, I knew that everything would be alright. And the best part was that, so did she.

I vowed to never put anything or anyone before my children ever again. Today, I am a proud dad of four beautiful little girls whom I love with all my heart. The mother of the girls still struggles and is in and out of jail. I speak to her once in a while, but all I can do is show her what works for me, and hopefully one day she'll find something that works for her.

I continue to work on my recovery and work the 12 steps. It may be hard to believe, but I sponsor men now, and I work as a parent mentor, side by side with Steve, the man who was and continues to be my mentor. I also work alongside an awesome group of seven other mother and father mentors. My role as a mentor is to give hope to the fathers who are currently going through what I went through. As a mentor, I show them the way and share my story of hope with them. I show them every day that no matter what the circumstances are in their lives, they can reunify with their families and live a clean, sober and healthy life.

My girls are the most precious things in my life. I now have the pleasure of being able to stay overnight with them and, once again, I get to sing to them the Sunshine song. To my oldest daughter, that song is more than just a song. It's our way of expressing our love to one another. Other times, I get the chance to be able to bring my girls to my apartment. I love it. I get to spoil them with some pizza and movies. And as I sit there with my beautiful girls, I think back to where I was in my active addiction and where I am at today. I'm glad I never lost my faith in a loving God. I know that it was by His mercy and grace that I am the person I am today. I am so very grateful for my family, who has helped me out in so many ways. I am grateful to my parents, Jose and Lupe, for taking my girls in and adopting them, and for making sure they would continue to stay in the family. My sister Janie has made such a huge contribution in my daughters' lives in so many ways. They love their Tia so much. My Aunt Olga donated a lot of her time in supervising visits so I could see my youngest daughter every week. So many people gave up their time and energy and homes to help me out. I owe these people so much and I will never be able to repay them for all that they have done for me and my family. To everyone who gave their time and put their lives aside for my daughters and me - I love you and thank you for believing in me.

PART I
THE PROFESSIONAL PERSPECTIVE ON FAMILY DRUG COURTS

The Judges
The Santa Clara County Model Court[11]

By Judge Katherine Lucero

A. Dependency Court

There is a court in each of our systems, in your county, your parish or state, which oversees the country's most vulnerable children in the nation. There are just fewer than 450,000 children in the foster care/court systems in the United States of America[12]. Just under a half a million children that have come to the attention of the authorities due to allegations of child abuse and/or neglect that are supervised by a judge in your community. In some places this court is called Dependency Court, Children in Need of Protection Court, Family Court or Juvenile Court. The names may differ, but their purpose is the same: to protect children from a home that has become so neglectful or abusive that the State must intervene to steer the family back, if possible, to wholeness and health. If the family

---

11   The National Council of Juvenile and Family Court Judges have 36 Model Courts that are used for the development of best, evidence-based practices throughout the nation.

12   Child Welfare Information Gateway, "Foster Care Statistics 2009", U.S. Department of Health and Human Services, Children's Bureau, Washington, DC, (pub. 2011).

cannot be steered back towards wholeness and health, the child must be placed in a new forever home to be adopted, placed in a guardianship with a family member or a non-related foster parent, or, as is often the case for the older child, left in a plan that keeps them in the foster care court system until they emancipate.

There are very serious abuse and neglect cases: shaken babies, battered children, children who are sexually abused by their parents or designated caretakers and the extreme neglect often caused by a parent's substance abuse or mental health disorder(s). However, what is witnessed day to day by many judges throughout the nation is that children enter the foster care system largely due to parental or guardian neglect, often generated by substance abuse. Parents end up incarcerated because of drug use; they leave their children with inappropriate caretakers. They leave their children alone at home or in cars. They make very dangerous decisions about the care and safety of their own children because they are afflicted with the disease of addiction. And many of these same parents often have complex mental health disorders, many caused by years of trauma.

The Child Welfare/Court division is one of the most important divisions in the court system. It is the most important division because it impacts the life of a family and, ultimately, the life of their child(ren). It impacts the life of a child who did not have anything to do with their parent's poor choices, the circumstances which led them to be in court because of overt abuse or a byproduct of addiction or poor mental health. Being removed from their homes will change their life forever, sometimes for the better, but more often, not. What is clear is that the State is not a good substitute for a family and we sometimes find ourselves in the quandary of actually having done more harm than good - especially when children are raised in one foster home after another before reaching the age of majority.

All can agree that foster care is not a "silver bullet" solution. In fact, recent studies show that children and youth who do grow up in the foster care system and "age out" have horrible outcomes: higher incarceration rates, higher incidences of unplanned pregnancies and, sadly, of homelessness.[13] We are finally "getting it" that we need to develop programs that help families; not just separate the child from the family and pretend that we have done our jobs.

Santa Clara County has been a National Council of Juvenile and Family Court Judges (NCJFCJ) Model Court for the last fourteen years. A Model Court is a court which commits to three court practice innovations a year that will improve the lives of families and children in their jurisdiction's system. Santa Clara County has made a commitment to at least 42 different types of innovations in the last 14 years. This effort has transformed the court from a standalone law and order court, to a collaborative justice court which values families and children as consumers of its services as much as it values each of the stakeholder partners and judicial leaders in its midst.

To emerge as a champion of therapeutic jurisprudence which is family-centered and trauma-informed is no small feat. In fact, the process has been sometimes painful, sometimes joyful, and often very slow. But, the hope for all of us has been made clear: we must make a go of it because it saves money, it creates government efficiency, most importantly it saves families, and, I would argue, that it actually saves lives.

---

13   Chapin Hall's Midwest Study provides a comprehensive picture of how foster youth fare during this transition since the Foster Care Independence Act of 1999 became law. Foster youth in Iowa, Wisconsin, and Illinois were eligible to participate in the study if they had entered care before their 16th birthday, were still in care at age 17, and had been removed from home for reasons other than delinquency. The study showed that those who emancipate at age 18 were more likely to become homeless, experience early and unwanted pregnancy, incarceration and joblessness. http://www.chapinhall.org/sites/default/files/Midwest_Study_ES_Age_23_24.pdf

B. Whose Children are in Foster Care?

I have traveled all over the world with my own family. We have seen so much with our own eyes. We have been uncomfortable in the country sides and the inner cities of South America, Mexico and India. We witnessed the extremely impoverished living conditions of families and we have held the orphaned children of Calcutta while volunteering at one of Mother Teresa's orphanages. It is clear that we live in the greatest country in the world. One day I asked a woman from India, "What's up with Calcutta"? "Why are there so many children living on the streets without their families"? She said that these were the children of the incarcerated, the mentally ill, drug addicts, the poverty-stricken and those forced into the sex trade industry. I had to reflect a moment on that because of my own work. I suddenly understood the magnitude of what the United States is preventing with its efforts to take care of our nation's most vulnerable children through the child welfare system. When I traveled to the inner cities of India I saw immediately, with my own eyes, the importance of sound public policy on child protection.

In the United States we have a fairly elaborate child welfare system. Since 1974 Congress has passed a series of acts to oversee the nation's abused and neglected children.[14] There have been well-meaning attempts since the 1800's in the United States to rescue children from abusive and neglectful homes. In fact, the earlier Good Samaritan agencies were called "Child Rescue Organizations." There are several interpretations of what exactly we were trying to do, but let us agree that we thought the motivation was to "save the child" from an unfortunate circumstance at best, and, at worst, we were horribly misguided as in the case of the relocation of our Native American Children.

What has clearly evolved is a system where a majority of the children in our courts today are indeed the children of the mentally ill, of drug addicts, incarcerated parents and sometimes parents who have been forced into the sex trade industry in order to survive.

---

14 Appendix I: Child Welfare Timeline prepared by the Child Welfare Information Gateway

But more significantly, they are the children of the poor and of our African American, Latino and Native American families. Four hundred years of institutional racism, social barriers and budget cuts, has resulted in our courts becoming the only social safety net some families can fall back on as the "last house on the block" or the "last ditch effort" to heal. And of course, this all occurs on the government's timeline, which does not vary nationally but may vary from state to state.[15] There is the government's heavy-handed consequences, because giant bureaucracies are neither nimble nor always able to administer justice in a fashion that would meet the needs of the complex social issues of the day. At the very least it is a high-priced, complicated way to address the human condition. In 2009 the Federal Government reimbursed $6.714 billion to states in 2009 to run these systems under what is referred to as a Title IV-E entitlement.[16] The money is supposed to cover social worker (case management) and foster care payments to foster placements for the children and youth. The Title IV-E money is not supposed to be spent on the services that these families and children so desperately need, such as drug treatment, medication for mental health stabilization or housing which would put the family back together. Those funds are obtained from a much smaller pot of money called Title IV-B for family preservation which added up to $629 million in 2009.[17]

C. Courts as Change Agents

At least 70% of the Dependency Court caseload is the result of drug and alcohol addiction and/or mental health problems of the parent.[18] It has been pointed out that we do not take children from a parent with diabetes or high blood pressure, but we do for the disease of addiction. Not only do we take their children, but then we give them a specific amount of time to get their children

---

15   California has what is called a "fast track" for children under the age of 3 years-California Welfare & Institutions Code Section 366.21(e).

16   NCJFCJ Child Welfare Finance Reform Policy Statement 2011

17   NCJFCJ Child Welfare Finance Reform Policy Statement 2011

18   Across the country 40-80% of foster care children are removed for substance abuse. (Voices for America's Children, Issues Brief, Nov. 2004)

back, or their parental rights can be terminated and they will be forever both physically and legally separated from their children. The Termination of Parental Rights is often referred to as the Civil Death Penalty. If asked, most parents would say that they would rather be incarcerated than lose their child forever. Of course they would. What has resulted, in its most unfavorable light, is that we are taking children from their families forever because their parents are sick and they do not get better in the time we tell them to get better. Even worse, we do not provide access to resources like housing, medical care, drug treatment, transportation and mental health treatment so that they can succeed in getting their children back. As a result, we end up raising thousands of children in foster homes and group homes across the nation.

Recognizing this social and legal dilemma some Child Welfare courts have adopted the Criminal Justice Drug Court Model[19] and have begun to overlay that into their Family and Dependency Courts. This has been a virtual revolution of how we deal with our families in abuse and neglect courts. It has been a transformation from the separation of families to the saving of families. To say that we are resurrecting families from a very dark place with previously grim outcomes is not an understatement[20]. In Santa Clara County, which is consistent with Family Drug Courts all over the nation, the family reunification rates are over 70% as compared to less than 50% for the non-drug court families. Cost savings in foster care placement alone are in the tens of thousands of dollars.[21]

Simply put, Dependency Treatment Courts are courts whose main focus is to champion the recovery of the addicted and/or mentally ill parent. In Santa Clara County we are in our eleventh year of running our Dependency Drug Treatment Court. In 2008,

---

19 Appendix III: Conference of Chief Justices Conference Of State Court Administrators, CCJ Resolution 22, COSCA Resolution IV In Support of Problem-Solving Courts

20 Appendix IV: Family Treatment Drug Court Evaluation-Final Report NPC Research March, 2007. See selected graphs

21 Appendix V: Sacramento County Cost Benefit Analysis for Dependency Drug Courts

we added our Family Wellness Court, which was developed to focus on babies and toddlers born addicted to or exposed to drugs/alcohol. Both of these courts have one thing in common: they seek to heal families through a "Whatever It Takes" methodology.

At first it seemed that perhaps this was judicial leadership run amok, but after a confidential survey of all the local stakeholders from Santa Clara County, it was determined that this was, in fact, the political will of the leadership. The survey showed that every one of the professionals affiliated with the Dependency Drug Court Systems' expansion and enhancement, very much wanted the model to be sustained and in fact was committed to doing whatever it took to keep the model going. The model works. It is, in fact, government at its best.

The Judge asked the Department of Alcohol and Drug Services, the Mental Health Department, the Department of Family and Children's Services, the Social Services Agency, the Attorney firms for both the children and the parents, Court Appointed Special Advocates (CASA), County Counsel and the Santa Clara County FIRST 5 Commission to come together to participate in a comprehensive systems overhaul necessary to best serve children and families of addiction. They all rose to the occasion.

The courthouse itself has been transformed. The courthouse is a community courthouse in every sense of the word. Co-located are Drug and Alcohol Treatment Assessors, a CalWorks Eligibility Worker, psychiatrist to perform emergency mental health assessments and dispense medication if necessary, FIRST 5 family partners and a Social Security Income (Public Assistance) evaluator from the Mental Health Department.

The hallways are lined with bulletin boards with valuable information for the parents, children and youth. Each of the six bulletin boards has important resource topics: Mental Health, Drug Treatment, Dental, Vision, Housing, Food, Jobs, Education, etc.

No space is wasted and no moment should go unresourced. A computer terminal is available with a printer so that the parent can do job and housing searches while they wait for their case to be heard. The waiting rooms have wall-sized flow charts describing the "life of the Dependency case" in three different languages so that not only are people aware of the resources available, but of exactly what is happening to their case and the State and Federal timelines that they have in which to operate and accomplish the court orders. This is a full disclosure, full support, "we want you to succeed" model.

D. Dependency Drug Treatment Court (DDTC)

Wednesdays are busy in San Jose, California for Department 67. There is a lot of buzz and paper is being stacked in the judge's Drug Court files so that she can be prepared for the morning staffing. At 8:30 a.m. she calls the calendar. The judge and the lawyers present go over the day. From 8:30 a.m. to 10:30 a.m. they handle Dependency Court legal hearings. These hearings are the formal mandated statutory reviews[22] that must be held on each case that is in the Dependency Court. What is different about these reviews is that they are often simple and straightforward because the family is in the DDTC program and is seen frequently on a review calendar which is not statutorily mandated. Usually the judge is making findings of compliance, returning children or dismissing cases that have come to a completion with the family intact.

From 10:30 a.m. to 12:00 noon, a larger crowd gathers. The Housing specialist, the Drug and Alcohol assessors, the Resource Specialist, the Drug Court Coordinator who specializes in both the parent's Criminal and Dependency cases where both exist, the lawyers, the FIRST 5 case worker, the CASA team member, the Cal Works Eligibility Worker, the Drug Court and the case carrying Social Workers, a paralegal from the parent's attorney agency and a few Mentor Parents come in to conduct a staffing on each of the reviews or nominations of new cases that will be conducted after the lunch hour.

The reviews are for existing clients and the nominations are for new clients seeking to get into DDTC. Their lawyer or social worker can petition the DDTC court team to allow the new client into this volunteer court. The entire team must agree that they are appropriate

---

22   California Welfare and Institutions Code Section 300, et. seq.

and motivated. The standards are not particularly stringent with the understanding that anyone who wants to get clean and sober and heal their families should be given a chance.

Carefully and in a concerted way, the team begins to go over each parent's current case compliance and treatment status for the review. In one afternoon, the team will review up to 20 parents over a three and a half to four hour period. Each person's case is discussed to determine if they are still clean and sober, drug testing, have transportation, a place to live, clothing, food, and contact with their children, whether their children's needs are being met, educational or vocational progress, financial literacy program compliance, medical health access, mental health access, medication compliance, dental health, criminal court compliance and working their 12-step program with their sponsor. No parent is excluded from this multi-disciplinary approach regardless of race, gender, socio-economic status, language, legal status or sexual orientation.

We take a lunch break at noon where many of the professionals follow up on details that need tidying up before the afternoon session. At 1:30 p.m. they reconvene, and the group grows even bigger: a Public Health nurse and a Community Recovery coach joins the session so that they can help people right there in court when necessary. The Public Health nurse takes blood pressure, consults on everything from the common cold to skin rashes and reproductive health.

One day in 2010 she actually sent one of our fathers straight to the hospital and when he arrived there he was admitted with serious heart problems. The Public Health nurse was credited with saving his life. The Community Recovery coach helps people find sponsors, meetings that fit their schedules and gently guides parents in the sometimes confusing work of recovery.

At 1:40 p.m.-ish, the current case reviews and new case orientations begin. These are conducted in a team setting and are not recorded by any court reporter. The courtroom clerk and bailiff remain in the courtroom, but the court reporter may retire to their office and is placed on standby just in case there is something that the team believes should be put on the record. 95% of the time the court reporter is not used. Other DDTC parents are allowed into the courtroom, which is a departure from the ordinary court hearing where a family is taken one by one. A parent may request that their review be held separately, but by and large this is not requested because the parents get to know and love one another from coming to court over the many weeks and months. The parents cheer for one another, routinely offer rides, meeting tips and other resource information to one another. In fact, the parents have started their own 12-step meeting called "The Family Afterwards" which meets every Wednesday at noon next to the courthouse. Children are welcome at these meetings. The parents from DDTC chair, run and record the 12-step meeting and have developed comprehensive information and social networks with one another. Indeed, they feel as though they all had a seat on the Titanic and have now been pulled out of the sea of despair and rejoice together in their new found luck-to be in DDTC.

The Team spends five to ten minutes with each parent and allows each team member to sing their praises, point out possible relapse behavior and suggest tips for moving forward as well as problem solve and eliminate any obstacles that may stand in the way of their day at a time success. We have done everything from hand out and help organize calendars, role play speaking up for what they need in a job setting, solve transportation quandaries, housing, medical and dental needs to organize rides from the jail to the sober living environment at 6:00 a.m. when someone was released and afraid they would not make it from the jail to their new home!

If a need is stated we try to get at the heart of the matter that could make or break that person's success. No obstacle is left without discussion and a bonafide attempt for every brain in the room to chime in to eliminate it. I call it the Rubik's Cube of the day. We are resolved to address each issue no matter what. To take a phrase from Susan B. Anthony, "Failure is impossible." How can 15 professionals *not* figure it out? Rarely do we leave the room without some solution, sometimes only temporary until the next review, but it buys the team the time needed for the parent to stay clean and sober for another week and for us to do what we can to find a long-term solution. And guess what? We usually do. It is magical.

E. The Natural Evolution of a Good Idea

After realizing the value of this court and having the experience with Ms. Parker that I spoke about in the Introduction of this book, I made it my mission to expand it so that each parent who came into Dependency Court in Santa Clara County could have the benefit of this wraparound model. We stakeholders put our heads together and we applied for grant funding through the federal government. We got the money! Between the federal government and FIRST 5 of Santa Clara County we launched our Family Wellness Court with the promise of $6.3 million. As supervising judge of Dependency Court, I worked on comprehensive systems change while Judge Yew implemented the new collaborative court itself. The next chapter is written by the Honorable Erica Yew. She made our vision come true with her relentless work and her tireless commitment to expanding this amazing service to more families and children in Santa Clara County. Our work with the Family Wellness Court also made DDTC better, stronger and sustainable.

What Can Judges Do In Dependency Drug Treatment Courts And Why?

By Judge Erica Yew

"How wonderful it is that nobody need wait a single moment before starting to improve the world."
~ Anne Frank

Family Wellness Court is a collaborative justice court. It is a state-of-the art extension in the continuum of drug courts that has evolved from the nation's first drug court established in 1989 in Miami, Florida. Collaborative justice courts, also known as problem-solving courts, were implemented to address challenging and recurring social problems – like addiction, domestic violence, homelessness, and juvenile delinquency – that come through courtroom doors daily. As our social safety net both constricts with diminishing resources and is strained with increasing need, more and more people dealing with life's challenges find themselves in the courts. For many, there is no place else to go and they are compelled to come by arrest warrants and protective custody warrants that remove their children from their care. In response to the influx of repeat offenders who are grappling with generational problems, the courts are situating social services in the courtroom where people can receive direct and immediate assistance. This allows the court to better serve litigants dealing with complex issues and it allows the court's community partners to leverage their resources by working within a multi-disciplinary team (MDT).

In terms of the history of collaborative courts, California's deinstitutionalization of the mentally ill in the 1970's and 1980's led to increased homelessness in the state. In response, California established the country's first homeless court in San Diego in 1989. By mid-2005, the state had over 265 collaborative courts with names such as: Homeless Courts, Drug Courts, Mental Health Courts, Peer Courts, and Dating Violence Courts. According to a 2005 study from the California Judicial Council and the Administrative Office of the Courts (AOC), the common guiding principles of collaborative courts are:

- Integrated services with the justice system,

- Purposeful avoidance of the traditional adversarial court process,

- Early intervention and prompt placement of litigants in programs,

- Access to a continuum of care,

- Coordinated strategies of sanctions and incentives,

- Ongoing judicial interaction,

- Monitoring and evaluation to measure effectiveness of treatment, services, and other programs,

- Continuing interdisciplinary education,

- Partnerships and collaboration to increase availability of services,

- Local and community support, and

- Emphasis on the team's and individual's commitments to cultural competency.

Interestingly, drug courts evolved along a similar path as medical interventions for adults. As medical research for heart disease focused initially on men and their response to medications, criminal drug courts were first geared toward men. Dr. Rivka Greenberg, a psychologist who trained FWC team members and partners, provided the FWC team with the progression of drug courts in relation to women and their needs. First, drug courts were formulated to respond to men's needs. Then women were included in criminal drug courts. Next, women and men brought their children to drug courts when their cases were heard. These children waited underfoot without direct or coordinated attention from the court or its partners. Today, there are drug courts that are child-focused, using the parent's desire to keep their children as a tool to motivate the parent's course of treatment and promoting the children's well-being.

As a child-focused court, FWC's physical environment is configured for the child's comfort in the courtroom. A First 5 family specialist is a key member of the court team and regularly shares insights about each child's developmental needs with the parents during FWC review hearings. Parents receive support from home visitors and public health nurses as well as mental health therapists; the latter through the form of dyadic therapy, parent-child interactive therapy and other modalities. Unlike traditional criminal drug courts, where the focal point for discussion is the parent's recovery, FWC also includes regular discussions about the child – all to reinforce the parent-child relationship and to use that relationship to motivate the parent in his or her recovery.

FWC's approach works and parents experience a high rate of success. In 2011, a federally-funded audit of FWC showed that the court has a 75% success rate in reunifying previously addicted parents with their children. Even where the parents fail to reunify, 100% of FWC's children benefit from the child-focused approach because of early screening, assessments and interventions. But it is not just FWC that is successful. Numerous studies have found that drug courts work and save money. A 1998 study showed that nine drug courts saved the state of California approximately $9 million in avoided criminal justice costs for every year a new set of participants entered these programs. A 2010 Substance Abuse and Mental Health Services Administration (SAMHSA) study demonstrated that for every $1.00 spent on drug services, our society saves $12.00. A 2002 study found that drug courts also reduce recidivism. For example, arrest rates were 85% lower for defendants in the two years after their entry into drug courts and 70% of drug court graduates were employed whereas 35% of these defendants were employed upon entering drug court.

In Family Wellness Court, we have experienced successes that are extraordinary when you consider the demographics of our population. All FWC cases are fast-track cases where parents have initially a short six months of services to prove that they can care for their children, all of whom are under the age of three years.[23] We know that most of our parents have prior referrals or involvement with the child welfare system. In addition, 40% of our FWC parents were dependent children in the foster care system, 90% have a criminal history and 80% have committed or have been a victim of domestic violence. A high number have an extensive trauma history where they have suffered abandonment, physical abuse, sexual abuse, emotional abuse, and multiple losses with deaths of close family members – sometimes right before their eyes. Sixty-five percent of our parents satisfy the definition of chronic homelessness. Our FWC parents also come from extreme poverty with 66% having an annual income of less than $10,000. The average income in California is $61,017; in the United States, it is $52,019. The federal poverty level for a parent with one child is $14,579.

Not surprisingly, because the FWC grant was sought to assist parents dealing with addiction to methamphetamine, most of our parents drug of choice is meth. In Santa Clara County, 64 to 67% of drug users identify methamphetamine as their drug of choice.

---

23   The definition of a fast-track case is one where the child is under the age of three years at the time the child is removed from the parent's care. If the child is three years or older at the time of removal, the parent has more time. The legislative policy for fast-tracking babies and toddlers is to allow those children, who may not yet have attached to their birth parents, to be in homes where they can form the healthy attachments and bonds that all humans need to establish lasting and loving relationships.

The addiction that we see in FWC is complicated by the fact that many of our parents are polysubstance users. National, state and local data indicate that 75 to 80% of child welfare cases stem from drug and alcohol related problems. The number of drug users in the United States is staggering. A study in 2004 captured the following statistics: 22.5 million Americans, 12 years and older, abused illicit drugs within the preceding year. Of that number, 3.4 million abused alcohol combined with drugs, 3.9 million abused drugs, and 15.2 million abused alcohol. Also in 2004, 19.1 million Americans, 12 years and older, admitted to abusing illicit substances in the preceding month.

With such daunting numbers, why do treatment courts work? Judges presiding in collaborative courts gave their opinions in the AOC's 2005 study mentioned above. They found the following interventions to be successful:

- Proactive and problem-solving oriented judges,

- Frequent judicial interaction with the defendant, litigant, parent,

- Ongoing judicial supervision with regular court reviews,

- Integration of social services,

- A team-based and non-adversarial approach, and

- The use of sanctions and incentives.

Family Wellness Court incorporates these approaches and more. It is state-of-the-art in terms of collaborative justice courts. It has become the next iteration of such courts by intentionally incorporating a trauma-informed approach. What does trauma-informed mean? The premise is that all of us – judges, professionals, team members, and litigants – have suffered some trauma in our life experience. Not all of us, however, have had the opportunity to process and heal from our traumatic histories. In serving our parents, and in dealing with one another, FWC's goal is to be trauma-informed in all aspects of a case. FWC and its larger system of grant-funded partners even performed a 360 degree evaluation to ensure that we were providing trauma-informed services at all times. We recognize that failing to hit the mark risks triggering or re-traumatizing our parents.

And what does a trauma-informed courtroom look like? We were fortunate to have Dr. Vivian Brown, the founder and CEO of PROTOTYPES, a multi-service agency in California and Washington, DC consult with us. Dr. Brown has more than 30 years of experience working with parents like those who come to FWC. In observing our court team in action, Dr. Brown concluded that we were the most trauma-informed court she had ever witnessed. What do we do that works? We create the illusion of time. Even if we know that time is quickly passing on our court calendar, we try not to rush a parent through the court review. We reduce extraneous activities and noise in the courtroom so that everyone on the multidisciplinary team is singularly focused on the parent. The courtroom is uncluttered, light, clean, and quiet and we even have a sign that expressly says "Welcome" on the door to our department. We do not have other parents in the courtroom, but rather see each parent individually. We listen and validate where possible. We use strength-based, positive language even while staying reality-based. We assure the parents explicitly that there is no negative judgment in the room for them. We demand honesty of the parents and we exact honesty from ourselves. We communicate that honesty authentically and with respect. We explain our expectations and processes to achieve transparency as much as we can. We honor the parent through praise, rewards, incentives and a fair and timely imposition of sanctions. We rave about the parent's children. We provide tangible support such as bus tokens, diapers and recovery books. We consistently come from a place of hope and non-judgment. Stephanie Covington, another consultant who trained FWC team members, said that our parents are often hopeless when they enter our child welfare system. It is our job to be their beacons of hope until they learn to hope for themselves. I believe they also present with shame, guilt and self-loathing. It is mandatory that we treat our parents with the utmost respect until they learn to respect themselves.

Based upon three years of such practices, we know that this approach works. FWC opened its doors on March 14, 2008. As of April 2011, we had served 290 parents and 350 children. While California's foster care system experiences an annual 11 to 12% reentry rate after reunification, as of April 2011, FWC had three new petitions filed for children where the parent had previously successfully completed FWC. Where the general rate of reunification in Santa Clara County was 48% in 2009 and 53% in 2010, FWC achieved a reunification rate of 75% in 2011 for fast-track cases. One hundred percent of all the children in FWC received extraordinary services such as early assessments, regular follow up assessments, mental health, medical, dental, vision, and physical therapy services, home visitation services, consultation with public health nurses, and linkage with community based resources and services. In fact, each FWC child receives approximately $6,000.00 worth of services at no cost to the parents through First 5 of Santa Clara County. First 5 pledged to match grant monies awarded by the federal Children's Bureau when these funds were granted to incubate FWC. The statistic that we are most proud of, however, is related to the impetus for starting FWC – the elimination of repeated positive-toxicity (pos-tox) births.

In continuing the Drug Dependency Treatment Court started by Judge Leonard Edwards ten years prior, Judge Katherine Lucero was stuck by the increasing number of pos-tox births. She witnessed mothers delivering one pos-tox baby after another year after year, and she was spurred to find a means to stop this revolving door. In applying for the FWC grant, Judge Lucero and our grant partners hoped to extinguish this recurring and generational problem. In the three-plus years that FWC has been in existence, we have seen our mothers give birth to many children. Of these babies delivered over the past three years, only one has been a pos-tox birth.

So how does FWC work? Our multidisciplinary team (MDT) is comprised of the following: the judge, a court resource manager, the courtroom clerk, the courtroom deputy or bailiff, county counsel who represents the Department of Family and Children's Services (DFCS) and its social workers, a social worker liaison who is present when the case-carrying social worker cannot participate, counsel for the parents and the children, a drug and alcohol rehabilitation counselor and assessor, a liaison from the County Mental Health Department, a resource specialist from First 5/ Gardner, an eligibility worker, a liaison from Child Advocates of Silicon Valley, a domestic violence and trauma therapist, and a liaison from Victim Witness. The most important member of the team is the parent. The parent is also accompanied in the FWC review by his or her mentor parent[24].

And what services do we offer our parents and children? FWC has 28 partners and 82 resource providers working together to form a strong network of support for our families. We strive to provide comprehensive services and holistic support. We also learn from our parents and endeavor to meet needs that they identify. As a result, we are ever-expanding our partnerships. This is what we offer at this time:

- A therapeutic court environment with an emphasis on establishing a therapeutic alliance between the parent and the team,

- Regular and frequent court reviews,

- Integration of services with the exchange of regular written reports from service providers and comprehensive staffing,

- Early connection to government financial aid such as TANF and food stamps,

- Case management by the court, DFCS, the Department of Alcohol and Drugs Services (DADS), and/or the County Department of Mental Health (MH),

---

24   Mentor parents are exemplary individuals who have successfully addressed their substance abuse and achieved the return of their children. These parents have participated as litigants in DDTC, FWC and Family Court. They are living proof to others that collaborative justice works and they befriend and support parents who have pending cases.

- Connection to SSI-related services,

- Legal representation,

- Early drug and alcohol assessments,

- Residential inpatient treatment for men and women, with the latter including the opportunity for mothers to live with their children in inpatient settings,

- Transitional Housing Units for men and women, either with or without their children,

- Outpatient drug services,

- Connection to 12-step meetings and generally accepted alternatives,

- Connection to same-gender sponsors,

- Connection to shelters and housing,

- Some assistance with rent and deposits through DFCS and community partners,

- Connection with resources for furniture and household items,

- Connection with Victim Witness for funds related to relocation, safety, and therapy,

- Connection with community agencies that provide financial assistance for food, supplies and PGandE,

- Mentor parent support,

- Domestic violence advocacy and services,

- Access to domestic violence classes and support groups,

- Assistance with obtaining restraining orders,

- Transportation assistance such as bus passes and bus tokens, as well as bicycles and car seats,

- Limited funding to assist with barriers such as funding for recovery books, obtaining parents' birth certificates,

- Linkages to employment services,

- Coordination with criminal court partners,

- Coordination of drug testing requirements,

- Assistance with criminal fine conversions to help people address debts,

- Budget information and connection to budgeting classes,

- Criminal Records Clearance services to enhance people's employability,

- Therapeutic services such as individual counseling, groups, dyadic therapy, parent child interactive therapy, family counseling, WRAP services,

- Psychiatric evaluations,

- Medication evaluations and connection to psychiatric medicines,

- Family planning education,

- Home visitation services,

- Consultations with public health nurses,

- Comprehensive developmental and behavioral screening, assessments and interventions for all children,

- Court-appointed child advocates for FWC children and their parents,

- Linkage to health care coverage and primary care physicians,

- Connection to dental and vision care through charitable organizations,

- Coordination with agencies funded by San Andreas Regional Center (SARC) where applicable,

- Access to an array of basic and specialized parenting classes,

- GED assistance,

- Language assistance,

- Information about nutrition and self-care,

- Information about stress management,

- Coaching for time management,

- Linkages for tattoo removal,

- Connection to community resources for food, clothing, hygiene products, shoes, and other items,

- Provision of tangibles such as diapers, wipes, umbrella strollers, children's clothing and shoes, children's books, developmental toys and games, and

- Family Team Meetings and Team Decision Meetings facilitated by DFCS.

Presiding over FWC as a judge is a uniquely satisfying experience. It also requires the judge to enter uncharted territory. All drug courts work best when the bench officer forms a therapeutic alliance with the participant. Indeed, twenty years of criminal drug court research shows us that the number one incentive for drug defendants is their relationship with their judge or their probation officer[25]. In FWC, not only is the judge charged with forming that alliance, the judge must model good parenting skills in his or her interactions with the parent. The judge must motivate the parent to do more than attend a criminally court-mandated drug program since parents in dependency court are required to complete much more than criminal defendants. These parents must complete drug programs, but they must also complete parenting programs, participate in an array of therapy, participate in home visitation, locate and maintain housing, and learn about time management, budgeting, nutrition, and the developmental needs of their children. These parents must also navigate sometimes Byzantine governmental, or inter-governmental, systems to acquire benefits and coverage for themselves and their children. They often must find employment to achieve financial stability to have their cases successfully dismissed. Their most intimate relationships are scrutinized for domestic violence, power and control, abuse, and the setting of healthy boundaries. They may be required to attend support groups, domestic violence classes, and couples' counseling. To keep a parent motivated in such a complex and taxing arena is a challenge since many addicts have survived in chaos and find it difficult to master the organization needed to live a life they never were raised to experience. Indeed, we know that stress and substance abuse often compromise the brain's executive functioning needed to be organized and timely.

The uncharted territory for the judge in FWC, however, is that the process works best when the judge relinquishes his or her control and status, or at least some of it, to the MDT. Nothing in law school, and very little in legal practice, prepares a judge for the experience of not acting like a judge. We are taught to be in control of our courtroom and those who come before us. Traditional legal education emphasizes detached analysis for judges. Judges are trained to value independence. While independent thinking serves judges well in other assignments, heeding the counsel of others in FWC allows the court team to come to the best approach and

---

25 Vivian Brown shared that studies show 50 to 60% of a successful outcome rests upon a positive therapeutic alliance. Only 1 to 2% is related to the treatment model or methodology used.

outcomes for our parents. In addition, while detachment and making decisions without being influenced by emotions is essential to traditional judging, the recognition of and mastery of emotions is key to good drug court judging. In dependency drug court, EQ – or emotional intelligence quotient – is as important as IQ – intelligence quotient.

In identifying our collective goals for FWC, the Oversight and Strategic Planning Committees determined that we wanted to "take the lawyers out of the courtroom" – meaning excise the adversarial legal posturing that is so often found in court. By extension, we also wanted to "take the judge out of the courtroom." Thus, the FWC judge is team mom, team leader, team follower, coach, cheerleader, parent, guide, sherpa, hostess, facilitator, mediator, and more. The FWC judge is not the traditional, forceful, omnipotent leader at the apex of an effort. As the Chinese philosopher Lao Tzu said, "A leader is best when people barely know that he exists; not so good when people obey and acclaim him; worse when they despise him. Fail to honor people, they fail to honor you; but of a good leader who talks little, and when his work is done, his aim fulfilled, they will all say 'We did this ourselves.'"

I relished the expanded role available to me in FWC, but I was discomforted by the undefined and sometimes amorphous role for the judge. Rather than sitting higher in the courtroom – as with a standard courtroom configuration[26] – and rather than keeping a distance from the attorneys and litigants, the FWC judge is required to bond with the team and form the therapeutic alliance with the parents. And the new territory also caused confusion for the litigants and service providers. Parents would stop me in the street to chat or confess – often touching upon improper ex parte communications which required abrupt termination of the interchange (hard to do while being trauma-informed). Eager and on-the-ball service providers would email updates to me about the litigants – again improper ex parte communications. Despite the disorientation stemming from my fuzzy – and often warm and fuzzy – role as a

---

26   Our juvenile dependency courtrooms have the bench positioned lower than in other courts and counsel table is configured in a horseshoe as opposed to separate and disconnected counsel tables.

judge, I found my tenure in FWC to be satisfying to the core. And I learned little lessons, and adopted some terminology, along the way that may prove useful to other bench officers.

1. **"Love In The Room"**: It is imperative to be non-judgmental. There should be no negative judgment and no shame. The judge should try to love each parent unconditionally. The judge needs to lead on this because there will be judgment from others and the judge must not allow it to seep into the courtroom in any way. Initially, it was challenging to talk about love, particularly when parents would say they loved us, since I wanted to remain professional, and demonstrate good boundaries. Yet I wanted to acknowledge that love actually is very important to the parent's healing process. Thus, it worked for me to talk about the "love in the room" for the parent. One father at the FWC Second Anniversary Party said, "Judge Yew always talked about the love in the room for me and I always felt it and left the room feeling better." The love uplifts the parents and helps to buoy hopes. All good parenting requires genuine love – love spurs children to please their parents and gives power to a parent's disapproval or sanction. If we are to properly re-parent our parents, we need to talk about love in the room and among the team for our parents. We need to demonstrate that love. One perinatal social worker, Margery Pentland, said that we are expanding our parent's capacity to love by praising them, accepting them, teaching them they are lovable, opening their hearts, and by modeling the unconditional positive regard we want them to show their children. Ann Louise Wagner, our first FWC therapist assigned to provide counseling for our parents, said, "If we don't love our clients, we re-wound them." It might help to keep this quote from David Hawkins in mind: "Love is misunderstood to be an emotion; actually is it a state of awareness, a way of being in the world, a way of seeing oneself and others."

2. **"Honesty In All Things"**: Addicts can be ever so smart and manipulative. Manipulation is a strong survival skill. The judge and MDT need to hold addicted parents accountable without imposing shame or judgment. We always tried to be strength-based in our

communications. Accountability does not mean being derisive. It means being straightforward with someone, advising them of what expectations exist for them, what they did wrong and why they are receiving a sanction. We tell our FWC parents that the first requirement upon them is to be honest at all times because we know that honesty is key to their recovery. We also promise the parents that we will always be straight with them.

3. **"Incentives Work"**: We have been fortunate to have a number of incentive items that we have received through donations and that we have purchased with grant money. Nearly anything presented with some fanfare and respect is going to serve as a motivator and incentive. Just two thoughts about incentives: First, it is very important to use them to break through the parent's distrust of the professionals in the system that has removed their children. Second, I believe that it is very important for incentive items to be new and to be in good condition. Our parents are accustomed to cast-offs and they often are provided with used items in residential programs or THU's. They can also acquire used items through community partners. An incentive item has to make the parent feel special and rewarded. It needs to be as sparkling new as possible.

4. **"Sanctions Also Work"**: Interestingly, incentives work for long-term behavior modification and sanctions work best for short-term behavior modification. In a successful drug court, the judge and MDT need to employ both. The issue of sanctions in FWC is challenging since we do not have the tool of flash incarceration which is such a useful tool in criminal drug courts. We use the following sanctions: requiring the completion of self-tests with a mentor and some questioning or follow up at the next court review, additional court reviews, dropping off meeting slips, doing make-up or extra meetings, writing essays, writing a good-bye letter to one's child, the MDT's expression of disapproval or disappointment in the courtroom, expression

of concern for the parent's situation, withholding the fishbowl[27] and other incentives.

5. **"The MDT Needs To Work Together"**: Comprehensive clinical staffings are also essential. Staffings often take time because everyone on the team talks and brainstorms. At our staffings we discuss drug testing, status in the recovery program, supervised visitations, home visitations, housing and employment needs, the child's needs, the availability of public benefits, the need for medical, dental, or vision care, domestic violence-related issues, challenges arising from the parent's relationship with foster parents or extended biological family members, transportation needs, nutrition and much more. Riccardo Carrillo, another FWC trainer, said FWC has the most comprehensive clinical staffings he has ever seen in his career. Staffings help the team to collaborate and reach consensus on an individualized plan for each parent before the parent comes into the courtroom. It is important for simplicity and clarity of message, among other things, and that the MDT speak in a unified voice.

6. **"FWC Is Not About Abstinence, It Is About Healing"**: Some drug courts are confrontational and seem satisfied with abstinence. FWC is not about abstinence, it is about healing. We want the parents to be in a place where they will never feel the need to use again. We tell the parents this and demand that they be clean in every aspect of their lives – their body and all their relationships. We say that when one is clean, things are as transparent as glass and one has nothing to hide. This is why

---

27   The fishbowl is FWC's way of motivating parents. If the parent is in full compliance, each time he or she comes into the courtroom for review, the parent can select a slip of paper from the fishbowl. The slips identify a practical incentive item that is earned by the parent. For example, the parent can pull a slip for a book of healthy recipes, sunglasses, a flashlight, a candle, or a CD of music. Alternatively, the fully compliant parent can choose a coupon. Saving coupons allows the parent to obtain larger incentive items such as a portrait with one's child, a digital camera with memory card, or a vacuum cleaner. As with parenting, it is important to be consistent when rewarding with the fishbowl and it is equally important to be transparent when a fishbowl is being denied.

Gandhi's quote is integrated into FWC documents given to parents: "Happiness is when what you think, what you say, and what you do are in harmony."

7. **"Eyes On Your Own Paper"**: As with many people in relationships, our parents are sometimes enmeshed in romantic or past romantic relationships where boundaries are muddied. In addition, with the high correlation of domestic violence in our cases, our parents are often living out the dynamics of power and control before our eyes. When it appears that one parent is unduly concerned about the progress, successes, failures, or visitation of the other parent, we remind the parent that recovery is about that parent's own status and internal work. The phrase, "eyes on your own paper" resonates with most people and conveys the message.

8. **"Relapses Are Understood But Not Excused"**: While we do not want parents to become mired in shame and despair after a relapse, we also do not want them to think that relapse is acceptable. The goal is to have parents not relapse, but if they do, it is better that they do while still in FWC as opposed to after the case has dismissed and when there are no safeguards in place for the child and the parent. In attempting to be both understanding and yet firm in holding parents accountable, we adopted the idea that relapses are understood, but not excused. In addition, we reminded parents that they should not lose hope and that it was never too late to change. We put Maria Robinson's quote on a board in the courtroom: "Nobody can go back and start a new beginning, but anyone can start today and make a new ending."

9. **"Come Back And Shine"**: At all times, it is most useful to maintain strength-based language and communication. Behavior modification includes failures and setbacks. After parents are told that they are failing or missing the mark, we tell them that we know they can do the work and we have faith in them. I tell them to "come back next time and shine."

10. **"Be Authentic"**: As judges, we are trained to remain detached and guarded – even inscrutable. For drug court to really work, however, the judge has to let down his or her guard. We have to be authentic and fully present. As Dr. Gabor Mate, author of *In the Realm of Hungry Ghosts*, said:

> "When my addict patients look at me, they are seeking the real me. Like children, they are unimpressed with titles, achievements, worldly credentials. Their concerns are too immediate, too urgent…. What they are about is my presence or absence as a human being. **They gauge with unerring eyes whether I am grounded enough on any given day to coexist with them, to listen to them as persons with feelings, hopes, and aspirations that are as valid as mine. They can tell instantly whether I'm genuinely committed to their well-being or just trying to get them out of my way.** Chronically unable to offer such caring to themselves, they are all the more sensitive to its presence or absence in those charged with caring for them.
>
> It is invigorating to operate in an atmosphere so far removed from the regular workaday world, **an atmosphere that insists on authenticity**. Whether we know it or not, most of us crave authenticity, the reality beyond roles, labels, and carefully honed personae. … [FWC] offers the fresh air of truth, even if it's the stripped, frayed truth of desperation. It holds up a mirror in which we all, as individual human beings and collectively as a society, may recognize ourselves. The fear, pain, and longing we see are our own fear, pain, and longing. Ours, too, are the beauty and compassion we witness here, the courage and the sheer determination to surmount suffering."

THE ADDICTION SPECIALIST

What Science Says About Drug Addiction

By Dr. Mark Stanford

In just the last ten years, advances in science have brought tremendous insights to our understanding of drug addiction and subsequently to improving treatment effectiveness. Based on this research, scientific evidence has defined addiction as a chronic, and for many people, reoccurring disease characterized by compulsive drug-seeking and use that results from prolonged effects of drugs on the brain (Dennis, 2007). A range of scientific research has demonstrated that chronic drug use changes the brain in fundamental ways that exist long after drug use has stopped. By using advanced brain imaging technologies, we can see what we believe is the actual biological core of addiction. What the science shows is that the brain of an addict is fundamentally different from that of a non-addict. Initially, when a person uses hard drugs like heroin or cocaine, the chemistry of the brain is not much affected, and the decision to take the drugs remains voluntary. But at a certain point, a "metaphorical switch" in the brain gets thrown, and the individual moves into a state of addiction characterized by compulsive drug use and continued use despite adverse health consequences.

These brain changes can persist long after addicts stop using drugs, which is why relapse is so common. Research has provided overwhelming evidence that not only do alcohol and other drugs interfere with normal brain functioning by creating powerful feelings of pleasure, but they also have long-term effects on brain metabolism and activity. Unfortunately, addiction as a chronic, relapsing disease of the brain is a completely new concept for much of the general public, for many policymakers, and sadly, for many health care professionals. The consequence of this informational gap is a significant delay in gaining control over the drug abuse problem. For example, there is the tendency for people to see addiction as a social problem that should be dealt with only by social solutions, and particularly via the criminal justice system. Science has demonstrated that drug addiction is as much a health problem as it is a social problem.

If we understand addiction as a chronic brain disease containing biological, behavioral, and social elements, treatment strategies must include bio-psychosocial methods using the principles of chronic illness care. Not only must the underlying brain disease be treated, but the behavioral and social elements must also be addressed, as it is done with other brain diseases, including stroke, schizophrenia, and Alzheimer's disease (Leshner, 1999).

The emerging paradigm views addiction as a chronic, relapsing brain disorder to be managed with all the tools at medicine's disposal. The addict's brain is malfunctioning, as surely as the pancreas in someone with diabetes. In both cases, "lifestyle choices" may be contributing factors, but no one regards that as a reason to withhold insulin from a diabetic. "We are making unprecedented advances in understanding the biology of addiction," says David Rosenblum, a public-health professor and addiction expert at Boston University. "And that is finally starting to push the thinking from 'moral failing' to 'legitimate illness'."

Herbert D. Kleber, M.D., the medical director of the National Center on Addiction and Substance Abuse in New York, says that the brain-disease concept fits with his experience with thousands of addicts over the years. "No one wants to be an addict," he says. "All anyone wants to be able to do is knock back a few drinks with the guys on Friday or have a cigarette with coffee or take a toke on a crack pipe. But very few addicts can do this. When someone goes from being able to control their habit to mugging their grandmother to get money for their next fix, that convinces me that something has changed in their brain." From the evidence of the new science of addiction, drug addiction is a brain disease expressed as compulsive behavior.

In laboratories funded by the National Institute on Drug Abuse (NIDA), MRI and PET scans are helping scientists discover more and more about the neurobiology of addiction. Geneticists have found the first few (of what is likely to be many) gene variants that predispose people to addiction, helping explain why only about one person in 10 who tries an addictive drug actually becomes hooked on it. Neuroscientists are mapping the intricate network of triggers and feedback loops that are set in motion by the taste—or, for that matter, the sight or thought—of a beer or a cigarette; they have learned to identify the signal that an alcoholic is about to pour a drink even before he's aware of it himself, and trace the impulse back to its origins in the primitive midbrain. And they are learning to interrupt and control these processes at numerous points along the way.

Among more than 200 potential medicines being developed or tested by NIDA are ones that block the intoxicating effects of drugs, including vaccines that train the body's own immune system to bar them from the brain. Other compounds have the amazing ability to intervene in the cortex in the last milliseconds before the impulse to reach for a glass translates into action. To the extent that "willpower" is a meaningful concept at all, the era of willpower-in-a-pill may be just over the horizon. "The future is clear," says Nora Volkow, M.D., the Director of NIDA. "In 10 years, we will be treating addiction as a disease, and that means with an array of evidence-based addiction medicines in addition to evidence-based counseling therapy.

Addiction Can Be Successfully Treated

Addiction is a treatable disease and, like other chronic diseases, can be managed successfully. Treatment enables people to counteract addiction's powerful disruptive effects on brain and behavior and regain control of their lives. Overall, treatment of addiction is as successful as treatment of other chronic diseases, such as diabetes, hypertension, and asthma. According to NIDA, drug treatment reduces drug use by 40 to 60% and decreases criminal activity during and after treatment by that amount as well. Research shows that drug addiction treatment reduces the risk of HIV infection by 6-fold and that interventions to prevent HIV are much less costly than treating HIV-related illnesses. Treatment can improve the prospects for employment, with gains of up to 40% after treatment. Combining treatment medications, where available, with behavioral therapy is a best practice standard to ensure success for most patients.

Data from NIDA shows that drug abuse treatment has a significant effect on reducing drug use. NIDA tracked 10,000 drug abusers in 100 treatment programs around the U.S. from 2001 to 2003 and found that methadone treatment cut heroin use by 70%. Only 28% of patients in outpatient methadone treatment programs reported weekly or more frequent heroin use, down from 89.4% prior to admission. The study also found that outpatient treatment resulted in a 50% reduction in weekly or more frequent cocaine use after one year of follow-up. Reductions were greatest for those patients in treatment for at least three months.

Relapse Is Not A Sign Of Treatment Failure

The chronic nature of the disease means that relapsing to drug abuse is not only possible, but likely. Relapse rates (i.e., how often symptoms occur) for drug addiction are similar to those for other well-characterized chronic medical illnesses such as diabetes, hypertension, and asthma, which also have both physiological and behavioral components. Treatment of chronic diseases involves changing deeply imbedded behaviors, and relapse does not mean treatment failure. For the addicted patient, lapses back to drug abuse indicate that treatment needs to be reinstated or adjusted, or that alternate treatment is needed.

Comparison of Relapse Rates Between Drug Addiction and Other Chronic Illnesses

Percentage of Patients Who Relapse

Type 1 Diabetes	30 to 50%
Drug Addiction	40 to 60%
Hypertension	50 to 70%
Asthma	50 to 70%

Because addiction can affect so many aspects of a person's life, treatment must address the needs of the whole person to be successful. This is why the best programs incorporate a variety of services into their comprehensive treatment regimens. Treatment counselors select from a menu of services for meeting the individual medical, psychological, social, vocational, and legal needs of their patients to foster their recovery from addiction.

About 22% of general health care patients report they have a comorbid substance use condition of some level of severity (SAMHSA, 2005). This large percentage of patients is likely related to the pervasiveness of a myriad of physical sequelae that result from untreated substance misuse and dependency. Additionally, the presence of substance use conditions often complicates the treatment of a variety of common medical disorders, such as diabetes.

Substance Abuse Treatment Reduces Health Care Costs

As drug use patterns change, addiction specialty treatment programs in the U.S. are seeing an increase in patients with serious medical problems, including HIV, HCV and HCB related to intravenous drug use (CDC, 2008; 2009), as well as patients with cardiovascular problems and lead poisoning associated with methamphetamine use (Burton, 1991). A study of adolescents entering drug treatment also reflects a similar increase among their group in health problems and health care costs (Mertens et al., 2007). In addition to the health problems associated with persons with substance use conditions and associated higher costs, research has shown that family members of persons with substance use conditions are also more likely to have medical conditions and to have higher medical costs as a result of living with addicted persons (Ray, Mertens, Weisner, 2007). The data is clear that health care costs, particularly the costs of chronic disease, substantially increase annually and over the lifetime of persons with untreated substance use, alcohol and other drug disorders. Substance abuse treatment has been found to be associated with individual's decreased subsequent health care costs, compared to the time before treatment. One study found a decline of more than one-third in both per capita inpatient and emergency room costs following the receipt of treatment. Other similar studies have reported more than a 50% drop in total per patient per month medical costs (Weisner, Parthasarathy, Moore and Mertens, 2010).

Science has shown, beyond a reasonable doubt, that addiction is a disease of the brain, and that our genes contribute close to half of the risk for becoming addicted. Addiction results from profound disruptions in the function of specific neurotransmitters and brain circuits. It involves an expanding cycle of dysfunction, first in the areas of the brain that process reward, followed by alterations in:

- complex cognitive functions, such as learning (memory, conditioning, habits);

- executive function (impulse inhibition, decision making, delayed gratification);

- cognitive awareness (interoception); and

- emotional functions (mood, stress reactivity).

These circuits work together and change with experience. Eventually, with repeated drug exposure, they become recalibrated, tilting the balance away from volitional control over one's behavior toward behaviors driven by drug cues and drug cravings. The result is compulsive drug use, despite severe health and social consequences – the hallmarks of addiction.

Promising Approaches: Trauma-Informed Treatment In Substance Abuse Services

Trauma means experiencing, witnessing, or being threatened with an event or events that involve actual serious injury, a threat to the physical integrity of one's self or others, or possible death. The responses to these events include intense fear, helplessness, or horror (Finkelstein, VandeMark, 2004). The relationship between interpersonal violence/trauma and substance use disorders is significant and complex. The prevalence of physical and sexual abuse among women in substance abuse treatment programs is estimated to range from 30% to more than 90%, depending on the definition of abuse and the specific target population (Moncrieff, Drummond, Candy, Checinski, and Farmer, 1996; Najavits, Weiss, and Shaw, 1997; Rice et al., 2001; Root, 1989). In addition, alcohol and drug problems have been shown to increase women's vulnerability to violence through exposure to unsafe situations (Parks and Miller, 1997).

The Effectiveness Of Trauma Treatment

Since the late 1980s, studies on the use of psychotherapeutic treatments have demonstrated reductions in PTSD symptoms, depression, and anxiety in combat veterans and victims of war and crimes (Hembree and Foa, 2003; Sherman, 1998). Trauma treatment models aimed specifically at persons with mental and substance use disorders are in its early stages (Zlotnick, Najavits, Rohsenow, and Johnson, 2003). Nonetheless, preliminary findings on the effectiveness of integrated models of treatment in reducing substance abuse and related problems, general mental health problems, and PTSD symptoms are promising (Brady, Dansky, Back, Foa, and Carroll, 2001; Fallot and Harris, 2002; Najavits, Weiss, Reif, Gastfriend, Siqueland, and Barber et al., 1998; Rosenberg et al., 2001; Talbot et al., 1999; Zlotnick et al., 2003).

Najavits and colleagues (Najavits, et al., 1998) followed a sample of 27 women who met the DSM-IV criteria for PTSD and substance dependence participating in *Seeking Safety*. At three months following treatment they found a significant increase in abstinence from substances and significant decreases in trauma-related symptoms and depression as compared with pretreatment symptom levels. In a separate study, 86 women with histories of childhood sexual abuse being treated in a mental health setting were assigned to a treatment as usual group versus a psychoeducational group intervention aimed at improving safety and self-care. In this setting, researchers found statistically significant reduction in mental health symptoms in the experimental group compared with the treatment as usual group (Talbot et al., 1999).

Researchers investigating the effectiveness of an individual exposure-based treatment (approaches that reactivate cues or memories associated with the traumatic event) in conjunction with a cognitive-behavioral relapse prevention model recruited 39 men and women seeking substance abuse treatment who had current diagnoses of PTSD and cocaine dependence. They found that those who completed 10 sessions of exposure treatment sustained statistically significant positive change six months later in alcohol and drug use, as well as employment (Brady et al., 2001).

Addressing trauma in substance abuse treatment involves both "trauma-informed" and "trauma-specific" approaches. Trauma-informed systems and services take into account knowledge about trauma—its impact, interpersonal dynamics, and paths to recovery—and incorporate this knowledge thoroughly in all aspects of service delivery. The primary goals of trauma-specific services are more focused: to address *directly* the impact of trauma on people's lives and to facilitate trauma recovery and healing. Ideally, substance abuse treatment programs will create trauma-informed environments, provide services that are sensitive and responsive to the unique needs of trauma survivors, and offer trauma-specific interventions.

In San Jose, California, the Santa Clara County Superior Court's Family Wellness Court has successfully integrated trauma informed approaches in its operations. By creating a setting within the courtroom clients are empowered to creatively problem solve and access community services with the assistance of a care coordinator. The court's preliminary experience with this approach is very promising and overall, they see that:

- People want to do better, but don't believe they can

- The human spirit is strong

- Genuine, constant positive regard penetrates pain and builds trust

- Don't discount "bribery" or the power of incentives

- People love their children

References

Dennis, M. L., Scott, C. K., Funk, R., Evaluation Program Planning, 2003; pp. 26, 339-352.

Web Of Science -An experimental evaluation of recovery management checkups (RMC) for people with chronic substance use disorders.

National Institute of Drug Abuse, The Science of Addiction; www.drugabuse.gov/scienceofaddiction/

Substance Abuse and Mental Health Services Administration; www.samhsa.gov

Weisner, C., Ray, G. T., Mertens, J. R., Satre, D. D., and Moore, C. (2003); Drug and Alcohol Dependence, 71(3), pp. 281-2. Short-term alcohol and drug treatment outcomes predict long-term outcome.

THE DOMESTIC VIOLENCE EXPERTS

Domestic Violence, Drugs and Alcohol

By Nancy Marshall, LMFT[28] and Kimberly Sanchez, Mentor Parent, Survivor

Addiction/Substance abuse does not occur in a vacuum. Most individuals struggling with addiction have histories that include violence and/or neglect, or other forms of trauma, often dating back to childhood. In Santa Clara County's Juvenile Dependency drug treatment courts (Dependency Drug Treatment Court and Family Wellness Court for Infants and Toddlers) there is a 78% to 82% overlap with domestic violence and substance abuse. These statistics reflect individuals with adult histories of domestic violence. This chapter will focus the victim/survivor experience, interweaving Kimberly's story with the more general information being provided.

---

28   Nancy Marshall, Marriage Family Therapist, is the Director of Domestic Violence Intervention Collaborative and has over 20 years of experience working with domestic violence. She has been the domestic violence specialist and trauma specialist with both the Family Wellness Court and Dependency Drug Treatment Court.
Kimberly Sanchez is a Mentor Parent with the Dependency Advocacy Center, supporting parents recovering from addiction and domestic violence. Kimberly is a recovering addict, a survivor of domestic violence, and works daily with clients, telling her story and using her experience to help parents successfully navigate the challenges involved in recovery, survival and healing, so their children can safely return home.

Cases entering the Child Welfare System in Santa Clara County are initially brought to the attention of the Department of Family and Children's services because of drugs and alcohol related issues (birth of a positive toxicity baby, arrests for being under the influence, accidents), child abuse, neglect, or police responses to domestic violence and resulting reports to the Department of Family and Children's Services. It is rare for a case to come under Court jurisdiction in Santa Clara County <u>solely</u> because of domestic violence.

Kimberly:

> *I came in to the dependency system in 2004 because my youngest daughter was born positive for cocaine and meth. I delivered my daughter at home because I was so loaded on drugs I did not realize that I was in labor. After I delivered my daughter, I was taken to the hospital and she was taken to the ICU because she weighed less than 5 lbs. I was so scared, because I knew they would test her for drugs and possibly take her that day. The reason why I knew they would test her is because prior to her birth, on October 3rd 2003, I had been in a car accident where my car had flipped over five times. (The accelerator was stuck and I couldn't stop the car). My older daughter was two and I was five months pregnant with my younger daughter. The ambulance took us to the hospital where I was tested for drugs and alcohol per the hospital protocol. That was my first encounter with a Social Worker. She was very nice and supportive, and she provided me with support and resources. At one point, she came to my house, and we talked about my getting into treatment. However, I managed to squirm my way out of that when I told her that I had moved to Watsonville - which of course was a lie!*
>
> *I had hidden my drug addiction from the father of my kids until after my baby was born. On some level I believed he had some suspicions or knew, but he never mentioned anything to me. He was too busy cheating on me, drinking and staying out all night with his friends.*

As I had predicted, my baby was tested for drugs at the hospital following her birth. But she was not tested until the third day after her birth, when mothers and babies are typically discharged from the hospital, so I was able to take her home with me. I was so relieved that I thanked GOD and promised to stay sober.

A couple of days later, I got a visit at home from another Social Worker. She explained to me that I was very lucky to walk out of the hospital with my daughter, and that she wasn't going to remove her, but that I had to get into an outpatient program. I also had a visit from a public health nurse who explained to me that if I used drugs I should not breast feed because it would be like injecting my daughter with drugs like an IV user. My daughter was born on the January 15th 2004. I got clean on January 16th, and stayed clean until January 27th. On January 27th the father of my children took me to the Doctor for my baby's first health check The Social Worker I had encountered when I flipped my car was there and, in front of the father of my daughters, she asked me how many days I had clean. He said he had no idea that I had been using. He stormed off, and left me at the hospital.

I was sobbing and it took a while for me to calm down. The Doctor and Social Worker wouldn't allow me to leave until I calmed down. I knew the wrath I would have to deal with when I got home – name calling and the silent treatment. So, I did what I knew best and used, and yes, I continued to breast feed my baby (It took awhile for me to clearly know how cunning, baffling and powerful the disease of addiction could be). The day after the Doctor's visit, a Social Worker came to my home and performed a random drug test. She didn't say much while she was at my home. The day after her visit, January 29th, my baby daughter was removed and my oldest daughter was picked up at her grandmother's house. I immediately called "Gateway" (the entry point for services through the Department of Alcohol and Drug Services) to see if I could get into residential treatment. I was so afraid of facing the father of my kids. My first real sober date is February 6th 2004; this was also the first day that I appeared in dependency court.

Domestic violence is complex! There is no "one size fits all." And domestic violence crosses all socio-economic lines. Perpetrators of domestic violence can be male or female, and the same is true for domestic violence victims. In the overwhelming majority of reported cases, women are the victims of domestic violence and men are the perpetrators, and this is mirrored in the majority of cases coming under the jurisdiction of the Santa Clara County Juvenile Dependency Court. For this reason, victims will be referred to as she/her in this chapter. And for the sake of brevity, victims/survivors will be referred to as victims.

Although there are many common threads for individuals who have experienced domestic violence, each individual must be recognized as unique, and their experience as being unique. When assessing risk factors and emotional impacts, individual context is critical. Context should include cultural background – including non-ethnic cultural impacts such as gang involvement, poverty impacts, religious beliefs, abuse history, standing in the community, immigration status, mental health, addiction, professional background, and history of childhood trauma.

Abusive Behaviors

The laundry list of abusive behaviors that occur in domestic violence relationships is diverse. In some cases there may never be an incident of physical assault.

A single incident of the more overt forms of abuse (physical, sexual, intimidation, threats) can define a relationship as domestic violence. Repetition of the more subtle forms of abuse (emotional abuse, minimizing-denying-blaming, isolation, abusive attitudes) is generally necessary to categorize a relationship as domestic violence. In most domestic violence relationships, the repetition of more subtle abuse results in the most emotional harm to victims over time. Some of the behaviors that typify domestic violence are as follows:

- <u>Physical Abuse</u> can include: pushing, hair pulling, slapping, punching, kicking, burning, being spit on, and attempted strangulation.

- <u>Sexual Abuse</u> can include: forced or coerced sex (rape), violence sex, attack on the victim's genitals, attack on the breasts, unwanted use of objects during sex, coerced sex with others, and withholding sex.

- <u>Intimidation</u> can include: threatening looks, gestures (making a fist, getting right in her face, throwing things, breaking things, etc.), displaying a weapon (e.g. gun, knife, club, belt), destruction of personal property (clothing, photographs, driver's license, green card, etc.), and hurting pets.

- <u>Isolation</u> can include: being cut off from friends and family, not being allowed to go anywhere alone, being followed, having one's mail opened, listening in on phone calls, destroying the phone, interfering with work, demanding to know where she is at all times, irrational jealousy, disabling her car, and calling her constantly.

- <u>Economic Abuse</u> can include: interfering with her job – resulting in job loss, preventing her from working outside the home, taking her money, and ruining her credit.

- <u>Emotional Abuse</u> can include: name calling, putdowns, mind games, double standards, blaming, false accusations, projection, and guilt trips.

- <u>Minimizing, Denying, Blaming</u> can include: denying the abuse happened, minimizing the seriousness of the abuse, denying or minimizing the seriousness of the resulting harm, refusing to allow medical intervention, blaming his behavior on her, refusing to accept responsibility for what he did, refusing to accept the reality of what he did (I didn't push you – you tripped).

- ■ <u>Threats Used for Control</u> can include: threats to harm her, her family, her friends, or her pets, threats to property, threats to report her to police, welfare, child protective services, or immigration, threats to kill himself, to kill her and/or the children.

- ■ <u>Using Children</u> can include: threatening to hurt the children, threatening to take the children, putting her down to her children, sending messages through the children, using visitations to harass her

- ■ <u>Abusive Attitudes</u> – often internalized by both men and women: male privilege (women's job is to serve men, service men, men are in charge, make all the decisions, men are superior to women), double binds and double standards (men who cheat are being men, women who cheat are whores, etc.), (men can go out for beer with their buddies, women who go out are neglecting their husbands, children), rigid gender roles (raising children, keeping house, cooking – that's women's work, men are worth more money on the job than women).

The majority of domestic violence victims entering the Child Welfare System in Santa Clara County do not recognize or acknowledge domestic violence as impacting their relationships. Many grew up witnessing/exposed to domestic violence, and might perceive the abusive behaviors they are subjected to in their adult relationships as "normal." Without a history of police responses for domestic violence, or self-reports about domestic violence, domestic violence may not be recognized as a problem. For those victims who do recognize domestic violence, it is usually minimized.

Kimberly:

> *I have to agree with the above statements. As a Mentor Parent, I know that there are a lot of cases of unreported domestic violence, especially in the Mexican/Latino cultures. I had been exposed to DV as a child and a teen. My stepfather started calling me a piece of shit when I was about 9, and continues to do so to this day. He was also very verbally abusive to my siblings and my mother. I'm not sure if this was a factor in my mother's ongoing use of drugs and alcohol. Today, I can see that this experience as a child is part of the reason I got caught up in an abusive relationship.*

> *Two of the things that were really hard to deal with were the double binds and the double standards. He would go out drinking and picking up women with his friends at night. When I would tell him I wanted to go out with friends, he would accuse me of wanting to go out and pick up men – which I now realize is called projection – and he would tell me I needed to stay home and clean the house – which was clean, or watch my daughter, or some other home-based reason. He would complain if I didn't cook his dinner, and when I would cook he would complain and say the food tasted like shit. No matter what I did it was wrong. In his eyes I couldn't do anything right. At times the double binds and double standards would make me feel like I was losing my mind.*

Although domestic violence may not be what brought them into the system initially, in Santa Clara County addressing domestic violence concerns is integrated into case plans for both victims and offenders, and is critical to safely returning children home. It is the policy of Santa Clara County's Department of Family and Children's Services and the Juvenile Dependency Court to recommend/order appropriate services to both victims and offenders, and to order separate case plans and services in cases where there has been a history of domestic violence. When providing services for victims, successful interventions are strength based, trauma informed, non-blaming, and are geared to help them recognize what constitutes domestic violence.

Kimberly:

> *I explained to the Emergency Response Social Worker who initially*
> *interviewed me that there had been a domestic violence incident in*
> *November of 2002 that resulted in the father being arrested, and*
> *that there was a peaceful contact order in place. I told her that he*
> *had thrown a phone at my back and that I had reacted by slapping*
> *him across the face. He then put me in a head lock, and I was afraid*
> *he would snap my neck or that I would be choked to death. I had*
> *abrasions on my face when the police officers arrived and they took*
> *pictures. I had been pushed, thrown on the floor, choked, and he*
> *attempted to suffocate me. Despite his violence to me, which I felt*
> *somewhat responsible for because I had slapped him, I was hoping*
> *that the girls would be placed in their father's care rather than be*
> *placed in foster care. I did not realize what torture I would have*
> *to endure in order to see my daughters because they did get placed*
> *with their father.*

Types Of Violence

Domestic violence is not a "one size fits all" phenomenon. Ellen Pence and Shamita Das Dasgupta identified five distinct categories of domestic violence. (*Re-Examining 'Battering': Are All Acts of Violence Against Intimate Partners the Same?* Praxis International, Inc., June 20, 2006; www.praxisinternational.org):

- Battering (Intimate Terrorism): an ongoing patterned use of intimidation, coercion, and violence as well as other tactics of control to establish and maintain a relationship of dominance over an intimate partner.

- Resistive Violence: victims of battering often retaliate and resist battering by using force themselves in order to escape and/or stop the violence used against them, and as a method of protecting themselves or their children. A woman who cannot access any resources may use violence to self-protect more readily than those who can access alternative resources or recourses.

- <u>Situational Violence</u>: intimate partners often use violence against each other to express anger, disapproval, or to reach an objective. But here the partner being violent does not use a pattern of intimidation and violence to establish control or dominance. The victim of an episode is typically not fearful of the partner. The position of victim and perpetrator may shift and change continuously.

- <u>Pathological Violence</u>: individuals use violence against others, including their intimate partners. It is clearly secondary to alcohol or drug use, mental illness or physical disorders, or neurological damage. In this type, when the cause is removed or successfully treated, the violence ends.

- <u>Antisocial Violence</u>: violence is not typically focused on any particular person or gender.

Approximately 85% of women under Dependency Court jurisdiction in Santa Clara County, who have been ordered to participate in women's domestic violence support groups, have experienced the type of violence defined as "battering" or "intimate terrorism." By providing them with the laundry list of abusive behaviors, and explaining the cycle of violence, victims are able to identify the type of relationship they have experienced, make informed decisions about their relationships, about safety planning, take the steps necessary to promote healing and safety for themselves and their children, and support their recovery.

Kimberly:

During the time that I was working to reunify with my daughters, they had been placed in their dad's care. He was telling me that he thought the girls should be placed in my care. At the same time he was telling the Social Worker that the girls would be at risk if they were returned to me. I believed at that time that he had the right to decide when I could visit.

And he would only let me see the girls if I had sexual intercourse with him. The Social Worker was unaware of this initially because I had so much shame about the fact that I was doing this. I learned in my domestic violence group that this was emotional blackmail. Realizing this, I was freed from the shame and I was empowered to tell my attorney what was going on, and we were able to file a 388 petition.

Even though my Social Worker was aware of the domestic violence history, it wasn't until I showed her the text messages and started documenting how much time dad was allowing me to have with my daughters that she started to believe me and understand the power and control dynamic I was still in.

The Cycle Of Violence

Initially defined by Lenore Walker, PhD. ("The Battered Woman", 1980) the three stages of the Cycle of Violence are: escalating tension, violence, and loving reconciliation. The Cycle of Violence is a core aspect of most education about domestic violence, and defines the power and control dynamics that typify a battering/ intimate terrorism relationship. Based on two decades of work with women actively experiencing battering relationships, Dr. Walker has developed the following description of the cycle of violence:

HOW DOMESTIC VIOLENCE IMPACTS EMOTIONAL WELL-BEING
BATTERING / INTIMATE TERRORISM, Resistive Violence, Antisocial Violence

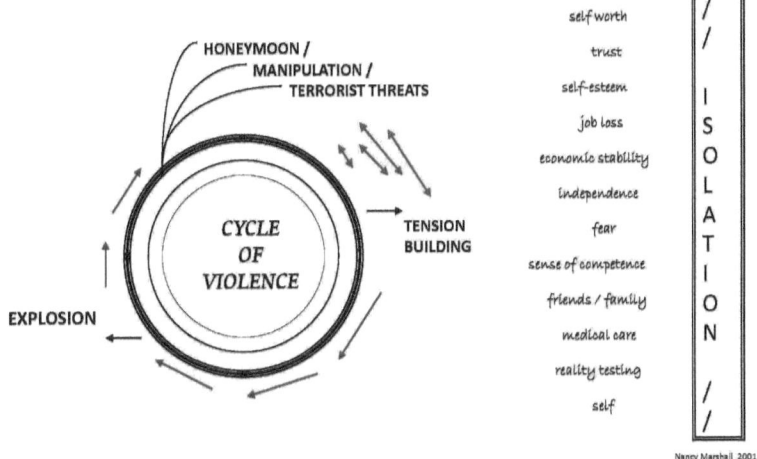

Nancy Marshall 2001

The composite of stories from victims of domestic violence is as follows:

Honeymoon: He comes along, sweeps her off her feet – it feels almost too good to be true. He wants to know all about her, tells her all about himself (usually how awful his last relationship was, or his troubled childhood, or how no one has ever understood him before, or has ever made him feel as good as she makes him feel, or he has never loved anyone like he loves her, etc.) He tells her he will never hurt her, will take care of her, and support what she wants to do, and so on.

- She becomes vulnerable, and he gains power.

Tension Building: Sometimes he would get mad, or sad, or withdraw. She would try to make it better, try to figure out what she had done wrong, and try to do things differently. Nothing would work. So she would distance herself.

- She becomes less vulnerable, and he loses power.

The dance between "honeymoon" and "tension building" continues to escalate during the initial phases of the relationship. As he loses more power and control, the tension building escalates until there is an explosion. The initial explosion may be him calling her a bitch. She sets a boundary, says "no one calls me that," and is less vulnerable. To regain control, he works to reconcile with her, promising to never repeat the offense involved in the explosion, and telling her how much he needs and loves her. His apology often includes "but" – if you had not…" in essence, blaming her for his behavioral choice.

As the cycle repeats, the abusive behaviors become more overt, and more volatile. The victim tends to isolate from family and friends. The isolation may result from the perpetrator creating problems with family and friends, refusing to go to events involving family and friends, and/or creating problems for the victim if she goes. Isolation may result from family and friends, in frustration, telling the victim they are tired of her leaving the relationship and returning to him. She may isolate because she does not want family or friends to see her bruises. Because she is often being blamed for all of the problems in the relationship, being told she is fat, stupid, a lousy mother, etc. - and she is internalizing these messages - her self-confidence is being eroded, she is losing trust in her own judgment, and she is often living in fear; walking on egg shells to avoid problems and stay safe. The more isolated she becomes, the more she is impacted emotionally. She becomes more vulnerable and he gains more power and control over time.

It is not unusual in long term relationships for the honeymoon phase to become ineffective. Victims can hear "I'm sorry, but" only so many times before the honeymoon tactics lose their effectiveness. Honeymoon tactics can then become tactics of manipulation, terrorist threats, and violence, and the cycle can become a two-stage cycle, with the dance between tension building and explosion defining the relationship.

When working with victims of domestic violence, it is important to remember that how the victim presents is often the direct result of her experience, and *contextually* tends to be a logical response that facilitated survival of traumatic experiences. To avoid making judgments or drawing erroneous conclusions, consider the following:

- What is her perception of self as a woman, and her perception of her roles and responsibilities in the context of a relationship?

- How severe is the traumatic impact, and her emotional reactions?

- What is her level of fear?

- How safe is she? How safe does she feel? (Emotional and physical safety).

- What abusive behaviors and threats has she been subjected to?

- Is there a recurring pattern and escalation of abusive behaviors?

- What are the coping skills she has learned to be able to survive the abusive behaviors?

- What are the degrees of isolation and the economic impacts that might keep her held hostage in the relationship?

- The most dangerous time in a battering relationship is when the victim is in the process of leaving and just after she has left. Threats of what will happen if she leaves will often keep the victim locked into the relationship.

Kimberly:

Even though <u>domestic violence was not the reason</u> my daughters were removed from me, I was referred to a women's domestic violence support group. I remember the first day I attended because it was the first time I had so many moments of clarity. That day, I knew I wasn't the only one - that there were others who had experienced the same craziness. I learned that I had not been the cause of his unhappiness, nor did I ask for, or *deserve to be treated the way I had been by him. The abuses that described domestic violence finally explained the behaviors that I had experienced. I would describe certain behaviors and to my surprise, find that it fell squarely in the category of DV. Looking back, I can tell you that even while we were going through the list of behaviors I was still minimizing.*

Oh, the freedom that my mind and soul experienced was so phenomenal! I felt so empowered to know that I had options, that there were ways to get through the web of lies! I wanted to know more. The empowerment I felt was amazing!

Typical Symptoms/Reactions

Victims who learn about domestic violence, the cycle of violence, and the impacts begin the journey from being "victims" toward empowerment that moves them to "survivors." Understanding their symptoms or reactions are "typical" and to be expected as a result of their experiences moves them from feeling guilty, stupid or crazy, to feeling better about themselves and more able to make informed decisions.

Typical symptoms and reactions include:

- Sleeping too little or sleeping too much.

- Changes in eating patterns.

- Difficulty concentrating, or intense concentration to keep intrusive thoughts at bay.

- Hypervigilance to surroundings, or a decrease in awareness of surroundings.

- Avoidance of thoughts, feelings, places, activities, people and/or conversations that remind her of her abuser and/or the trauma she experiences, or a need to repetitively talk about the trauma and think about the places, activities, and situations related to the trauma.

- Irritability, or absence of emotional responsiveness/reaction.

- Feeling detached - from her experiences, from other people in her life, *from* her life.

- Dissociative features – gaps/partial gaps in memory for significant traumatic events.

- Loss of interest, loss of hope.

- Apathy or outrage.

- Lack of ability to recognize or experience more than a limited range of emotions (e.g. anger, sadness, guilt and/or shame).

- Anxiety – feeling restless; keyed up; on edge. Anxiety can range from mild to panic attacks.

- Flashbacks – being flooded with memories. This can be emotional, physiological, and/or cognitive (with and without visual and/or auditory flashbacks of the trauma).

- Fear: for physical, emotional, or economic safety; for her children's safety; for the ability to recover and provide for one's self (and any children) in the future.

- Feeling like she is losing her mind.

- Substance use/abuse.

Drugs, Alcohol And Domestic Violence

Drugs and or alcohol are involved in the majority of Juvenile Dependency cases where there is domestic violence. Most victims referred for domestic violence services initially believe that the drugs or alcohol caused the domestic violence, and once they or their partner stops using, the relationship issues will be resolved. This is one of the most challenging aspects of working with victims of domestic violence in the child welfare system. Once victims have gained an understanding of the types of violence, what behaviors typify domestic violence, and the concept of the cycle of violence, providing them with the following information can be helpful in assisting them to look objectively at the impact of drugs and alcohol on the power and control tactics they have been subjected to in their relationships.

- Substance use/abuse can and often does contribute to impacts of domestic violence.

- As disinhibitors, drugs and alcohol can contribute to increased levels of violence.

- With the exception of true pathological violence, drugs and alcohol do not <u>cause</u> domestic violence.

- Victims are often coerced into using drugs and/or alcohol by their partners.

- Drugs and/or alcohol are a way to escape the nightmare of domestic violence.

- Batterers can gain an increased level of power and control over victims if they become "hooked" – especially if the batterer is their connection.

- Batterers will often use the excuse of being high/loaded to justify their abuse.

- Batterers will at times get victims high, knowing their victim won't call the police while under the influence.

■ There can be a circular (cyclical) pattern of reengaging in a power and control dynamic that can trigger relapse for victims in recovery. Relapse can make victims vulnerable to reengagement in a domestic violence relationship.

Victims of domestic violence in the Child Welfare System often attribute their partner's behavioral choices to drug or alcohol use (pathological violence), or see their relationship as defined by situational violence. Most women in the system who have used physical violence in their relationships identify themselves as the "batterers," or see the violent episodes as situational. In a small percentage of cases, pathological violence and situational violence does apply. And in a small percentage of cases, women are in fact the dominant aggressors.

Helping victims to determine if the violence in their relationship is pathological – caused by alcohol or drug use – or if it falls more in the battering category, and the abusive behaviors employed by their partners are intentional, can be traumatic for the victims. Most want to believe that their partners would never hurt them intentionally, and that the Mr. Wonderful from the honeymoon phase of their relationship is the "real" partner.

Using a list of abusive behaviors can be a key element in helping victims gain an in-depth understanding of the role of drugs and alcohol in their relationships. The first step is to identify the behaviors they have been subjected to, and note which behaviors have occurred only in private or primarily in private. For the purposes of this step, private is defined as occurring only in front of children, or only in front of his family members who condone the behaviors, or his friends who condone the behaviors. The second step is to have them identify the severity of behaviors in public vs. private. (He may whisper in her ear she is a slut in public, and get in her face and scream it at her in private.) Third – explore if he ever drinks or uses, or is under the influence in public, where the behaviors do not occur or do not occur in an overt manner. Most victims will identify behaviors as occurring primarily in private while he is under the influence. And most will indicate he is around others in public when drinking or using or under the influence, yet he only exerts the abusive behaviors in private. This exercise helps them to understand that use of drugs or alcohol do not cause the violence or a loss of control, and the fact that the abusive behaviors happen primarily or only in private suggests that he knows exactly what he is doing and has control over his behavioral choices.

With pathological violence, the abusive behaviors will be directly linked to substance use and will result in the inappropriate behaviors only occurring while under the influence (or when there are unmedicated mental health issues). With antisocial violence, the behaviors can occur any time, any place, with anybody, whether or not the perpetrator is under the influence.

(Note: Assessing for reactive/resistive violence can also be done using the abusive behaviors check list and employing a timeline to determine when the abusive behaviors occurred, if the violence was in reaction to what her partner was doing to her, or if she was trying to exert power and control over her partner by using abusive tactics.)

Recovery is necessary for the therapeutic process to be effective. Revisiting incidents that cause trauma can be intense and potentially triggering for relapse if new and healthy coping skills for intense emotions are not in place. Fear, feelings of helplessness and hopelessness, emotional numbing, emotional flooding, lethality risk (whether rooted in childhood or adult experiences, or both) can be debilitating. For the recovering addict, having the supports of intensive outpatient treatment while addressing trauma can be critical.

Kimberly:

> *I take full responsibility for my addiction. By doing so, I also take full responsibility for my recovery. I learned that their father's drinking did not cause the violent episodes we experienced, and that my addiction did not cause the violent episodes. I was able to figure out that our*

relationship was about power and control - about him believing that he had a right to have power and control over me, and that the name calling and putdowns and blackmail were behaviors he believed he had the right to use. He would try to intimidate me with looks, or throwing things around to get attention. There were moments that I just felt defeated by the flooding emotions I felt when he would assert power and control. The fear, intimidation, and the level of power he held while my kids were in his care would paralyze me.

He would also make it impossible for me to get a job, because I was never allowed to use the truck, and he would make me beg for money – which I now know were forms of isolation and economic abuse. When I had my truck accident, I was so afraid to call him and tell him what happened because I was afraid of his reaction. And when I was finally able to muster enough courage to tell him, he called me a fucking bitch and asked me how could I have done this to him? For the longest time, I believed that the truck was more valuable than my own life.

I have flashbacks, and I can tell you that the last time this happened I cried from 12:00 p.m. – 9:00 p.m. I saw my therapist and asked her to give me the number to the suicide hotline and to the mental health department. I remember thinking that I should just give up my parental rights and give him the girls. This was after he slandered me in court while I was trying to get a restraining order. I remember him speaking so fast and that all the slander that came out of his mouth so quickly and easily blew me away and paralyzed me completely. Other than my moments of complete defeat and despair in my addiction, this is the only other time I wanted to crawl into a fetal position and die. I needed to completely detach from him; and giving up the girls seemed like a good option for me at that moment. It's hard to describe the feelings he triggered in me. It was just so intense and overwhelming - it felt unbearable.

It is amazing how our minds work to protect us. One time, when he punched me in the face, I started crying. He said "Why are you crying – we were just playing around." I actually bought into that – it was safer than arguing with him. When he tried to suffocate me, I honestly believed I was going to die. I cannot begin to describe how terrified I was. Part of my mind still dissociates from the reality of that experience because it was so terrifying, and when I talk about it I find that I tend to chuckle, because it is just too painful to let the real feelings come to the surface.

My case plan ordered me to participate in individual therapy, outpatient treatment, and domestic violence support groups. Because of these services, I learned to recognize a lot of relapse triggers that would occur when he would do things to try to control me. I was also able to recognize that a lot of these relapse triggers kept me from addressing my addiction during the relationship; that I would use drugs to escape from the trauma his behaviors were causing. Some of his behaviors triggered childhood memories of my step-father's ongoing emotional abuse of my mother and me. And many of his behaviors were traumatic to me as an adult. When I stopped reacting with fear or guilt or shame, I was able to start responding by setting healthy boundaries, by developing my safety plan, and by reaching out for support from people I trusted.

There have been many layers of trauma for me to work through. I continued to participate in therapy and domestic violence support groups for the entire length of my Dependency case, far beyond the requirements of my court-ordered case plan. To this day, I continue with therapy for my daughters and myself as we need it, especially when we are impacted by their dad's ongoing attempts to regain power and control.

Children And Domestic Violence

There is no question about the potential impacts of domestic violence and substance abuse on children and their development - both physiological and psychological. Children exposed to drugs and alcohol prenatally can experience a range of permanent physiological harms. And exposure to violence prenatally and during the first five years can impact how a child's brain is hardwired. The number of children living in families with domestic violence is staggering. *Futures Without Violence* (Family Violence Prevention Fund, www.endabuse.org) reports:

- 15.5 million U.S. children live in families in which partner violence occurred at least once in the past year. 7 million live in families in which severe partner violence occurred.

- Two-thirds of U.S. non-fatal intimate partner victimizations of women occur at home.

- In a single day in 2007, 13,495 children were living in a domestic violence shelter or transitional housing facility.

- Children who have been exposed to family violence suffer symptoms of PTSD, such as bed-wetting or nightmares, and are at greater risk than their peers of having allergies, asthma, gastrointestinal problems, headaches and flu.

- Children of mothers who experience prenatal physical domestic violence are at an increased risk of exhibiting aggressive, anxious, depressed or hyperactive behavior.

- Females exposed to their parent's domestic violence as adolescents are significantly more likely to become victims of dating violence than daughters of nonviolent parents.

- Children who experience childhood trauma, including witnessing incidents of domestic violence, are at greater risk of having serious adult health problems (e.g. tobacco use, substance abuse, obesity, cancer, heart disease, depression, unintended pregnancy.)

The Alabama Coalition Against Domestic Violence's (www. acadv.org) excellent outline of age-specific indicators in children exposed to domestic violence follows. Many of these indicators are also true for children living in families with substance abuse.

- Infants: their basic need for attachment is disrupted, routines around feeding/sleeping are disturbed, they may experience injuries while "caught in the crossfire," experience irritability or inconsolable crying, frequent illnesses, difficulty sleeping, diarrhea, developmental delays, and lack of responsiveness.

- Preschool: they will present somatic or psychosomatic complaints, regression, irritability, fear of being alone, extreme separation anxiety, developmental delays, and sympathetic displays toward mother.

- Elementary: vacillation between being eager to please and being hostile, verbal about home life, experience developmental delays, externalized behavior problems, inadequate social skills development, and conflict/ confusion regarding gender role modeling.

- Preadolescence: behavior problems become more serious, increased internalized behavior difficulties, depression, isolation, withdrawal, emotional difficulties, shame, fear, confusion, rage, poor social skills, developmental delays, protection of mother, sees her as "weak," and is guarded/secretive about family.

- Adolescence: internalized and externalized behavior problems can become extreme and dangerous, including drug/alcohol use, truancy, gangs, sexual acting out, pregnancy, running way, and becoming suicidal; dating relationships may reflect violence learned or witnessed in the home.

Over the past two decades of working with adult victims of domestic violence in the Child Welfare System, mothers have reported a variety of ways that their children are used in power and control relationships. They are used as spies ("Who is Mom seeing"? "What time does she come home"? "Who does she talk to"? "What kind of underwear is she wearing"? "Where does she work"?) Children are often used to coerce Mom into coming back home/reengaging with Dad through emotional appeals, through Dad undermining her authority as a parent, through sending messages via the children which can range from "Tell Mom I love her" to "Tell Mom she is being mean to me by staying away" and other emotional appeals.

Kimberly:

> *Their dad would send messages through my daughters and undermine my authority. He would say things like, "Don't listen to your Mom, she doesn't know what she talking about." or "She's crazy." In addition, when I would discipline the girls, he would completely go against what I would say, or tell them things like "Tell your Mom to shut up."*

Putting children in the middle causes confusion for them, creates guilt, and can make them feel like they have to choose one parent over the other. Where there are multiple siblings in a family these tactics can create havoc in the sibling relationships as well.

It is important to note that some children are very resilient and are minimally impacted. Some children show no symptoms initially, and may be "perfect" children, with behavioral indicators of trauma surfacing over time. Some show immediate symptoms which then dissipate over time.

Providing an environment that is emotionally and physically safe, with clean and sober parents, and reaching out for appropriate supports for children and for the family when safe and appropriate; all of these can make a notable difference in the healing process and long-term outcomes for children exposed to domestic violence, and substance abuse.

So many victims of domestic violence have stated that even though their significant other is not a good partner, he is a good dad. The offending parent may be loving towards the children, may play with them and attend to their basic needs. However, when the offending parent exposes his or her child to abusive behaviors toward the non-offending parent, children are negatively impacted. And there are concerns about the parenting styles of the offending parent in domestic violence relationships.

Jeffrey Eddleson and Oliver Williams report in "Parenting by Men who Batter" (Oxford University Press, 2007) report:

- Men who batter were more likely to have used negative child-rearing practices, such as spanking.

- Men who batter were also more often angry with their children.

- Many battered mothers report that their abusers purposefully involve the children in violent events.

- 48.6% of Mothers reported that they were intentionally hurt at least sometimes when they intervened to protect their children

- 38.7% reported that their perpetrator frequently or very frequently hurt them for their children's acts.

- 22.5% reported that the perpetrator frequently or very frequently blamed them for the perpetrator's own excessive punishment of the children.

Kimberly:

Both my daughters have been affected by domestic violence. Both my daughters would have nightmares, and sleepwalk for six to twelve months following an incident. It has been an extremely difficult process.

My children's dad continued to drink when the children were in his care, and after they were returned to me. He also continued to perpetrate the power and control tactics in front of the children with new girlfriends, and made attempts to perpetrate them with me.

My youngest daughter felt she had to defend her dad, and showed her loyalty more to her father. Recently, while on our way to the bowling alley, she started crying because the last time she was there was with her father, and he told the girls not to talk about me because he hates me.

It has been challenging to support the love and loyalty my daughters feel for their dad in a way that also stresses they have to be safe when with him. It was hard to find the right words that let them know they had to be safe with me, and with anyone they love, and that it is important for them to let someone know if they do not feel safe with people they love. It is important for my children to feel free to talk about their dad when they are with me, and to know I support their ongoing relationship with him.

Before I left their dad, my oldest daughter saw her father on top of me and told him that if he didn't get off me she would call the police on him. She was only 2 years old, and at that time it was clear to me that she sensed danger. For some time after she was returned to me, she was so afraid of her dad that she didn't even want visits with him. Most of her parent teacher conferences up to 3rd grade were about her inability to speak up or sit up straight - her whole demeanor showed fear, low self-esteem, and no confidence, and she was easily startled.

Both my daughters have claims through the Victim/Witness Assistance Center which pay for their therapy. They have established relationships with a wonderful therapist whom they trust and feel safe to be open with. When issues come up, she is there for them. Although I don't participate in their therapy, the therapist does provide me with guidance in how to support them and their relationship with their dad while keeping them safe and presenting my concerns in a way that does not put their dad down.

> *Thanks to the support system, I've been empowered to go back to court and file orders that keep our family safe. I'm forever grateful to my great teachers then and now who continue to inspire me to speak up. They saved my life and left an imprint upon my heart!*

For additional reading on the impact of domestic violence on children please consider "The Batterer as Parent: Addressing the Impact of Domestic Violence on Family Dynamics" (Lundy Bancroft and Jay G. Silverman, Sage Publications, Inc., 2002 and "When Dad Hurts Mom: Helping Your Children Heal the Wounds of Witnessing Abuse", Lundy Bancroft, The Berkley Publishing Group, March, 2005).

Safety And Empowerment

Some couples choose to live together, and to work to keep their families intact. Some may choose to separate and hope for a friendly relationship for the sake of their children. And some will choose no contact with the offending parent, with visitation arranged in a public place or through a third party.

There is never a guarantee that someone completing batterer intervention services will change their core beliefs and remain violence-free. Perpetrators of domestic violence may say and do everything they know is expected of them while involved in the legal system, or are on probation. Those who embrace the change process and change their core beliefs will generally continue with the new behaviors once their legal cases have ended. Sadly, many will make the appropriate presentations until their legal case is dismissed; and then revert to their old behaviors.

Some individuals participating in batterer intervention services become more sophisticated in their abusive tactics, learning how not to leave evidence trails, marks on their victims, and learning how far they can go without getting caught up in the criminal justice system for their behaviors.

Providing victims with basic information about domestic violence – the laundry list of behaviors, the cycle of violence, the impact on her self-esteem and independence, the impact on her children - will help the victim understand her experience. Information provides a context for her to begin to ease the guilt and sense of responsibility she has for her partner's abusive behaviors. Information helps her to recognize the subtle and overt red flags suggestive of abusive behaviors and/or power and control tactics, and supports her efforts with safety planning for herself and her children. Information encourages and supports the empowerment needed to make informed decisions about her relationship, and to set healthy boundaries.

The way information is provided will, to varying degrees, impact the victim's ability to hear/receive it. Service providers need to be strength-based, trauma-sensitive and trauma-informed; non-judgmental and non-blaming. Replicating the power and control dynamics the majority of victims have been subjected to does not support empowerment. Encouraging victims to make informed decisions; offering suggestions rather than advice; applauding their courage and strength and providing other reflections that are the opposite of their abuse histories make all the difference as they move from victims to empowered survivors.

Safety planning is integral to working with victims of domestic violence. Safety plans need to be unique to each individual and her situation, they need to be fluid, and they need to be maintained in a safe place not accessible to the domestic violence offender. Safety planning should address a range of potential concerns: escape; how to reach out for help and to whom; local shelter based agencies; involvement or exclusion of children in the process of safety planning; abuse prevention; saving evidence; addressing concerns about impacts on children post-separation. Perpetrators who have access to detailed safety planning guidelines may be able to anticipate what their victim is planning. It is recommended that victims of domestic violence work directly with one of their local shelter-based organizations or with a domestic violence advocate on safety planning. To locate a shelter-based domestic violence agency, talk to an Advocate, or to get help with safety planning, the National Domestic Violence Hotline is available 24-hours a day, 7 days a week. (1-800-799-7233 or 1-800-787-3224 TTY).

Kimberly:

> *The legal process has ended, and visitation orders are place. Safety planning never ends, though, and power and control tactics continue around the children. In the years since my case with the Juvenile Dependency Court was dismissed, I have had to make many trips to Family Court to ensure visitation orders are clearly enforced, and to obtain a restraining order to keep us safe. Safety planning, like breathing, is an ongoing and essential part of my daily life.*

> *It is my responsibility to keep my children safe at all times. That means I have to keep myself safe. Both of my girls know about safety planning. We talk about code words to use, we talk about them calling me from the bathroom and turning on the water if they are at their dad's, or anywhere else where they don't feel safe. I continue to document concerns, power and control tactics, and violations of the restraining order and visitation orders. If I have to go back to Family Court again to ensure the safety of my children, I will have the evidence I need to support the legal process.*

> *Safety planning is also about prevention. Having learned about power and control tactics, I now know that they are not restricted to an intimate partner relationship. Power and control tactics can occur with platonic friends, with siblings, in work and educational settings. I am always alert for behaviors that could suggest power and control, and I am empowered enough to set healthy boundaries in any situation.*

> *In my experience as a Mentor Parent, I have seen first-hand the changes in the women who benefit from services that include drug treatment programs, domestic violence services and therapy, and the support of drug treatment courts.*

My heart breaks for the women who fall through the cracks. Some do not get domestic violence services because it was never reported and they are still with their perpetrator. Some are simply so deeply in denial about domestic violence, their addiction, or both, that they don't engage in all of the required and available services. These ladies come back into our system again and again, or they don't reunify.

It is so important to be aware of the trauma that we experience both as children and adults. Domestic violence causes trauma. Oftentimes, because we are using drugs, or we relapse to escape from current or historical trauma in our lives, we don't recognize domestic violence is playing a major role in our family dysfunction.

My life has dramatically changed because of the services that I received as part of my case plan. The combination of therapy, domestic violence support groups, and all of the services related to addiction were essential to my recovery, to my ability to stay sober and to heal. The frequent reviews and ongoing support of the Dependency Drug Treatment Court team provided additional incentive and support for me to stay enthusiastic and determined in my recovery process. The pieces came together for me, and have created a sense of wholeness in my being.

And my children: thanks to our continuing work on domestic violence and trauma prevention, my girls - especially my oldest daughter - has found her voice now, and not just with me but others as well. My youngest daughter has a voice, and does not mind using it. They continue to heal and thrive, and I have great hope for their futures. And in mine.

THE CHILD WELFARE WORKER

Why Does DDTC Work?

By Michele Dove, Drug Court Social Worker

I've been working in Child Welfare for more than 17 years; more than six of those years have been in the Dependency Drug Treatment Court (DDTC) Unit. As a the continuing social worker for the families I work with, I'm responsible for providing referrals to families, arranging placements, monitoring compliance and progress and ongoing risk and safety assessments (among other tasks). The majority of the families I work with are DDTC participants; however, I have also worked with a family in Family Wellness Court (FWC). I was a continuing worker in the mid-1990s and the job was basically the same. However, I have seen more parents succeed and more families reunited now because of DDTC and FWC than I saw previously with families who were not participants in DDTC.

So what's the difference? Why does DDTC Work? Is it me? Well, it's partly me, but it is also the holistic team approach that is the hallmark of successful treatment courts. I have to say that all of us have changed—social workers, attorneys, treatment providers, support persons and judges. Not only do we all work together and communicate more effectively with each other, we include the parents as part of the team. I have learned so much about addiction and recovery and some of my best teachers have been the parents in recovery.

There are a lot of support services for the parents, increased access to free services (such as individual therapy) and a lot more interaction with the parents. But it's not just that. Parents are given more support but are also held more accountable. I think personal accountability is one of the most important things for anyone in recovery, combined with having the support and services necessary to become a clean and sober person who can safely provide for their children.

I can honestly say that I have seen miracles happen. It's very rewarding to work in a treatment court and see parents reunite with their children, successfully have their case dismissed and <u>not come back into the system</u>.

THE SUBSTANCE ABUSE AND PARENTING EXPERT

How Addiction Impacts Children

By Rosemary Tisch

<u>Chemical Dependency: A Multi-Generational Family Disease</u>

"After supper pap took the jug, and said he had enough whisky there for two drunks and one delirium tremens...I judged he would be blind drunk in about an hour... all of a sudden there was an awful scream and I was up. There was pap looking wild, and skipping around every which way and yelling about snakes. He said they was crawling up his legs and then he would give a jump and scream, and say one had bit him on the cheek—but I couldn't see no snakes... By and by he rolled out and jumped up on his feet looking wild and he see me and went for me. He chased me round and round the place with a clasp-knife, calling me the Angel of Death, and saying he would kill me, and then I couldn't come for him no more. I begged, and told him I was 'only Huck' but he laughed such a *screechy* laugh, and roared and cussed, and kept on chasing me up..." ~ Mark Twain

For centuries we have known from our literature, and in our souls, the impact of chemical dependency on children and families. Today, parental substance abuse commonly involves alcohol in combination with other drugs (prescribed and illegal) as well as mental health problems, poverty, and violence. Addiction runs in families on one or both sides, from generation to generation. For families seen in Dependency Drug Treatment Courts and the child welfare system, the adult addict/alcoholic often will be the child or grandchild of an alcoholic/addict. Thus, it is likely they did not experience nurturing or a healthy family and probably have few innate parenting skills.

Addiction can have strong negative effects on marital relationships, including a high correlation with separation, divorce and family violence - adding to the impact on children. Addiction affects every member of the family, although each member may be affected differently. Think about a family sitting outside around a wood fire. There's a strong wind blowing from one side to the other. Children sitting with their backs to the wind love the smell of burning wood and looking at the stars. Children sitting with the wind in their faces have tears running down their faces from the smoke. Same place, same fire, but a very different experience!

Parents with the disease of chemical dependency love their children, but may not have the skills or abilities (even when sober) to express this love appropriately. Their parenting often is inconsistent, chaotic, and unpredictable. Multiple caregiving placements for a child are the norm. Consequences for children can include a lack of attachment to a significant adult; physical and emotional abuse or neglect; inadequate supervision; multiple separations and changes in residence; toxic substances in the home (meth labs and marijuana grow houses); interrupted and unsupported education; poverty; and exposure to criminal and inappropriate adult behavior. Parental substance abuse can compromise a child's development, as well as their mental, emotional and physical health at every stage from conception onwards.

Prenatal Exposure

Fetal alcohol spectrum disorders (FASD) are the leading cause of preventable mental retardation in the United States (Centers for Disease Control and Prevention, 2009). Yet, prenatal exposure to alcohol and other drugs has many significant harmful effects that may not rise to the level of mental retardation. Research shows negative impact on children's:

- Language skills, impulse control, visual attention (Pulsifer, Butz, O'Reilly Foran, Belcher, 2008).

- Memory deficits (Richardson, Ryan, Willard, Day, Goldschmidt, 2002).

- Cognitive deficits and altered brain structure, with shorter attention span, delayed memory, poorer long-term spatial memory and visual/motor integration (Chang, Smith, LoPresti, Yonekura, Kuo, Walot, Ernst, 2004).

Prenatal exposure to tobacco is particularly concerning, as many expectant mothers smoke—by one estimate, over 10 percent in the United States (Hamilton, Hamilton, Minino, Martin, Kochanek, Strobino, Guyer, 2007). In utero exposure to tobacco by-products has been linked to:

- Cognitive deficits (Dwyer, Broide, and Leslie, 2008).

- Greater visuospatial memory deficits (Jacobsen, Slotkin, Westerveld, Mencl, Pugh, 2006).

- Attention deficit hyperactivity disorder (ADHD) (Pauly and Slotkin, 2008).

Childhood

SAMHSA (Substance Abuse and Mental Health Services Agency, 2003) found that younger children are slightly more likely than older children to live with a parent with substance-abuse or substance-dependence. Why? Is the rate of addiction increasing? Are adults of child-rearing age more likely to be addicted? Have older children been removed from the families due to abuse/neglect? Have older children run away? Have parents entered recovery as they (and their children) age?

Having parents active in their addiction during a child's development can have long-term impact, as the basic, biological organization of the brain occurs principally between the ages of 0-5 (Commission on Children at Risk, 2003). At its peak the cerebral cortex creates an astonishing two million new synapses every second (Zero to Three, 2011). Brain development continues throughout our lives, proceeding to keep the synapses that are used and pruning away those that aren't. All of these processes - critical to emotional, physical and mental health - need to occur in the context of a relationship with another human, another brain. Some researchers now say that neglect can be more damaging to brain development than abuse (Randall, 2010).

"This relational context can be growth-facilitating or growth-inhibiting; imprinting into the developing brains either resilience against or a vulnerability to later forming psychiatric orders." (Commission on Children at Risk, Hardwired to Connect, 2003; Anda and Felitti, 2002).

Children of alcoholics are four times more likely than other children to develop addiction due to environmental and genetic factors. Children of alcoholics/addicts (and grandchildren and great-grandchildren) are more likely to:

- Exhibit symptoms of mental health disorders including depression, anxiety, ADHD (Attention Deficit Hyperactivity Disorders), compulsivity, and panic attacks more than children of nonalcoholics/addicts (National Association for Children of Alcoholics, NACoA, 1999).

- Experience greater physical and mental health problems, 1.5 times more injuries, and have a 32% greater rate of total health care costs (NACoA, 1999).

- Have difficulties with learning, memory and language, believe they will fail even if they are doing well, and score lower on tests measuring cognitive and verbal skills than children of nonalcoholics/addicts (NACoA, 1999).

- Have greater difficulty with abstraction and conceptual reasoning (important in problem solving), requiring very concrete explanations and instructions, especially if prenatally exposed to alcohol (NACoA, 1999).

- Are highly distrustful of others (NACoA, 1999).

- Tend towards dangerous play, early sexual promiscuity (and related teenage pregnancy), and engage in delinquent or criminal behavior (NACoA, 1999).

Parents with a chemical dependency focus on their alcohol or drug addiction, not their children. They, too, are more likely to have poor cognitive abilities and provide environments lacking stimulation. Some studies have found that learning disabilities are genetically linked with addiction. (Blum, Cull, Braverman and Cummings, 1996). Hence, parents cannot (not will not) provide supportive environments.

Yet somehow, some of these children bounce back resilient, learning to cope with life's difficulties. Why? How?

Teens

By the time a child of alcoholic/addict (COA/A) becomes a teen, the consequences of their childhood can include depression, hopelessness, suicide, and self-mutilation (NACoA, 1999). Often teen COA/As join gangs (to gain a sense of family), become sexually active and pregnant (in order to find relationships or love), drop out of or do poorly in school, have friends that smoke and use, or become involved in crime. One study found that two thirds of juveniles arrested reported a member of their family was abusing substances (Pritchard and Payne, 2005).

Adolescence is a tough time when one comes from a healthy family! It is a period of significant brain growth, maturation, and remodeling. Maturational changes are occurring in the prefrontal cortex and regions of the brain critical for cognitive functions such as judgment and insight. Adolescent risk-taking and novelty-seeking are connected to these changes in brain structure and function. 85% of all deaths among U. S. adolescents result from homicides, suicides and accidents (Commission on Children at Risk, 2003).

Adolescents need family values, limit-setting, structure, lots and lots of communication, and mentors, along with models for having fun that are safe and don't involve the use of alcohol and drugs. Parents active in their addiction have great difficulty providing these essentials.

Abuse, Neglect and Foster Children

Violence and child abuse are tightly related to substance abuse:

- Perpetrators are often under the influence of alcohol and other drugs with alcohol being a key factor in 68% of manslaughter, 62% of assaults, 54% of murders and attempted murders, 48% of robberies, and 44% of burglaries (At Health, 2011).

- Parental substance abuse is an underlying factor in as high as 80% of child abuse/neglect cases (CASA, 1999).

- The Dept. of Justice found that 61% of domestic violence offenders had substance abuse problems and that 36% of victims in domestic violence programs also had substance abuse problems (Collins and Spencer, 2002). Individuals with an alcohol or drug addiction and a problem with violence need treatment for both issues. Even if they become sober, the violence will not automatically stop (Center for Substance Abuse Prevention, 2004).

Studies indicate that youth who had been in foster care had higher rates of any illicit drug use than youth who had not (33.6% vs. 21.7%) (National Survey on Drug Use and Health, NSDUH, 2005):

- Older youths were more likely than younger youth to use alcohol or any illicit drug in the past year (NSDUH, 2005).

- White youth who have ever been in foster care were more likely than their black counterparts to have used alcohol (41.4% vs. 29.8%) or any illicit drug (36.2% vs. 26.7%) in the past year (NSDUH, 2005).

- There was little difference in alcohol or any illicit drug use by gender (NSDUH, 2005).

- Youth who have ever been in foster care had higher rates of need for substance abuse treatment compared with youths who have never been in foster care: 17.4% versus 8.8% (NSDUH, 2005).

- 81% of youth in foster care in 2003-04 needing treatment did not receive it, although foster care youth were more likely to have received treatment: 19.1% received treatment in the past year versus 7.2% of youth who have never been in foster care (NSDUH, 2005).

Percentages of Youths Aged 12 to 17 in Need of Substance Abuse Treatment, by Foster Care Status: 2002 and 2003. (National Survey on Drug Use and Health, NSDUH, 2005). Latest available data:

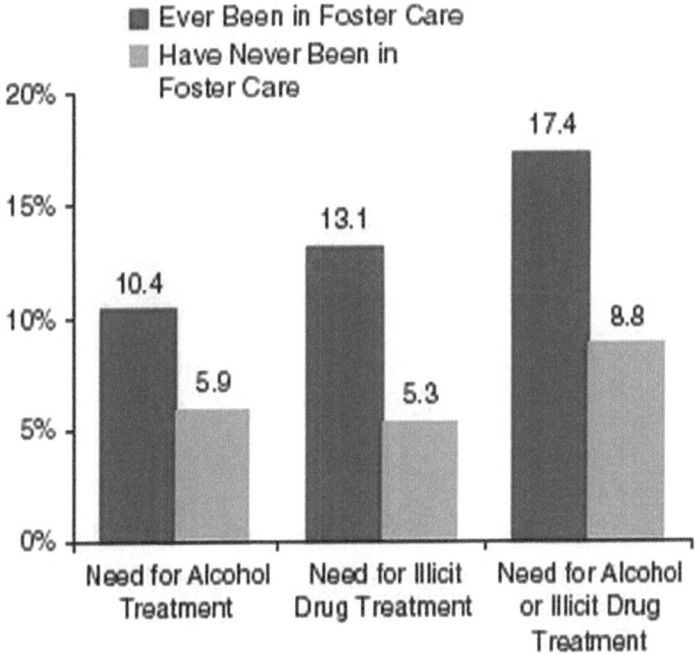

Currently, child welfare professionals working with youth from alcohol and drug abusing environments are seeing more respiratory distress (allergies, asthma), sleep disturbances, auditory and visual disturbances, seizures, and eating concerns (over/under eating and other food and trauma presentations). They urge professionals working with children of alcoholics/addicts, exposed in utero, and in the child welfare system to be cautious about:

- The use of aggregate scores (averages) for reporting testing results for cognitive disabilities, as they may give misleading results due to the "Swiss Cheese" profile of these children (Randall, 2010).

- The generalization of testing results into the indefinite future, as child outcomes can be affected by the child's development and other mediating factors referenced elsewhere in this chapter. Generalizing results can lead to the misinterpretation that findings are predictive into the indefinite future (Randall, 2010).

Links between childhood maltreatment and later-life health and well-being are well-documented in a study by the Center for Disease Control and Kaiser Permanente's Health Appraisal Clinic. This study identified key traumatic events which affect children's neurodevelopment and social, emotional, and cognitive impairments:

- Abuse: emotional, physical, and sexual

- Neglect: emotional, physical

- Witnessing domestic violence

- Growing up with parental substance abuse

- Mental illness, and

- Discord or crime in the home

The researchers labeled these experiences "Adverse Childhood Experiences" or "ACEs" (Anda, 2010). ACEs were found to lead to increased risk of unhealthy behaviors of violence or re-victimization, disease, disability and premature mortality. Related to addiction and families:

- The likelihood of injection of street drugs increased strongly and in a graded fashion with the ACE Score: a male child with an ACE Score of 6, when compared to a male child with an ACE Score of 0, has a 4,600% increase in the likelihood of becoming an injection drug user sometime later in life. (Felitti, 2003).

- The likelihood of adult alcoholism <u>increased 500%</u> in a strong, graded manner to adverse childhood experiences (Felitti, 2003).

"Our findings indicate that the major factor underlying addiction is adverse childhood experiences that have not healed with time... The ACE Study provides population-based clinical evidence that unrecognized adverse childhood experiences are a major, if not the major, determinant of who turns to psychoactive materials and becomes 'addicted.'" (Felitti, 2003).

Court Services, Child Welfare and Social Services

Foster children and children "at risk" for abuse/neglect are primarily children of alcoholics/addicts with environmental exposure and greater genetic vulnerability for cognitive deficits, mental and physical health problems, substance abuse, and other acting out behaviors (teen pregnancy, breaking the law). Research now shows a clear relationship of preschool age children's cognitive delays, abnormalities in brain systems, neurological development and abuse/neglect (Commission on Children at Risk, 2003; Chasnoff, 2010).

Dependency Courts, Child Welfare Agencies and Departments of Social Services are in a unique position to make a significant contribution in the lives of children with parents with substance abuse disorders. Although research has clearly shown the relationship of abuse/neglect and alcohol and other drugs, Family Court judges note it is often <u>not</u> included in the allegations contained in the neglect petition (New York State Office of Children and Family Services, 2008). Not identifying substance abuse/chemical dependency hampers service providers' ability to provide essential needed services for parents and children. Left unserved:

- Parents continue their addiction

- Parents relapse

- Children continue to be abused/neglected

- Children become addicts and addicted teenage parents

- Families continue to suffer

- Chemical dependency continues to progress and spread

So, What Can Be Done?

"We know that COAs are at greater risk in their lives. But we also know what to do to help them avoid repeating their families' problems. We can break the generational cycle of addiction" Charles G. Curie, former Administrator of SAMHSA (SAMHSA, 2003).

"Attachment may be the key to breaking the multi-generational cycle of addiction and abuse." (Felitti, 2003).

"New scientific findings are teaching us to marvel at how nature and nurture interact...Social contexts can alter genetic expression...Even neuronal regeneration is possible given the right 'environment.'" (Commission on Children at Risk, 2003).

Addiction is a brain disease with environmental and genetic components. Although children may be *predisposed* by their family environment and genetics, they are not *predestined* to become alcoholics or addicts. Environmental strategies can make a difference.

All work with children and families has to be done with respect and collaboration, validating their experiences without judgment or discrediting statements. (Remember, parents are likely adult children of alcoholics/addicts). Offer alternatives and provide coaching, while being careful to avoid telling participants what is best for them to do. Punitive approaches and shaming are not appropriate.

First, provide a safe, nurturing and consistent (structured and predictable) environment, free from violence, threat of violence, and substance abuse. Minimize the number of placements children experience, as several studies show the importance of keeping this number as small as possible. Help families create Family Safety Lists covering various emergency situations, including parental relapse. These lists can be posted wherever the family is living. Work <u>with</u> families, helping them to learn how to create their own solutions.

Second, help families identify the addiction and develop the ability to talk about it. This alone could lead to recovery for the parent(s). It is imperative for children to know that their parent's addiction is a disease that they (the children) did not cause, cannot cure, and cannot control. All family members need to learn:

- The characteristics of a "safe person"

- What is appropriate touch; what are their personal boundaries

- How to ask for help and how to say "no"

Third, identification of one or more safe people is critical for each family member. A safe person is someone they can turn to for support, nurturing (relationship, unconditional love), help, and safety. This may be a sponsor, relative, neighbor, social worker, coach, a Sunday school teacher or then neighborhood's "cookie lady." Guide children and family members to identify their safe person by asking questions: "What happens when they are angry"? "Can you talk with them about your friends"? "Do they judge you"? "Does this person use drugs or drink alcohol"?

My Kind and Loving Grandfather

My name is Rob. I'm 75 years old. When I was two and three years old, I lived a few blocks from my grandpa. He loved me with a devotion and consistency like no one else I ever knew. Grandpa took me to the duck pond; he took me to the roundhouse to climb into a train locomotive. In late 1939, when I was three and a half, he had a bad heart attack, and had to lie in bed all the time. That's when he taught me the 23rd Psalm and the Lord's Prayer. Most of all, every single time he saw me, Grandpa said, "Robbie, I love you up to the skies and back again."

He loved me, and I loved him! Always!! In 1941, my world darkened. We moved to Berkeley. Grandpa died. The Japanese bombed Pearl Harbor. My dad was a Regular Army officer. He was sometimes really nice, but a lot of times got really mad, really fast. Living with him was like living in a minefield. When I was a grown-up, married and had my own kids, my mom blew her brains out. I didn't see it happen, but I saw her a little while later.

Many years later, I was able to heal my heart and soul. Some people say I am strong and wise. I have two younger brothers. They have never healed. They never will. Neither of them ever knew my Grandpa. I could always feel my Grandpa's love and kindness – it convinced the Little Boy in me that I was lovable (Lancefield, 2011).

Resiliency research has shown that having one person that a child can turn to can make a difference (Henderson, 2007). Don't ever underestimate the impact that one person can have in the life of a child.

Critical Family Factors

The United Nations Office on Drugs and Crime (UNODC, 2009) identified the following critical family factors that may help protect children from substance abuse:

- Secure attachment with safe individuals

- Secure and healthy parent/child attachment

- Parental supervision, with consistent, fair discipline and monitoring

- Communication of pro-social family values

- Parental involvement in child's life

- Supportive parenting (emotionally, cognitively, socially and financially)

- Organized family environment with consistency of activities (e.g. bedtimes), family meals and rituals

- Encouragement to become independent

- Family problem-solving and coping skills, especially when under stress

Professionals Can Make The Difference

You can help your families succeed by providing:

1. Family skill building programs that serve the whole family. Programs should be developed for parents, caregivers, and ALL children - not just the identified alcoholic/addict and their partner. The entire system around a child needs to reinforce the same behaviors (skills) and be able to talk about addiction, family violence and abuse/neglect. Include any significant caregivers or adults in the child's life, such as foster families or extended relatives that are raising the children. Family skill-building programs have been found to be effective in preventing many risky behaviors and to change family functioning and parenting practices in long-term positive ways. Parent education programs have not been found to be as effective (UNODC, 2009).

2. <u>Services utilizing multi-modal, interactive teaching strategies</u>. Most family members in your programs will have some level of cognitive deficits due to chaos, stress, detoxing, in-utero exposure, or abuse. Programs need to be appropriate for individuals with limited cognitive abilities and learning disabilities or differences. Many of the individuals you are working with cannot (versus will not) comprehend what you are asking them to do.

3. <u>Services teaching basic social skills.</u> Instructional techniques need to utilize specific skill steps, role plays, practice and feedback with everyone in the family learning the same skills in developmentally-appropriate ways. (It is critical that staff in sober living environments, group homes, juvenile hall or prisons, also learn these skills in order to reinforce individuals' attempts to use the skills.) As chemical dependency can impact multiple generations, programs need to teach <u>basic</u> social skills, including:

   - Simple centering or stress reduction – taking four deep breaths when feeling overwhelmed or before attempting difficult conversations or situations

   - Communication and listening

   - Understanding what healthy and abusive relationships/ friendships are; how to make friends; and understanding the impact friends have on our values and behavior

   - Social competencies of anger management/conflict resolution, decision making, goal setting, and the ability to say "no" (refusal skills)

   - Individual and family values or norms, family rules and consequences

4. <u>Programs reducing a family's risk factors, enhancing their protective factors, and increasing Developmental Assets.</u> Curricula need to specifically address Risk Factors (Hawkins, Lishner, Catalano, and Howard, 1986):

- Availability of alcohol, tobacco, prescription and illegal drugs at home

- Parental drug use (role modeling)

- Permissive parental attitudes towards use (limit setting with consequences)

- Child's early mental health needs

- Peers who use drugs

- Child's favorable attitudes toward drug use

- Social isolation of families

- Family management problems (lack of supervision, severe or inconsistent discipline)

- Lack of family rituals and dinners

- Poor family management and communication

Family Rituals may be a part of their daily routine (e.g. meals, weekend sports, church) as well as holidays and occasions that are special in the culture of the family:

- Christmas, Easter, Passover, Independence Day

- Birthdays, graduations, weddings, funerals, baptisms, bar mitzvahs

- Family holiday trips, community or school events

Establishing safe, drug/alcohol free, family rituals is not easy for families riddled with addiction. Relatives may have to be told not to come or that they must not be under the influence. (Sometimes a family has to disconnect from other family members). Parents may have *never* before eaten a quiet meal or played with their children.

Services need to help parents learn how to talk with their children and model mealtimes free of phones, texting, television/internet, and chaos.

Even if the addiction continues, if families can safely continue traditions it makes a difference for the children.

> *"…..On Christmas Eve, Dad took each of us kids out into the desert night one by one…I was five that year, and I sat next to Dad and we looked up at the sky. Dad loved to talk about the stars. He explained to us how they rotated through the night sky as the Earth turned. He taught us to identify the constellations and how to navigate by the North Star. Those shining stars, he liked to point out, were one of the special treats for people like us who hiked out in the wilderness.*
>
> *"Pick out your favorite star," Dad said that night. He told me I could have it for keeps. He said it was my Christmas present. "You can't give me a star!" I said. "No one owns the stars." "That's right," Dad said. "No one else owns them. You just have to claim it before anyone else does."* (Walls, 2005, pp.39-40).

While addressing Risk Factors, programs also need to increase <u>Protective Factors</u>, many of which have already been discussed. The development of strong bonds between parents and children, critical to children's' healthy brain development, is risky, difficult, and essential. Skills helping to establish bonds that can be taught and nurtured are:

- Development of parents and caregiver's ability to set clear, nurturing limits/rules with consistent enforced consequences

- Clear, honest respectful communication

SEARCH Institute has identified 40 Developmental Assets critical for young people to thrive (SEARCH Institute 2002; 2006). Thankfully, many are similar to Protective Factors. Unique is the emphasis on providing a "reason to be":

- Sense of purpose, hope, self-esteem, and a positive view of personal future and power

- Purpose (being of service to others and valued; having high expectations and values of integrity, honesty, restraint, and respect)

- Ability to see beauty in the world

- Connection with caring and religious communities

5. Help children develop attachment to their parent, who may have lacked (or still lacks) the ability to care for them due to their disease. Children need to believe their parent loves them (no matter what) and that they can depend on the parent to keep them safe. Steps in this process for parents are:

- Learning how to tell each child "I love you" at least once a week (to begin). Service providers need to work with parents about their feelings of fear and rejection. (Remember they too are probably children of alcoholics and may never have heard these words from their parents). Help them identify a safe time to share with their children and talk about their expectations. (Children may not respond or may respond with anger when they hear these words).

- Developing "parting rituals" – how to say good-bye whether for a short time (a meeting) or when their child returns to the foster family after a visit. (There is a lovely book called *The Kissing Hand* by Audrey Penn that may be helpful).

- Learning skills to build consistent, safe, predictable relationships. Utilizing strength-based, empowering models, service providers need to teach the importance of consistent schedules (bedtimes, mealtimes), and limit-setting with consequences, based on children's developmental stage. Consistency helps build trust and brains!

- Developing their own relationships with safe individuals, which increases their chances of staying clean and children's chances of living a safe, healthy, addiction-free life.

6. And, if your role allows, <u>help individuals develop empathy and to expand their world view</u> by learning to give to others and to see beauty in the world:

- Provide opportunities to be of service to others (doing a kind thing for someone else, such as helping a neighbor carry groceries, washing dishes when not your turn, reading a story to a younger child).

- Help each family member see the beauty of the world around them. Share about something that touched you. Ask about an experience that "touched" them – baking cookies, wildflowers in bloom, a caterpillar moving up their arm. Do this regularly.

- Be a model. Be of service yourself; regularly see beauty in your world.

These skills seem abstract, but with guidance and modeling, professionals and other safe people can draw children and adults to these assets. It may seem strange for a judge or social worker to be asking or sharing at this level. Drug court judges know the importance of developing a relationship with the individual. (The relationship between judges and offenders is central to Drug Courts' success (Tauber and Huddleston, 1999). Addiction is about the brain (dopamine reward systems), which need to re-calibrate in recovery. These activities and observations are small steps in this process.

Conclusion

Although children of alcoholics/addicts are at extremely high risk both environmentally and genetically, they are not pre*destined* to repeat the cycles of substance abuse and family violence. Child Welfare Agencies, Departments of Social Services, and the Courts are critical players in helping children develop the skills that protect and repair their brains and their lives. There are simple things you can do to make the difference for a child's future mental, physical, and emotional life:

- Practice acts of kindness and compassion: be available to listen, discuss their feelings, share interests and support children's efforts to make friends. Let them know they matter to you.

- Encourage children to ask for help: Assure them that getting help is a sign of strength. Ask whether they have a safe adult to talk with. Explain there are responsible adults available to help. Offer your own examples and be prepared to help them connect with caring, trustworthy adults.

- Be sensitive to clues about their friendships, achievements, and their home situation.

- Validate that they are not alone: one in four children grow up with a parent that abuses alcohol and other drugs. There are lots of people with similar life experiences who grow up to lead happy, healthy, satisfying lives.

- Share what you know about the disease of addiction.

- Help them understand that their parents have a disease. Explain their parents love them, although they may not be able to appropriately show it due to the disease. Repeatedly share that their family's problems are neither their fault nor their responsibility to solve.

- Remind them their job is to be a child. Help them to learn the facts about alcohol, tobacco and other drugs; to recognize their own risks; to learn how to avoid repeating their family disease of addiction; and to understand the 4 C's: You didn't <u>cause</u> the disease (of addiction), you can't <u>cure</u> it, you can't <u>control</u> it, but you can help take <u>care</u> of yourself.

Resources

Addiction Series – a feature length documentary available from www. HBO.com/addiction. Click on the far right link "The Films" to view online or purchase through the HBO Shop link at HBO.com.

Al-Anon Family Groups, "What's 'Drunk' Mama"?, Al-Anon Family Group Headquarters, Virginia Beach, VA, 1977.

Amen, Dan, - Has a number of DVD's and books that are valuable, including, "Which Brain Do You Want"? Available at www. mindworkspress.com.

Anda, Robert, MD, "Health and Social Impact of Growing Up with Alcohol Abuse and Related Adverse Childhood Experiences." Available at www.celebratingfamilies.net/pdf/RobertAnda_article.pdf.

Black, Claudia, Has a number of books and CDs, including "It Will Never Happen To Me"; "My Dad Loves Me"; "My Dad Has A Disease"; 3rd Edition, and "Straight Talk". Available at www. claudiablack.com.

Brooks, Cathleen, "The Secret Everyone Knows", Hazelden Educational Materials, Center City, MN, 1981.

Brown, Stephanie, Ph.D., and Abbott, Stephanie, M.A., *Children of Alcoholics* in "Family Therapy", 2005. Available at www. celebratingfamilies.net/pdf/Abbott-Brown_article.pdf.

"Celebrating Families!" is an evidence-based cognitive behavioral, support group model written for families in which one or both parents have a serious problem with alcohol or other drugs and in which there is a high risk for domestic violence, child abuse, or neglect. Available at www.celebratingfamilies.net.

Chasnoff, Ira, J., MD, "The Mystery of Risk: Drugs, Alcohol, Pregnancy, and the Vulnerable Child", NTI Upstream, Chicago, IL, 2010.

Children's Program Kit. Available through NACoA.

Dayton, Tian, Ph.D., TEP, "The Set Up: Living with Addiction", Available at www.celebratingfamilies.net/pdf/TianDayton_article.pdf.

"Faces and Voices of Recovery", available at www. facesandvoicesofrecovery.org.

Gould, Thomas, J., Ph.D., "Addiction and Cognition", Addiction Science and Clinical Practice, December, 2010.

Join Together, available at http://www.jointogether.org.

Krull, Kenny, Kevin and Helen, Sometimes My Mom Drinks Too Much. Raintree Children's Books, Milwaukee, WI, 1980.

McCloud, Carol. Have You Filled A Bucket Today?, (Paperback Edition), 2006.

National Association for Children of Alcoholics (NACoA) - www.nacoa.org.

National Center on Addiction and Substance Abuse at Columbia (CASA) - www.casacolumbia.org.

National Center on Substance Abuse and Child Welfare (NCSACW) - www.ncsacw.samhsa.gov.

National Clearinghouse for Alcohol and Drug Information (NCADI) - www.ncadi.samhsa.gov.

National Institute on Alcohol Abuse and Alcoholism (NIAAA) = www.niaaa.nih.gov.

National Institute on Drug Abuse (NIDA) - www.nida.nih.org.

Nurturing Parenting Programs (NPP) are family-based programs for the prevention and treatment of child abuse and neglect. Nurturing Families - www.nurturingparenting.com.

Penn, Audrey. The Kissing Hand, Child and Family Press, 1993.

"Recovering Hope: Mothers Speak Out About FASD", available at SAMHSA's FASD Center for Excellence -https://ncadistore.samhsa.gov/catalog/SC_ItemList.aspx.

"Recovering Together", a substance abuse treatment program for the whole family. Curriculum available on-line at http://www.claritycounseling.com/OpenRTPdisc.html.

Strengthening Families Program (SFP) is a family skills training program designed to increase resilience and reduce risk factors for behavioral, emotional, academic, and social problems in children 3-16 years old. Strengthening Families - www.strengtheningfamilies.org.

Substance Abuse and Mental Health Services Administration (SAMHSA) - www.samhsa.gov.

Sweeney, Joan. Me and My Family Tree, Crown Publishers, (Paperback Edition), 1999.

Yeh, Emerald, Lost Childhood – DVD available through the National Association for Children of Alcoholics (NACoA).

References

Anda, R., "The health and social impact of growing up with alcohol abuse and related adverse childhood experiences: The human and economic costs of the status quo", www.nacoa.org/pdfs/AndaNACoAReview_web.pdf, 2010.

Anda, R., and Felitti, V., "The Relationship of Adverse Childhood Experiences to Adult Health Status", U. S. Dept. of Health and Human Services, Administration for Children and Families, Child Welfare Information Gateway - www.childwelfare.gov/calendar/cbconference/fourteenth/presentations/ahdc/sld046.cfm, 2011.

At Health, "Children of Alcoholics: Important Facts", www.athealth.com/consumer/disorders/coafacts.html, 2011.

Blum, K., Cull J., Braverman E., Cummings D., "Reward Deficiency Syndrome", The American Scientist, March-April 1996; http://www.lifeskillsu.org/campus/campus_key/rdj/reward_deficiency.html, 2011.

Brookoff, D., O'Brien, K., Cook, C., Thompson, T., Williams, C., 1997. "Characteristics of Participants in Domestic Violence: Assessment at the Scene of Domestic Assault", Journal of American Medical Association (JAMA), 1997; pp. 277(17), 1369-1373; www.jama.ama-assn.org, 2011.

CASA, "No safe haven: Children of substance-abusive parents", Columbia University Center for Addiction and Substance Abuse, 1999; www.casacolumbia.org/templates/publications_reports.aspx, 2010.

CASA, "Family Matters: Substance Abuse and The American Family", A CASA White Paper, 2005; http://www.casacolumbia.org/templates/publications_reports.aspx?keywords=family, 2011.

Center for Substance Abuse Prevention (CSAP), Prevention Pathways Online Courses, "It Won't Happen to Me: Substance Abuse-Related Violence Against Women for Anyone Concerned About The Issues", 2004; http://pathwayscourses.samhsa.gov/vawc/vawc_10_pg1.htm, 2011.

Centers for Disease Control and Prevention, "Fetal Alcohol Spectrum Disorders Fact Sheet", 2009; http://www.cdc.gov/ncbddd/actearly/pdf/hcp_pdfs/FactSheets.pdf, 2011.

Chang, L., Smith, L., LoPresti, C., Yonekura, M. L., Kuo, J., Walot, I., Ernst, T., "Smaller subcortical volumes and cognitive deficits in children with prenatal methamphetamine exposure", <u>Psychiatry Research: Neuroimaging</u>, 132(2), 2004, pp. 95-106.

Chasnoff, I. J., <u>The Mystery of Risk: Drugs, Alcohol, Pregnancy, and the Vulnerable Child</u>. NTI Upstream, Chicago, 2010.

Collins, J., and Spencer. D., "Linkage of Domestic Violence and Substance Abuse Services, Research in Brief, Executive Summary", U. S. Department of Justice, 2002.

Commission on Children at Risk, "Hardwired to Connect", The New Scientific Case for Authoritative Communities. co-sponsored by YMCA of the USA, Dartmouth Medical School, and Institute for American Values, 2003; http://www.americanvalues.org/html/hardwired_press_release.html, 2011.

Dwyer, J. B., Broide, R. S., and Leslie, F. M., "Nicotine and Brain Development-Birth Defects Research Part ", <u>Embryo Today: Reviews</u>,84(1), 2008, pp. 30-44.

Felitti, V. J., "The Origins of Addiction: Evidence from the Adverse Childhood Experiences Study", Kaiser Permanente Medical Care Program, San Diego, CA, 2003.

Hamilton, B. E., Minino, A., Martin, J., Kochanek, K., Strobino, D., Guyer, B., "Annual summary of vital statistics: 2005", <u>Pediatrics</u>, 119(2), 2008, pp. 345-360.

Hawkins, J. D., Lishner, D. M., Catalano, R. F., and Howard, M. O., <u>Childhood Predictors of Adolescent Substance Abuse: Toward an Empirically Grounded Theory</u>. New York: Haworth Press, 1986.

Henderson, N., "Resiliency In Action: Practical Ideas for Overcoming Risks and Building Strengths in Youth, Families, and Communities", Resiliency In Action, Inc., 2007.

Jacobsen, L. K., Slotkin, T., Westerveld, M., Mencl, W. E., Pugh, K., "Visuospatial memory deficits emerging during nicotine withdrawal in adolescents with prenatal exposure to active maternal smoking", Neuropsychopharmacology, 31(7), 2006, pp.1550-1561.

Lancefield, R., "My Kind and Loving Grandfather Written in honor of Jacob Kanzler, 1876-1940", Unpublished private correspondence", 2011.

NACoA (National Association for Children of Alcoholics), "Children of Alcoholics Important Facts", 1999; http://www.nacoa. org/impfacts.htm, 2011.

National Survey on Drug Use and Health (NSDUH), "Substance use and need for treatment among youths who have been in foster care", www.oas.samhsa.gov/2k5/FosterCare/FosterCare.htm, 2005.

New York State Office of Children and Family Services, "Gearing up to Improve Outcomes for Children", Pub. 5073, 6/2008. New York State Collaborative Practice Guide Managers and Supervisors in Child Welfare, Chemical Dependency, and Court Systems, 2008; http://www.ocfs.state.ny.us/main/publications/Pub5073.pdf, 2010.

Pauly, J. R., and Slotkin, T. A., "Maternal tobacco smoking, nicotine replacement and neurobehavioural development", Acta Paediatrica 97(10), 2008, pp. 1331-1337.

Prichard, J., and Payne, J., "Alcohol, drugs and crime: a study of juveniles in detention", Research and Public Policy Series, No. 67, Canberra: Australian Institute of Criminology, 2005.

Pulsifer, M. B., Butz, A., O'Reilly-Foran, M., Belcher, H., "Prenatal drug exposure: Effects on cognitive functioning at 5 years of age", Clinical Pediatrics 47(1), 2008, pp. 58-65.

Randall, K. F., "Drug Endangered Children: Ecology, Psychological Profiles and Long Term Risk", 7th Annual National Drug Endangered Children Conference Presentation, 11.10.2010; http://www.nationaldec.org/goopages/pages_downloadgallery/download.php?filename=3828_7969669.pdfandorig_name=Psychosocial Needs of DEC ppt 9.17.08.pdf, 2011.

Richardson, G. A., Ryan, C., Willford, J, Day, N. and Goldschmidt, L., 2002. "Prenatal alcohol and marijuana exposure: Effects on neuropsychological outcomes at 10 years", Neurotoxicology and Teratology 24(3), 2002, pp. 309-320.

Search Institute. "The Asset Approach: 40 elements of healthy development", (2003; 2006); http://www.search-institute.org/developmental-assets/lists, 2011.

Substance Abuse and Mental Health Services Agency, "Children Living with Substance-Abusing or Substance-Dependent Parent", 2003; http://www.oas.samhsa.gov/2k3/children/children.pdf, 2011.

Tauber, J., and Huddleston, C. W., DWI/Drug Courts: Defining a National Strategy, 1999; www.maafirm.com/files/dwi_courts_national_stategy.pdf, 2011.

Twain, Mark, The Adventures of Huckleberry Finn (Tom Sawyer's Comrade). Harper and Brothers Edition, P. F. Collier and Son Company, 1912.

UNODC (United Nations Office on Drugs and Crime), Guide to implementing family skills training programmes for drug abuse prevention, United Nations 2009; www.unodc.org/pdf/youthnet/familybased/FINAL_ENGLISH_versionforPRINTINGreceived120209.pdf, 2011.

Walls, J., The Glass Castle – A Memoir. Scribner, New York, NY 10020, 2005.

Zero to Three, FAQ's on the Brain", http://www.zerotothree.org/child-development/brain-development/faqs-on-the-brain.html, 2011.

THE CHILD ADVOCATE

Child Advocates' Involvement in the Drug Treatment Courts of Santa Clara County

Vickie Scott Grove, Executive Director

Child Advocates of Silicon Valley has served abused and neglected children in the Santa Clara County dependency system since 1986. Our volunteers serve the dependency court as Court Appointed Special Advocates (CASAs) and spend time each week with their child, becoming a trusted friend, mentor, and consistent adult presence. Their court appointment allows them to work with foster parents, teachers, social workers, counselors and others to gain a complete picture of the child's life and needs. By knowing the child, the volunteer Advocate becomes a powerful, independent voice for the child when placement and other key decisions are being made.

Working with the family-focused drug courts over the years has given Child Advocates the opportunity to develop a more collaborative and system-informed approach. We have been able to join in the design of new initiatives such as the Family Wellness Court (FWC) to ensure that our volunteers (over 450 each year) can work effectively with other court partners while serving the youngest, and often most at-risk, of our children. We serve approximately 600 children a year, and almost 20% are ages zero to five years old. Our experience has also allowed us to understand the reservations that some volunteers bring to working with fragile families, who may be impacted by many stigmas – addiction, domestic violence, mental illness, illegal immigration status – and to begin to address their concerns. This support is provided from our very first CASA training sessions, continuing education workshops, discussion groups and individual staff support.

By building the capacity of our volunteers to work with very young children, their biological parents, extended family and the network of providers serving these families, we feel we have made a lasting difference in the lives of these children and many generations to come.

Special Concerns for Advocates

As our agency prepared for the launch of the FWC, essentially a second generation Dependency Drug Treatment Court (DDTC), we took time to review our ten years of experience in working with drug court families with a special interest in examining any demands and risks of a higher level of involvement with parents. Essentially, the focus was on evaluating whether Advocates could work effectively with families without compromising their ability to place a child's interests first. It was foremost in our minds to protect that role. We also wanted to identify ways to better equip our Advocates for the challenges of engaging with struggling families. We met with all of our partners to address these concerns and solicit their input on areas of expertise needed by our volunteers. The overriding conclusion of all parties was that Advocates working with FWC cases could act as a role model and provide support for parents while also keeping their focus on the child. The outstanding achievement of this program – 76% family reunification – certainly encouraged our consideration of these issues.

Family Wellness Court (FWC)

On November 13, 2007, the Santa Clara County Board of Supervisors granted the Department of Family and Children Services (DFCS) authority to work with specific community partners to create a dependency drug treatment court for mothers with children age zero to three.

This first of its kind program received a five-year federal grant with matching funds and in-kind services from FIRST 5. The FWC core team members evolved to include judicial officers, social workers, parents' attorneys, children's attorneys, attorneys for the DFCS, representatives from FIRST 5, Department of Alcohol and Drug Services, Department of Mental Health, Domestic Violence and Trauma Services, and Child Advocates of Silicon Valley. FWC also developed collaborative relationships with over 80 community partners, who offer services and support to children and families in the dependency system.

Goals of FWC

The Family Wellness Court has two overarching goals:

- To build on the success of the Dependency Drug Treatment Court (DDTC), which has operated in Santa Clara County for ten years. A national study has shown the DDTC to be highly effective for families in the child welfare system. The FWC adds additional enhancements to this model and targets 100 families per year who have a very young child (ages zero to three) and who are struggling with methamphetamine or other substance use. In addition to the expansion of services, the focus of the Court includes immediate access to services for the parents and access to developmental services for the child when appropriate.

- To assure sustainability through the integration of services and inter-agency fiscal planning.

Five Primary Objectives of FWC

The FWC offers a ground-breaking model for working with children and families. Its primary objectives are:

1. Early identification of and intervention for parents who are using/abusing methamphetamine and other substances and who have children ages zero to three.

2. Rapid engagement and successful retention in treatment and care for parents with children ages zero to three.

3. Reduction in subsequent births to mothers who are abusing methamphetamine and other substances and have children in the dependency system.

4. Early identification of and appropriate services for children ages zero to three who are exposed to parental substance abuse and have suspected/known developmental delays, disabilities and/ or other concerns.

5. To create a Comprehensive System of Care across all systems serving children who are in out-of-home placement or at risk of out-of-home placement as a result of their parents' methamphetamine and other substance abuse.

The development of the goals and objectives of the FWC was a collaborative process led by two dependency judges, which included all initial and potential court partners. All agencies participated in the extensive one year planning process and came to a share vision of the goals and objectives. They also participated in drafting policies and procedures, in understanding every partner's unique role and in considering ways to adapt their own services to better serve the participating families and children.

Child Advocates as a Drug Court Partner

Child Advocates works in partnership with the many members of the court team - social workers, substance abuse experts, mental health experts, housing experts, attorneys, service providers, and the judge, as well as other professionals. Staff and Advocates attend the weekly FWC pre-hearing team meetings, hearings and Family Team Meetings (case planning meetings with the parents and social workers). The opportunity for Advocates and professionals to meet and discuss a case in such depth is unique to these courts. Through these discussions, the entire team becomes invested in the success of the parents. Staff members also act as a liaison between the court and our Advocates, relaying current information about the child and family and providing feedback from other service providers and the Court.

The Drug Court Advocate's Role

We are often asked, "What does an Advocate do for such a young child? How do they help the Drug Court team"? As these families have a reunification plan in place, the Advocate's role is somewhat different than that of volunteers supporting children in long-term foster placement. Key responsibilities include:

- providing a consistent and affirming presence in the child's life,

- being vigilant of the child's development and surroundings, ensuring a safe, appropriate environment,

- showing parents how to stimulate development and engage an infant or toddler,

- assuring that the child is receiving all needed assessments and services,

- communicating with the child's caregivers, biological parents, and FWC team members and service providers,

- offering support to the family throughout the court case and supporting good parenting practices,

- after dismissal, following up with the family and child for post-termination check-ins.

Child Advocate Goals for Serving our Drug Courts

Although it would be ideal for each child under supervision to have an Advocate, the number of available Advocates is limited. To date, Child Advocates has met its goal of providing Advocates to 30 - 40% of our total drug court cases. Over the last three years, we have increased the number of very young children we serve from 13% of our caseload to over 18%. Due to the challenges of assigning volunteers mentioned above, we have added age-specific content to our required 30 hours of initial training and featured experienced Advocates who have worked effectively with drug court families as speakers.

Site-Based Advocacy for FWC

In addition to our drug court advocacy programs, Child Advocates has partnered with residential substance abuse treatment facilities for mothers and their children to provide site-based Advocates. These Advocates expand our capacity to serve as they are stationed at the facility and can work with two to five children at a time. They can also help prioritize children and mothers most in need of a volunteer Advocate. By collaborating with facility staff, site-based Advocates develop a close working relationship, become knowledgeable about the facilities' programs and procedures and are able to offer consistent support to the mothers and children.

Increased Training and Support

Given the unique role of the Advocate in the drug courts, the agency recognizes that providing increased support and specific trainings to these Advocates increases their ability to work with families and contribute to the drug court team. We coach volunteers to be forthcoming with parents about their focus on the best interests of the child. Over the last several years, the agency has offered workshops on early childhood development, attachment disorder, the effect of trauma on early childhood, working with very young children, working with parents recovering from addiction and related topics. In addition, notices of relevant community trainings are emailed to Advocates to attend at their convenience. The Court and its partners support an annual conference and periodic trainings on topics specifically related to families in the drug courts, which are offered at no cost to Advocates. All of these trainings count toward the Advocate's requirement of 12 hours of continuing education each year.

Child Advocates also offers a monthly discussion group focused on drug court cases facilitated by staff. This group offers Advocates a chance to discuss their children's cases with their peers and agency supervisors and to talk about their experiences on their case in relation to substance abuse, the treatment courts, and child development.

One Family's Story (names have been changed to ensure confidentiality)

Jenny grew up in Santa Clara County, California. She never met her father; she was raised by her mom; a single parent. However, her mom remarried, and Jenny's new step-father regularly beat Jenny's mom. Jenny regularly witnessed this abuse. Jenny started using drugs at 13 years old and had her first child at age 16. The child's paternal relatives assumed primary care of her first child. Jenny moved away from California, and over the next 11 years, she had two more children. The father of her children was incarcerated for possession of 400 pounds of marijuana, and Jenny moved back to California.

Now a single parent, Jenny's stress and desperation increased. She started using cocaine, marijuana, and methamphetamine heavily and soon became homeless for a period of time.

One December night, Jenny parked her car while both of her children were asleep. Jenny left one child asleep in the car as she took the other child in the house. Distracted by a phone call, she left her younger child in the car longer than she had planned. Someone called the authorities, and Jenny spent the night at the County Correctional Facility while the Department of Family and Child Services (DFCS) investigated. Jenny's children were removed from her custody and placed with their paternal grandparents. Prior to this incident, DFCS had already received reports of suspected abuse on the children. Despite the seriousness of her situation, Jenny was in denial regarding the severity of her drug use and was not compliant with her court-ordered services. Jenny continued to use cocaine, marijuana, and crystal methamphetamine. At that point, the courts stopped Family Reunification services; and Jenny's parental rights were terminated.

The following February, Jenny had a baby, Molly, with her new boyfriend, Adam. Adam also had a history of drug and alcohol abuse. Molly was born with a positive toxicology screen for methamphetamine. The family was determined to meet admission criteria and was entered into Family Wellness Court. In March Joanne, a Child Advocate was assigned to Molly. Joanne visited Jenny, Molly, and Adam regularly, offering support and a listening ear. She monitored Molly's development, helped Jenny and Adam bridge extended family relationships and watched Molly so Jenny could attend her support groups and classes. This time Jenny worked her way through the services ordered by the court. She attended substance abuse treatment, Alcoholics Anonymous groups, and parenting classes. Jenny enrolled in community college to become a lab technician and embraced her sobriety and her child.

Joanne continued to visit Jenny and Molly when they were placed at House on the Hill (temporary shelter placement facility), as they moved to a Transitional Housing Unit (THU), and as they moved into Adam's family home. Joanne supported the family as they went through many changes, cheered them on as they experienced success, and offered reflection when needed; she remained consistent, present, and accessible. The DFCS Social Worker reported, "Jenny has great insight into her past behaviors...she is strong and confident...Jenny is taking charge of her life...She is determined to remain clean, sober, and provide for her children..." Early in the following year, Jenny and Adam's Dependency case was dismissed, and they successfully graduated from FWC. Although the court case was closed, Joanne continues to receive updates and pictures from a very thankful Jenny. Molly is happy, safe, and doing very well in the care of her mother and father.

The judge overseeing the FWC at the time - Judge Erica Yew - made the following comment on Child Advocates' contribution to the Family Wellness Court, "The Advocates do so much -- like Joanne -- in supporting the child as well as the parents. Joanne helped the mother bridge with the grandmother and helped to heal their relationship. Since some of the children are so young, the Advocates are the court's eyes and ears and can provide additional tangible support like the diapers, clothes, and baby items that Child Advocates has donated. Thanks so much for all that you do!"

THE CHILD SPECIALIST

The Zero to Five Professionals: FIRST 5 Santa Clara County

By Melanie Daraio

FIRST 5 is an advocate for all young children in Santa Clara County. Of particular concern are children under the age of 5 who are abused or neglected and involved in the child welfare system. These children often lack loving, consistent caregiving that is necessary for oral language development, nurturing relationships, effective health care and early intervention services.

These are the county's most vulnerable children. Many are born premature or low birth weight and have been exposed to toxic substances like drugs or alcohol. They may have serious medical problems and developmental and/or behavioral challenges. If left unaddressed these children may drop out of school, become teen parents, homeless or become entangled in the criminal justice system (Dicker, 2009).

Jolene Smith, CEO of FIRST 5 explains, "We partnered with the dependency and child welfare systems because we wanted to impact the intergenerational cycle of children born to parents who experience trauma and struggle with substance abuse, many of whom are former foster youth themselves". In discussing existing drug court practices she states, "In general most of the drug treatment courts have been adult focused. We have the opportunity and more importantly the responsibility to shift the focus to a child centered, family focused approach embedded within a social ecological model".

In 2000 the Board on Children, Youth and Families, the National Research Council and the Institute of Medicine published the book <u>From Neurons to Neighborhoods: the Science of Early Childhood Development</u>. The publication sought to evaluate and integrate knowledge about the field of early childhood development. The study analyzed research in neurobiology, behavior and social sciences regarding young children and emphasized four core concepts as fundamental to understand the needs of young children:

- Importance of early life experiences as well as the inseparable and highly interactive influences of genetics and environment, on the development of the brain and the unfolding of human behavior,

- The central role of early relationship as a source of either support and adaptation or risk and dysfunction,

- The powerful capabilities, complex emotions, and essential social skills that develop during the earliest years of life,

- The capacity to increase the odds of favorable developmental outcomes through planned interventions (Shonkoff and Phillips, 2000, p.2).

<u>From Neurons to Neighborhoods: the Science of Early Childhood Development</u> provided FIRST 5 with key concepts informed by cutting edge national research combined with FIRST 5's local research to develop a comprehensive system of care with particular focus on the most vulnerable children involved in the child welfare system.

<u>Who We Are and What We Do</u>

FIRST 5 was established in 1998, when Californians voted to dedicate tobacco taxes to local health and education programs for young children ages birth-5, creating First 5 commissions in each county across the state. First 5 funding for children's programs is based entirely on local planning and decision-making specific to families' needs in the county and not on state mandates.

Research shows that a child's brain develops most dramatically during the first five years of life. During this critical period, a window of opportunity exists to help shape how a child's brain matures and to lay the foundation for all of the years that follow. While the early period in children's development is critical to their future success, unfortunately, it is also where public investments are lowest.

Our vision is to act as a catalyst for ensuring that the developmental needs of children birth through age 5 are a priority in all sectors of the community. Our mission is to support the healthy development of children ages 0-5 and enrich the lives of their families and communities.

FIRST 5 targets resources in the following four areas, each with a primary goal within an overarching goal of Systemic Change.

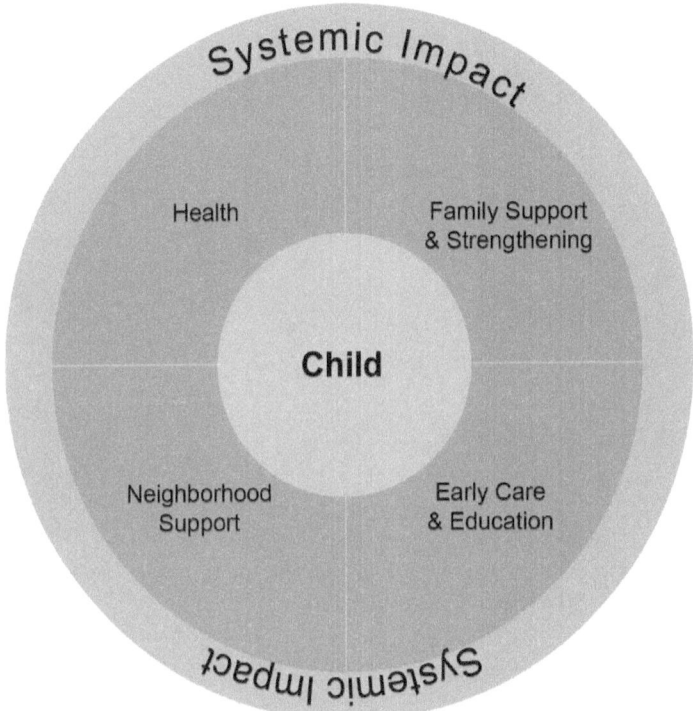

1. Health Access: Children are born healthy and experience optimal health and development.

2. Family Support: Families provide safe, stable, loving and stimulating homes.

3. Early Care and Education: Children enter school fully prepared to succeed academically, emotionally and socially.

4. Community Engagement: Neighborhoods and communities are places where children are safe, neighbors are connected and all cultures are respected.

5. Systems Change: Systems are responsive to the needs of children and families.

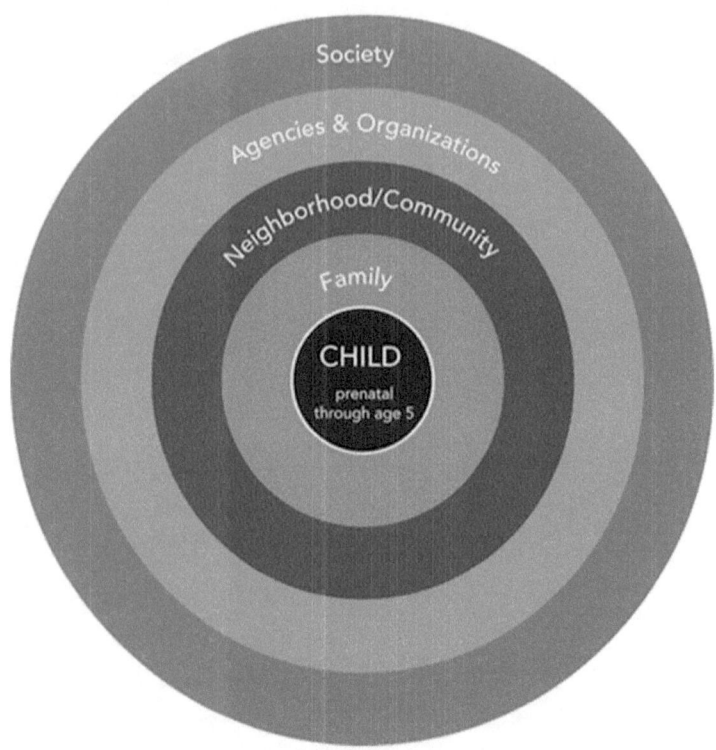

Based on Uri Brofenbrenner's social-cultural theory, FIRST 5 adopted an ecological framework for working with children and families

Social cultural theory approaches child development with the understanding that children do not develop in isolation, but rather within a set of social systems that are interconnected and dynamic impacting, individually and collectively, the healthy development of the child. This guides everything we do. We know that if all domains in which a child's development are healthy, relational based and inner-connected, a child is highly likely to grow healthy and able to reach his/her full potential.

In 2005, FIRST 5 released the results of 14 months of research and data analysis that supported the development of a comprehensive System of Care designed to support the healthy development of all children, birth through age 5—especially those children at greatest risk of poor developmental outcomes.

A critical component of this research was the geo-mapping of cumulative developmental risk factors for children birth-5 years. Data was collected on more than 20 risk factors. Of those, 8 (listed on map) were consistently prevalent and most relevant to the birth through age 5 population and were amenable to intervention through the FIRST 5 Investment Strategy.

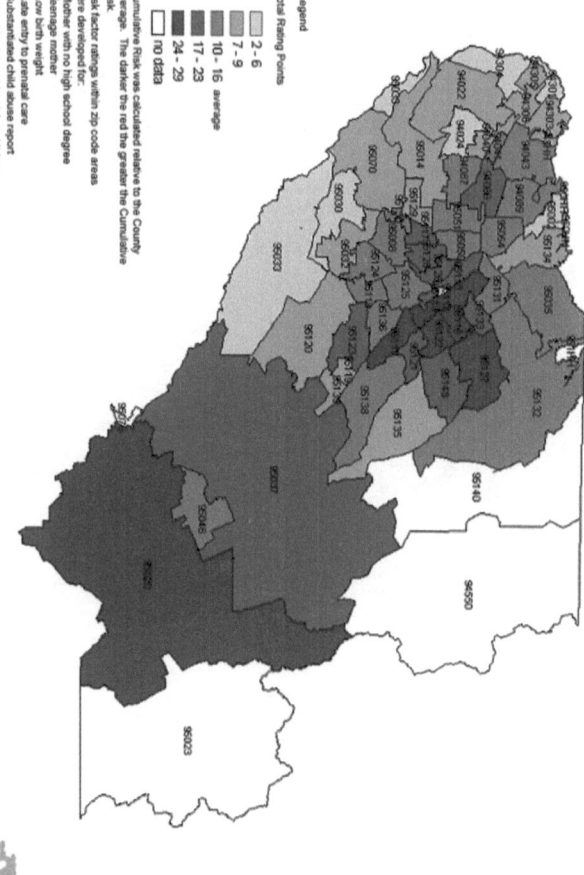

Combined Cumulative Child Risk Factors by Zip Code in Santa Clara County

Legend

Total Rating Points

- 2 - 6
- 7 - 9 average
- 10 - 16
- 17 - 23
- 24 - 29
- no data

Cumulative Risk was calculated relative to the County average. The darker the red the greater the Cumulative Risk.

Risk factor ratings within zip code areas were developed for:

- Mother with no high school degree
- Teenage mother
- Low birth weight
- Late entry to prenatal care
- Substantiated child abuse report
- Domestic violence involving children
- Medi-Cal
- Elevated blood lead levels

Copyright FIRST 5 Santa Clara County

FIRST 5

Children living in high/multiple risk environments are at greater risk of physical impairments, cognitive impairments, social, emotional and behavioral impairments, poor developmental outcomes and serious emotional problems.

National and local research defined what was essential for those children at greatest risk of poor developmental outcomes:

- Physical health

- Age and developmentally appropriate cognitive skills

- Positive/age-appropriate social, emotional and behavioral skills development

In 2006, FIRST 5 developed a service delivery system that included promotion, prevention, early intervention and treatment. We also developed a cross-disciplinary training program to build the capacity of all partners and the community to better serve children prenatal through five and their families. Additionally, we were guided by research and evaluation in an effort to document outcomes and continually improve our services.

FIRST 5 SCC Service Delivery Continuum For
Children Birth - 5 and their Families

FIRST 5 Santa Clara County Service Delivery Continuum

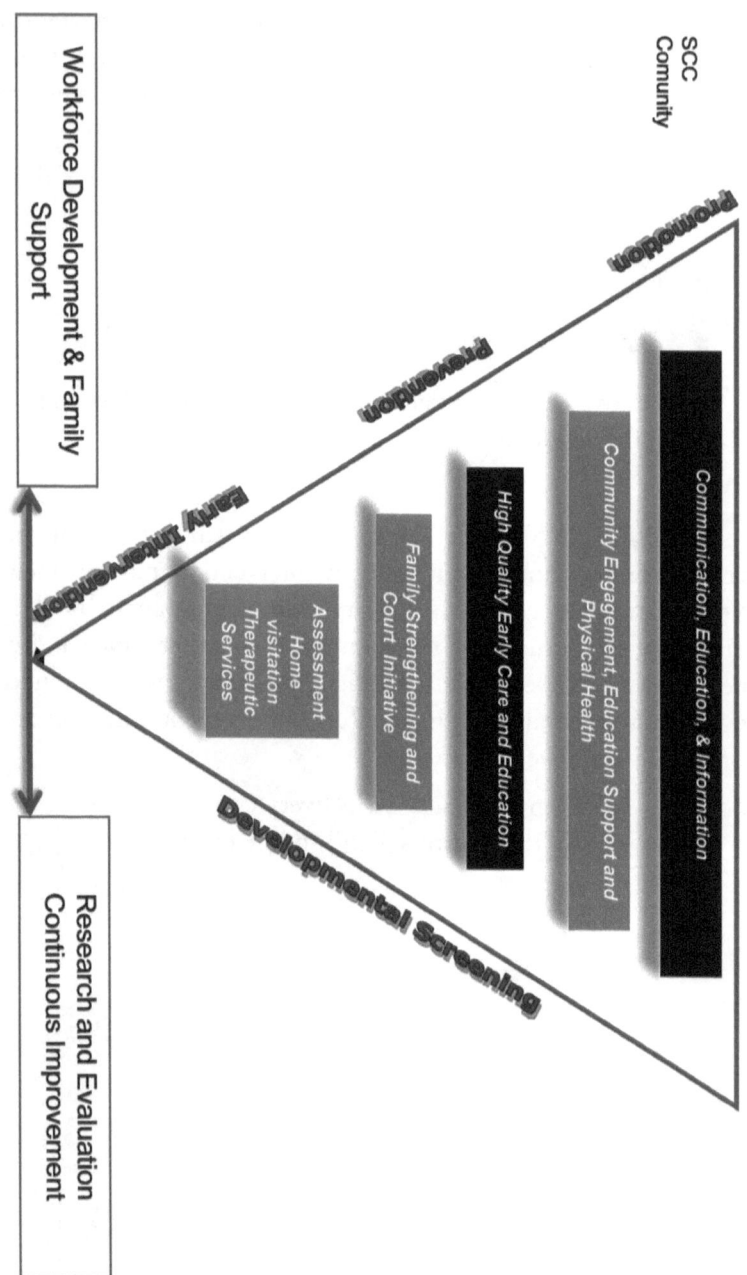

Once we had a determined approach in place we identified those systems in which collaborative projects were likely to result in systemic change:

- Social Services/Child Welfare

- Superior Courts

- County Office of Education

- County Health and Hospital Neonatal unit

- Public Health

- County Mental Health Department

How We Got Involved With the Dependency System

At the same time, our research and work to build a comprehensive system of care for young children and families was progressing, Superior Court Judges were concerned about the number and complexity of cases coming before them. Many involved pregnant mothers and/or parents with infants and toddlers who had been prenatally exposed, exposed at birth and/or in their home environment to methamphetamine and other substances and were struggling to address these concerns.

Data from the Family Treatment Drug Court Evaluation (2007) reported that, "From July 1, 2005 to June 30, 2006, 172 infants and children under the age of three were identified as being "positive toxicology" or "prenatally drug exposed" and were removed from their parents' custody. Many Mothers used more than one drug, so the total entries for drugs were 280 for 172 children." (NPC Research, 2007, Appendix A). Of note is that Santa Clara County Public Health Department experts indicated that the number of positive toxicology was significantly underreported.

The Substance-Exposed Infants/Toddlers Task Force was convened by FIRST 5 at the request of the Honorable Katherine Lucero,Supervising Judge of the Dependency Court System, to address the complex issues faced by pregnant mothers and/or mothers with infants and toddlers who had been prenatally exposed, exposed - at birth and/or in their home environment - to methamphetamine and other substances.

It was a perfect storm, we had all been working separately focused on the same issues and then at the request of the Judge all the county systems leaders got together and said, "Wait a minute how do we work together to best serve children and families who are involved in the dependency system"? At the same time that the task force was convened, a federal grant from the Administration of Children and Families was released to serve children affected by their parent's methamphetamine and other substance use.

In October 2007, FIRST 5 Santa Clara County began an exciting collaborative venture with the following agencies:

- Social Services Agency, the agency's Department of Family and Children's Services

- Superior Court

- Dependency Advocacy Center

- Department of Alcohol and Drug Services

- Mental Health Department

As a result of our history of working together, coupled with a substantial match from FIRST 5, this group was awarded a 5-year grant in the amount of $3,742,000 to serve children affected by their parent's methamphetamine and other substance use. The funding has been used to expand and enhance the Superior Court's successful Drug Dependency Treatment Court.

In March 2008, the Family Wellness Court for Infants and Toddlers (FWC) was implemented. FWC serves pregnant women and parents, with children birth through age 3, whose abuse of methamphetamine and other substances has placed their children in or at risk of out-of-home placement.

The new court built on the success of the existing Dependency Drug Treatment Court while enhancing and expanding services to better meet the needs of the population with intentional focus on the needs of the children.

The Family Wellness Court model added:

- Early assessment of substance abuse treatment needs.

- Early access to substance abuse treatment.

- Developmental/Behavioral screening and assessment for all children.

- Developmentally focused services.

The project, Family Wellness Court for Infants and Toddlers (FWC) includes a strategic planning process across all involved systems. It facilitates evidence-based practice, implementation by consensus, sustainability planning and creating the foundation to take the model to scale across the dependency system. This structure includes:

- Shared values, goals, mission and governance

- A comprehensive system of care

- Blended funding and other resources

- Cross-systems training and workforce development

- A willingness to change programmatic structures and policies

- A shared expectation that practice and service delivery will be:

- Child-focused/ family-driven

- Culturally appropriate

- Strength-based

- Developmentally appropriate

- Community-centered

- Evidence-based and data-driven

- Trauma-informed

- Recovery-oriented

A continuum of prevention, intervention, treatment and recovery support are incorporated into the daily practice of all systems, as well as a cross-systems multi-disciplinary team approach to serve children and families in need of services.

FIRST 5 Services for Children and Families in Family Wellness Court

The goal is for every child in Family Wellness Court (FWC) to have access to developmental screenings and appropriate early intervention services in order to optimize their development.

Since 2006, FIRST 5 Santa Clara County has partnered with the Mental Health Department, County Office of Education and a wide variety of community based organizations to implement a coordinated, community *Screening to Assessment, Referral and Treatment System* (STARTS) for children birth through age 5; especially those children at risk of serious social/emotional, developmental, and behavioral delays.

Studies show that children who receive early treatment for developmental delays are more likely to graduate from high school, hold jobs, live independently, and avoid teen pregnancy, delinquency, and violent crime, which results in a savings to society of about $30,000 to $100,000 per child (Glascoe and Shapiro, 2004).

Public Health Nursing Services

All children in Family Wellness Court receive immediate developmental and social-emotional screening, as well as bio-psycho-social assessment from a Public Health Nurse (PHN). Assessments include but are not limited to: Ages and Stages Questionnaire (ASQ) and Ages and Stages Social Emotional Questionnaire (ASQ: SE)[29], initial family intakes, evaluation of health and immunization status, and a review of any medical records. In addition, postpartum depression assessments are conducted for women who have recently delivered, and referral to appropriate Mental Health services are made.

Nurses assist families with linkage and follow-up to San Andreas Regional Center's Early Start program[30], the Santa Clara Valley Medical Center Infant Neurodevelopmental Clinic[31] and other medical services. PHNs provide home visitation services to medically fragile newborns and infants less than 12 months old, support their transition in placement and reunification processes and refer to Santa Clara County System of Care if necessary at the time their services close.

In addition, Public Health Nurses support parents/caregivers in securing and utilizing a medical home, provide information on ages and stages of early child development; educate and refer parents/caregivers to pregnancy planning, prevention and/or prenatal care; coach and mentor to foster a positive parent/caregiver and child relationship.

The Public Health Department recently added a Nursing Assistant to provide language and cultural support, assist with transportation and linkages made by the PHNs, and provide additional family planning and health education. In addition, the

---

29   The *ASQ* is a series of questionnaires designed to screen the developmental performance of children in the areas of communication, gross motor skills, fine motor skills, problem solving, personal-social skills, and overall development across time. The ASQ: SE is a series of 8 questionnaires designed to screen for social emotional challenges in the following areas, (self-regulation, compliance, communication, adaptive functioning, autonomy, affect, and interaction with others). The use of both tools is endorsed by the American Academy of Pediatrics.

30   Early Start is California's term for early intervention services provided under Part C of the Individuals with Disabilities Education Act (IDEA).

31   Infant Neuro-Developmental (IND) Clinic provides neuro-developmental assessments and interventions for intrauterine drug-exposed newborns and infants.

PHA provides application assistance for families to connect with Head Start[32], Early Head Start[33] and other school district services.

The Screening to Assessment, Referral and Treatment system is comprised of Santa Clara County's Kid Connections Network of Providers (KCN). The KCN includes eight community-based organizations located throughout Santa Clara County, that employ more than 65 professionals trained in the field of infant and early childhood development and behavioral health. The KCN receives screening results from the PHNs and provides appropriate assessment and treatment services for children and families. The KCN provides this multidisciplinary team approach by leveraging Medi-Cal's Early Periodic Screening, Diagnosis, and Treatment (EPSDT)[34] Program revenue, and through blended funding provided jointly by the Department of Mental Health and FIRST 5.

There are two levels of assessments available:

- <u>Assessment/Screening for Interventions</u> which are conducted by mental health and developmental specialists, and

---

32 Head Start is a federally funded program targeting children ages 3-5. It was introduced in 1964 by President Lyndon Johnson and adopted into law as part of the Economic Opportunity Act. It is overseen by the U.S. Department of Health and Human Services within the Administration for Children and Families. Head Start programs promote school readiness by enhancing the social and cognitive development of children through the provision of educational, health, nutritional, social and other services to enrolled children and families. They engage parents in their children's learning and help them in making progress toward their educational, literacy and employment goals.

33 Early Head Start was launched in 1995 by the Administration for Children and Families in the U.S. Department of Health and Human Services. The program, which now serves more than 63,000 children and families in over 700 American communities, was designed to serve low-income pregnant women, and families with infants and toddlers up to age 3.

34 The Early and Periodic Screening, Diagnosis and Treatment (EPSDT) benefit is a mandated component of the California Medi-Cal Program. Physical and mental health services are provided under EPSDT for full-scope Medi-Cal beneficiaries less than 21 years of age.

■ <u>Targeted Diagnostic Assessments</u> that are conducted by a multidisciplinary team that may include a developmental pediatrician, psychiatrist, mental health specialist, speech pathologist and occupational therapist.

Assessments and treatment may occur in the child's home, school, community or location of parents' or guardians' choice. The assessment team reviews the outcome of the assessment with the family, discusses conclusions and reviews recommendations for services. Based on the recommendations from the team the child and family are referred to home visitation and or therapeutic services.

Home Visitors use the evidence-based Program for Infant/Toddler Care (PITC)[35] model to engage parents/caregivers, provide information on ages and stages of early child development, and coach and mentor to foster a positive parent/caregiver and child relationship that contributes to the child's healthy development.

Therapeutic services span a continuum that includes: promotion of wellness, prevention of mental health disturbances and intervention and treatment of mental health concerns that may interfere with the healthy development of children. Therapeutic service providers utilize developmentally appropriate practices with the integration of substance abuse treatment and medication management.

To enhance their work with parents and children home visitors and therapists have also been trained on the evidence-based model known as Triple P Positive Parenting Program. Triple P draws on social learning, cognitive-behavioral and developmental theory, as well as research into risk and protective factors associated with the development of social and behavioral problems in children. This approach to the treatment and prevention of childhood disorders has the strongest empirical support of any intervention with children, particularly those with behavior problems (Kazdin, 1987; Sanders, 1996; Taylor and Biglan, 1998; Webster-Stratton and Hammond, 1997).

---

35   Grounded in the nationally recognized PITC philosophy, the PITC Home Visiting model integrates best practices in home visiting with the latest advances in child development.

Triple P Positive Parenting is designed to: 1) enhance the knowledge, skills, confidence and self-sufficiency parents; 2) promote nurturing, safe, engaging, non-violent and low conflict environments for children; and 3) promote children's social, emotional, language, cognitive and behavioral competencies through positive parenting practices (Sanders, M. R., Markie-Dadds, C., and Turner, K. M. T., 2003, p.3).

Additional FIRST 5 Services and Support

Children and parents also have access to FIRST 5 Family Resource Centers located throughout the county. The Family Resource Centers provide a continuum of programs, services and activities from prevention to early intervention services. Some of the services include but are not limited to the following:

- Early literacy and oral language development activities

- Art enrichment and creative expression activities

- Triple P Positive Parenting Program (levels two and three)

- Oral health information, resources, and screening

- School readiness activities, support and information

- Increased access to Early Head Start and Head Start programs

Preliminary Evaluation Results

In 2008, SRI International was contracted as the local evaluator for the FWC. A report was released in September 2011 that documents the implementation and effectiveness of the first 3 years of the FWC. Preliminary data shows promise in the child outcome areas below:

- Children remain at home

- Length of stay in foster care

- Rate of family reunification

- Rate of substance-exposed newborns

- Access to health care

- Access to developmental/behavioral screening and assessment and connection to intervention services

Children's Profile

Participants included 311 children and 276 adults (172 mothers and 104 fathers), representing 189 families. Almost half (48%) of the children were younger than 12 months at entry, 29% were ages 1–3, 8% were ages 4–5, and 15% were 6 or older.

More than a quarter (29%) of children entering FWC were born substance exposed. Data indicates that only one subsequent drug-exposed birth was reported on a 6-month follow-up survey.

Most (91%) of the children eligible for a developmental/emotional screening received one, and 48% of those screened received that screening in the first 90 days of FWC participation. Ninety-four percent of children who received a developmental screening also received an Assessment for Intervention, and 8% of children received a Targeted Diagnostic Assessment. Based on the screening results, a high proportion of children were identified as having concerns in one or more developmental area.

Of those children with a developmental screening, 16% received home visitation, and 17% received therapeutic services. In addition more parents reported having health insurance coverage for their children at follow-up than at program entry (79% vs.75%) and 95% of parents report their child receives routine medical care (SRI, 2011).

In a comparison between children in FWC and a similar group of children who received regular dependency services more FWC children remained at home and never spent time in foster care, more FWC children were reunified in less than 12 months, and more FWC children had at least one parent retain custody of them. In addition, the average number of days FWC children stayed in foster care was significantly shorter than children in the comparison group (194 days vs. 429)(SRI 20011 FWC Evaluation Report p. 25).

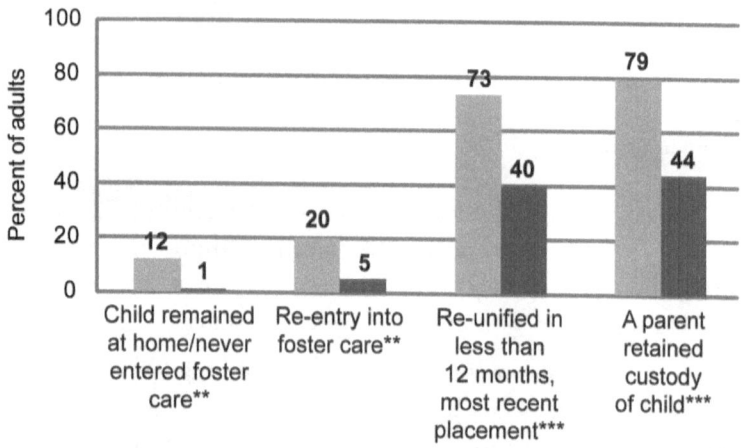

Child Welfare Outcomes Diagram, SRI International, 2011 Evaluation of Family Wellness Court for Infants and Toddlers, Year 4 Annual Report, p. 26.

Systems Improvements

The partnerships forged and strengthened by the Family Wellness Court project led to significant system enhancements to meet the needs of all young children and families in the child welfare system and across the entire Silicon Valley.

Four important changes must be highlighted:

- Expanded Public Health Nursing services in the foster care system

- A collaborative, coordinated effort to prioritize children for referral to Head Start

- Implementation of an evidence-based parenting program

- Early developmental/behavioral screening and access to early intervention services

In January 2012, Public Health Nursing (PHN) services for children and families were expanded to serve **all** children under the age of 6 and their families in the child welfare system. There is now a coordinated referral mechanism in place to connect children in foster care to Head Start programs. In July 2012 the Department of Families and Children Services will implement the Triple P Positive Parenting program, an evidence-based parenting support system designed to prevent and reduce child maltreatment.

The last highlighted system change is a collaborative effort with the County Mental Health Department and FIRST 5. Leveraging Medi-Cal and FIRST 5 funding and resources created the Screening to Assessment Referral and Treatment System (STARTS). The initiative includes eight community-based organizations located throughout Santa Clara County that employ more than 65 professionals trained in the field of infant and early childhood development and behavioral health, and allows for the expansion and increased access to screening, assessment and intervention services for children birth through age 5 in Santa Clara County. This leveraging strategy is critical in terms of local, statewide and national sustainability of screening, assessment and treatment services for very young children. FIRST 5 Santa Clara County is one of the first counties in California to leverage this funding.

Final Thoughts

The Family Wellness Court project was the catalyst that brought Santa Clara County systems leaders together to make possible that which could not be accomplished alone, the creation of a comprehensive system of care for the most vulnerable children and families in the county. Diverse agencies and individuals joined together in a unified effort to make young children the highest priority across all sectors of the community. Strengthened by the development of common values, clear goals, defined roles, effective communication and a continuous quality improvement process, the system leaders that oversee the FWC project have worked tirelessly to ensure its success and sustainability at all levels.

The success of Family Wellness Court is the result of the hard work and dedication of many individuals and agencies across multiple systems. However, none of the accomplishments would have been realized without the visionary leadership of three key individuals: Judge Katherine Lucero, Supervising Judge in the Dependency Court is a champion for children and families. She understands the importance of collaboration and service coordination between the courts, community-based organizations and government agencies. She says," It does not matter which role we are taking in this village of child welfare and court systems. We are all serving the same families and children and to be most effective we must work as a team". She believes in turning crisis into opportunity and in the influence of judicial leadership at every level in the community.

The Honorable Erica Yew was the first presiding Judge of Family Wellness Court. She embraced the philosophy of a therapeutic court room and transformed the courtroom experience for families from deficit-based to a collaborative, problem-solving approach to working with families to help them successfully reunify, stay clean and sober and build relationships to support their children's health and well-being. She describes what Family Wellness Court means to her: "This is really about your heart and soul and connecting with other human beings on an emotional level, really being with them every step of the way, caring very deeply about how they do".

Jolene Smith, CEO of FIRST 5 is tirelessly committed to ensuring the healthy development of our youngest children is viewed as a high priority in the county. She works closely with policymakers and elected officials to create the necessary change in laws and policies to improve the lives of children and families in Santa Clara County. She believes that, "In a comprehensive system of care all systems, institutions and agencies work together in a coordinated approach to ensure that children and their families have access to the services and supports they need to succeed, tailored to the individual needs of the child and family with respect to all areas of the child's ecology and is consistent with the family's culture and language".

The National Child Resource Center for Tribes (NCRC4Tribes) has a philosophy that illustrates the common value about children that is shared by all the partners involved in the Family Wellness Court project. It is a philosophy that should be shared with anyone who cares about children. "Children are sacred and entitled to be cherished in a safe and nurturing environment with strong family, community and cultural connections. Their happiness and well-being includes nourishment of mind, body and spirit in order to fulfill their dreams throughout their journey toward becoming a healthy Elder".

References

Brofenbrenner, U., "The Ecology of Human Development: Experiments by Nature and Design", Harvard Press, Boston, MA, 1979.

Dicker, S., "Reversing the Odds: Improving Outcomes for Babies in the Child Welfare System", Brookes Publishing Co., Baltimore, Maryland, 2009.

Glascoe, F. P., and Shapiro, H. L., "Introduction to Developmental and Behavioral Screening", Developmental Behavioral Pediatrics, 2004.

Kazdin, A. E., "Treatment of Antisocial Behavior in Children: Current Status and Future Directions", Psychological Bulletin, 1987, pp. 102, 187–203.

NPC Research, "Family Treatment Drug Court Evaluation, Final Report", 2007.

Sanders, M. R., "New Directions in Behavioral Family Intervention with Children", Ollendick, T. H., Prinz, R. J., (Eds.), Advances in Clinical Psychology, Vol. 18, Plenum Press, New York, 2006, pp. 283–330.

Sanders, M., R., Markie-Dadds, C., and Turner, K. M. T., "Theoretical, Scientific and Clinical Foundations of the Triple P

Positive Parenting Program: A Population Approach to the Promotion of Parenting Competence"; http://www.triplep-america.com/pages/evidence/Theoretical.html, 2003.

Shonkoff, J., and Phillips, D., (Eds.) "From Neurons to Neighborhoods: The Science of Early Childhood Development", National Academy Press, Washington, DC, 2000..

SRI International, "Evaluation of Family Wellness Court For Infants and Toddlers: Year 4 Annual Report", 2011.

WHEN TWO ROADS MEET:
HOW A PRIVATE-PUBLIC
PARTNERSHIP CAN SUPPORT
CRITICAL COMMUNITY NEEDS

By Gisela Bushey, Co-Founder

The Chris Shaheen Charitable Foundation

"Children in America lag behind almost all industrialized nations on key child indicators. The United States has the unwanted distinction of being the worst among industrialized nations in relative child poverty, in the gap between rich and poor, in teen birth rates, and in child gun violence."

Children's Defense Fund report
"The State of America's Children, 2010"

The impact of abuse, abandonment and neglect on our children is most profoundly apparent among children who become a part of the child welfare system in America. When the courts remove a child from his/her parents due to abuse or neglect, the child welfare system typically places that child in a foster care home; preferably with relatives. When a safe environment cannot be found among relatives, children enter non-relative foster homes or group homes.

Due to their maltreatment, children often enter the foster care system with medical, behavioral, and/or emotional problems. Children removed from their homes feel socially isolated and depressed, and these problems are exacerbated when children move from one foster setting to another. Foster children are more likely to do poorly in school and have physical and mental health problems. They are at risk for behavioral problems, drug and alcohol use, and delinquency. They are more likely to end up in the juvenile justice system, ultimately ending up fully engulfed in the "cradle to prison pipeline."

The challenges are especially acute for those who "age out" of the system. According to research, these youth face serious challenges and are at higher risk of homelessness, substance abuse, emotional difficulties, involvement with the legal system, and lower educational and career attainment. In the majority of case, this stems from a history of abuse and neglect, and the lack of a support system to aid in their transition to adulthood.

Nationally, nearly 470,000 children were placed in foster care. Of these:

- Infants are the most likely to be victims of abuse and neglect. Nearly one-third of all victims are younger than age four.

- 71.3 percent are victims of neglect; 16.1 percent of physical abuse; 9.2 percent of sexual abuse; and 6.8 percent of psychological abuse. Boys and girls are almost equally likely to be victims of abuse or neglect, with girls just slightly more likely.

- Close to 40 percent of child victims receive no services after the investigation.

- Approximately one in five child victims in 2008 was maltreated by someone other than his/her parents. More than half of the known non-parental perpetrators were either another male relative or a male partner of the parent. ("Child Maltreatment: 2008", (pub. 2009),

U.S. Department of Health and Human Services, Administration on Children, Youth, and Families; Child Welfare Information Gateway, "Foster Care Statistics 2009", U.S. Department of Health and Human Services, Children's Bureau, Washington, DC, (pub. 2011). Calculations prepared by the Children's Defense Fund.)

In California, 68,127 of these children entered foster care - 80.4% of children who entered foster care were removed from their families due to neglect; 10.8% due to physical abuse; and 3.5% due to sexual abuse. Twelve months after entering foster care, 44.3% were reunified with their families and 52.0% were still in care. Children in foster care in California spend an average of 14.1 months in the child welfare system.

Astoundingly, from 2006-2008, California infants entered foster care at nearly three times as high a rate as any other age group. Children of color are disproportionately represented in foster care in California [four times the national average] – and California ranks as one of the top 9 states in numbers of children in foster care overall. (CDF, "Children in Foster Care by State", 2008).

In Santa Clara County, local reporting data showed that 80% of parents involved in Santa Clara County Dependency Court have substance abuse problems. Of those, 58% report methamphetamine as their primary drug of choice, cocaine was the drug of choice for 7%; marijuana was the drug of choice for 8.6%; and alcohol was the drug of choice for 18.6% (Santa Clara County Department of Family and Children Services, 2000 - 2005.)

Our dependency court is one of the most important divisions in the court system, because it is the single consistent presence in the lives of the families and the children who come before them. Their decisions impact the entire family, not just the children involved, and must "stand in the shoes of the parent(s)" who – because of drugs, alcohol, their own personal histories of abuse, neglect, and mental health concerns – are unable to adequately care for and meet the needs of their children. The children played no role in the decisions or activities of their parents that led to their removal; however, their lives will be forever changed as a result.

When Chris Shaheen, a Silicon Valley realtor and corporate real estate entrepreneur first approached me with the idea of establishing a charitable foundation focused on local community issues - particularly those affecting disadvantaged youth - it quickly became apparent that his interests aligned very well with the critical issues and concerns faced by the abused, abandoned and neglected children that I had worked with for most of my career.

As a result, we decided that The Chris Shaheen Charitable Foundation would do more than just function as a financial support opportunity. We met with community stakeholders serving children in foster care; families and children affected by domestic violence, drug and alcohol addiction; local, state and national legal and advocacy groups; and non-profit organizations throughout Santa Clara County working with children and families in need. A particular theme emerged: with ever-constrained budgets and limits on their ability to identify and pursue alternative sources of funding, our local dependency courts - the common thread in the lives of our most vulnerable children and their families - were unable to adequately access available community services or financially assist families diligently working to reunify their families.

We certainly shared an affinity with the dependency court's mission to:

- Protect children

- Give them stability

- Keep families together

- Treat everyone with dignity

- Respect diversity, and

- Value every child like their own

We particularly wanted to help extend the reach and positive impact of two innovative model programs of our dependency courts that serve vulnerable, high-risk and underserved populations of children, youth and their families: Santa Clara County's Family Wellness Court (FWC) and the Dependency Drug Treatment Court (DDTC).

Our county's Family Wellness Court is an expansion and enhancement of the Superior Courts' Dependency Drug Treatment Court, which has been highly successful in assisting parents to achieve and maintain sobriety, overcome personal obstacles, become better parents and successfully reunify with their children. The additional resources provided by our Foundation for the FWC and DDTC would assist parents in having earlier assessments for and access to substance abuse treatment and ensure that their children receive in-depth developmental and behavioral assessments and services to improve their well-being. These programs seek to:

- Keep minors with their families and make the families stronger whenever possible.

- If the court removes a minor from the home for the child's well-being and safety or to protect the public, the court will work with the family and the minor to improve the home conditions so the child can return home.

- Ensure that the minor children, while in the care of the court, receive the care and assistance they need to be safe and protected.

By far the largest unmet expenditures encumbered by these programs relate to items and activities that, left unmet, impede the progress of family reunification, and in many cases, determine whether or not a child enters the foster care/dependency court system. These impediments, identified by the court, include the following (by no means an exhaustive list, as each case is unique and subsequent cases will have specific concerns that arise for them):

- clothing [baby, children's, school clothing];

- strollers and car seats to ensure child safety during transport;

- bottles, bibs, teethers, and child development tools;

- school supplies, educational toys and books;

- the inability to access or maintain medical, dental, vision or therapeutic assistance, and to remain on medications due to cost;

- transportation [bus passes, vehicle repairs needed, train fares];

- mentoring, tutoring and after school homework club access;

- post-emancipation independent living skills training;

- loss of housing due to unemployment/underemployment;

- job training and employment placement assistance;

- transitional or permanent affordable housing assistance

- Additional program goals included [1] preventing subsequent births of substance exposed newborns, [2] creating a unified system of care for the target population and [3] building capacity to take these programs to scale across the dependency system.

These innovative model programs complement the overall work of the Santa Clara County Juvenile Dependency Court system, which is responsible for determining the paths of the children and families in the county's foster care system. The system consists of the judicial officers of the Court, and the organizations that make up the quilt of legal and community services for families that by law have come under the oversight of the county (e.g. Department of Family and Children's Services, County Counsel, Office of the District Attorney, CASA, Department of Alcohol and Drug Services (DADS), and Dependency Legal Services.)

While anecdotally it was clear that impediments toward many of these cases progressing through the dependency system to a permanent resolution existed, a needs assessment was undertaken to obtain a more concrete measurement of the level and extent of the need among these children and families navigating the child welfare system.

In January/February 2009, 14 dependency court sessions were attended, and 200 cases observed. This was a representative sample of approximately 30% of the total cases heard by county court officers during this period of time. Assessors elected to only observe the proceedings rather than obtain court documents in advance of the cases.

- **68 of the 200** cases heard revealed issues that would have benefited from the resources we wanted to help the court to provide. Specific issues were identified by the judge/commissioner, the needs assessment observers, attorneys representing the child(ren), the parent(s) as well as social workers in attendance.

- **All 200** of the cases heard would have benefited from the ability of the court officers to have a resource to facilitate/collaborate on the resolution of those impediments identified that either were not being addressed by current participants in the proceedings, or were the responsibility of a participant, but the matter had yet to be satisfactorily addressed.

Subsequent to the court observations, assessors reviewed a random sampling of 10% of the cases actually heard. Assessors found issues **in every one of the documents reviewed** that would benefit from the presence and participation of our Foundation and proposed use of Foundation funding. **At least 1,768 children and families** would have benefitted from the kind of partnership assistance we sought to provide.

Two important prospective contributions by the Shaheen Foundation were additionally corroborated by this assessment:

1. In matters where an immediate need was identified and unaddressed (e. g. transportation, medical or therapeutic intervention, after-school activities, tutoring, mentoring), the Foundation would administer the funds and be a direct resource to bringing that specific impediment to resolution.

2. In matters that continued to be an impediment to a case's progress, and current case participants had, to date, failed to address them, the Foundation would function as an "extending reach" of the court officer to ensure that the matter is more expeditiously addressed by directing the Foundation to collaborate with the necessary party[ies] to bring the matter to closure.

Thus, the Chris Shaheen Foundation could act as both a bridge and an accountability "safety net" on behalf of the courts for the children and families that are trying to successfully navigate the dependency court system; obtain critical provisions for children and families appearing in the Juvenile Justice/Dependency Courts in Santa Clara County, California; and strengthen and restore families, preventing them from penetrating deeper into the juvenile dependency system. Foundation activities would not overlap with assistance provided by other agencies or organizations but would be complementary to their services. Our aim was to be at least an additive factor, if not multiplicative one.

Each day, the judges hear cases where it is apparent that the children or their caregivers have needs that are difficult but not impossible to overcome that function as persistent obstacles in their road out of the dependency system. Despite the gallant work of organizations (both government and non-profit) that make up the support services of the entire Santa Clara County child welfare system, the needs described above exist because of the "patchwork quilt" nature of the system, the fact that the dependency/foster care system is overloaded and underfunded for these needs, or they just don't fall into a current organization's mission.

After our assessment and review, and multiple meetings with our county's presiding judge and court staff, we agreed to partner with the Santa Clara County Juvenile Dependency Court to help children and parents overcome these persistently difficult obstacles that exist in virtually every case that comes before the court. The Chris Shaheen Charitable Foundation would provide all financial administration, reporting and documentation of expenditures of funds, and funds would be exclusively designated for use on behalf of the FWC and DDTC program's requests. Court officers would submit items/activities requiring funding to the Shaheen Foundation, and we would then process/facilitate the provision of the requested assistance.

And the results? In a letter to the Foundation, specialty court coordinator Deborah Dohse wrote:

"Over the past fiscal year 2010-2011, Dependency Drug Treatment Court (DDTC) and Family Wellness Court (FWC) was able to purchase 160 adult day pass tokens, 30 youth day tokens, and other various requests which included the following: California State ID cards, housing application fees, assistance with PG&E, copies of Birth certificates, registration fees for 12-Step study groups, and assistance with prescriptions with the funding provided by the Chris Shaheen Foundation.

Bus tokens assist parents without reliable transportation to attend their Court hearings, treatment services, and other necessary appointments to complete the program. Bus tokens are provided to participants when they have exhausted all other sources of transportation. Bus tokens have been useful in providing transportation to a parent to get their appointments such as visiting their children, substance abuse treatment, or doctor's appointments.

A single mother of one with 12 months clean and sober wrote a letter of gratitude to the DDTC. She stated that was thankful for the opportunity to share a little bit about her. She thanked all of us for this gift and the chance to become a grateful recovering addict. She appreciated all of the work and dedication to helping her and others like her to make the changes necessary to become the people we've always wanted to be. This participant was speechless for the all kindness which she has received as result from these incentives which has been graciously given to DDTC. In addition, this client received extensive dental care from Santa Clara County Dental Foundation. This client was very appreciative that she could smile and have self-confidence now.

In addition, the Chris Shaheen Foundation has provided food and clothing assistance to one of the graduates from DDTC over the Christmas holiday last year. With this gift, the family sustained their housing and they were very appreciative of this gift. Your Foundation also provided 150 gift cards for thanksgiving dinner at the 10th Annual DDTC/FWC Thanksgiving Dinner in November 2010.

The DDTC/FWC team and their participants are very appreciative of the Chris Shaheen Foundation and their generosity over the past year. The funds have made a tremendous difference in the families we served over the past year. Bus tokens and other requests to assist families in need are much appreciated by the families. It is the small things that make a tremendous difference in a family's life. Thank you for your generosity over the past fiscal year."

The Chris Shaheen Charitable Foundation was founded on the belief that at-risk children require our attention, advocacy and assistance, and vulnerable populations in particular need our support. Our mission is to support organizations and programs serving vulnerable populations and at-risk children through the advancement of education; to improve or develop individual capabilities; assist children who have special education needs; support services to children in foster care and their families; and identify the critical needs of children in our community and provide preventive investments to ensure the likelihood of positive outcomes for these at-risk populations.

Our partnership with FWC and DDTC and the dedicated judges, attorneys, court staff, and non-profit service providers who work on behalf of our most vulnerable families is a pragmatic, meaningful, and successful endeavor that every court across the country can adopt. It's just not that complicated – we all have a role to play in the health and well-being of families and children in need. Some travel down the public road; others, the private. When these two roads meet, and we travel together, our public/private partnerships can reunite broken families, help keep them whole, and provide a hope-filled future for <u>all</u> of our families and children. Together, we can weave that tapestry called community; and together, we will all be the stronger for it.

FAMILY DRUG COURTS: THE SOLUTION

By Judge Katherine Lucero

There are 10 key components to a successful criminal drug court[36]. The child welfare drug courts have embraced those 10 components and created a template for success when working with the *entire family*. Below are listed the 10 key Drug Court Components rewritten to be applied to healing the whole family in Family Drug Courts.

Key Component #1: Family Drug Courts must closely partner with the jurisdiction's alcohol and drug treatment agency in order to share confidential background information that is generally not available from one discipline to the other and partner in an integrative model which allows for cross training and cross assessments.

Drug and Alcohol Services should not just be a part of your team. They should be connected at the hip to the child welfare agency if at all possible. This key component takes the child welfare case to the next treatment intervention level. If there is no alcohol and drug treatment partner who is willing to sit with the team and go over each case for assessment, case planning, and referrals and follow up, the model is lost. This is the most critical partner after the social worker. It is highly likely that the parent in the case is receiving or has received drug treatment services in your jurisdiction in the

---

36   http://ndcrc.org/sites/default/files/PDF/TheFactsonAdultDrugCourts_0.pdf

past. Having the participation of the Drug and Alcohol Agency allows for informed decisions often based on data they have in their own systems as well. We actually have the Drug and Alcohol Assessors co-located at the courthouse. They have access to our court files upon the individual consent of the parent. The Drug Assessor will generally sit with the parent and have the information in front of them, along with the Dependency petition and any social studies that have been written to support the allegations of abuse and neglect as well as the drug and alcohol treatment history, *prior to making a decision about the level of treatment needed.*

We have developed protocols and consents for information sharing that allows all professionals to trust the indicated treatment intervention assessed by the drug and alcohol specialist. In the past, when the specialist did not have the child welfare file, the assessments were not readily accepted by all the attorneys and child advocates. Due to the close working relationships that we now have with the drug and alcohol specialist, and the exchange of critical information which impacts the child, the assessments are tailored and effective.

Our drug and alcohol assessors have also performed child safety assessments and mental health screenings. Much is learned at this initial contact which generally occurs within the first two weeks of the new child welfare case being petitioned. All of this information is passed along to the social worker and, together, the professionals discuss the next logical steps of the case.

Key Component #2: Using a non-adversarial approach, attorneys for parents, the state and the child promote child safety while first working to keep the child at home with the parent in treatment, and, if unable to keep the child with the parent, they work together to get the child home at the earliest possible time while setting up services to preserve the parent/child bond and at the same time protect each party's due process rights.

Dependency Court is the original problem-solving court. If there is a way to keep children at home safely, it is the law to do so. Taking a child from the home is the last resort. For the parent afflicted with substance abuse and in need of treatment, the need for collaboration is even more urgent. Significantly, these are not bad people trying to become good. These are parents who have an addiction to alcohol and/or drugs (many with mental health diagnosis) who are in need of a way to get well. Resources are always the key. True, some parents will not be in a stage of mental health illness or drug addiction that they are ready to get the help they need; but many will be after they have lost their children.

It is critical that the entire court case be driven by the desire to protect children and at the same time heal families. This can only be done when the entire court stakeholder team agrees on common values and does everything possible to address the issues in both the legal and resource forums. The child should remain with the parent if at all possible in residential treatment. The child who must be taken from the home should be placed in a concurrent relative foster care home first, and if not in a non-relative foster home. In the meanwhile all of our resource energy must be focused on the treatment services and the parent/child bond.

Key Component #3: All parents who have come to the attention of the Child Welfare Court System primarily due to substance abuse shall be directed into the Family Treatment Court model on the first day of court.

If the parent has lost their child due to substance abuse, they should automatically be placed in Family Treatment Court. The same day of the initial hearing after the child has been removed, the parent should be able to sign up and/or receive a drug/alcohol assessment to determine what level of intervention is necessary, including the ability to go into treatment with their children. The treatment services should be available to that parent that day or shortly thereafter. Prioritizing the child welfare population in your jurisdiction in this regard is critical. A drug addict without children in the system, who is waiting for a bed out of criminal court will not lose a child to adoption within as little as 10 to 16 months if they do not get treatment. The population we work with will have their parental rights terminated if the system does not move fast enough to help them access services.

The parent with a young child simply has no time to lose. If the parent and child are separated, the Adoptions and Safe Families Act (ASFA) kicks in and the parent is now on a very strict legal timeline to get better. The ASFA timelines and the addiction treatment timelines are different. However, the best hope for a parent to begin the process of recovery and family reunification is when they have same-day assessments and prompt treatment services delivery. Nothing except the most egregious cases of system negligence, will stay these timelines.

Key Component #4: Family Drug Courts provide access to a continuum of family-centered and trauma-informed resources including alcohol, drugs and other related treatment rehabilitation services as well as mental health, family violence and other family-centered services.

The success of healing an entire family is different than that of rehabilitating one individual. In the Child Welfare Court Systems we are tasked with healing an entire family. Every family is different, but I am sure that we can agree in most cases there is at least one parent and one child involved and each person in the family has very distinct needs. Therefore, the Family Treatment Court must also have components like substance abuse parenting informed classes, domestic violence services, mental health counseling and assessments for each member of the family and even services like housing and transportation as well as job placement and educational opportunities in order to help create long term success.

The goals of these family treatment courts is to help the parent get clean and sober, help the child understand it is not their fault and that they may be at risk for addiction in the future, and to set the family on a trajectory of growth and continuous healing. The best programming offers aftercare in all spheres, including mental health, physical health, housing and addiction.

We have FIRST 5 of Santa Clara County programming which follows the case for up to six months after case dismissal, and we also recently obtained an Aftercare Grant which follows the family for up to one year to make sure that they have all the support that they need and will develop a robust Family Treatment Court Alumni program so that folks can stay in touch with one other and continue to benefit from meaningful relationships that were developed as a result of the Court Team intervention. Our drug and alcohol services do not end as the parent can always call the treatment program that they graduated from and receive one-on-one counseling if necessary. We also bridge our families to a community health clinic where they can continue to get mental health intervention and counseling to maintain mental health interventions after their case is dismissed.

Key Component #5: A drug and alcohol free lifestyle is monitored by frequent alcohol and other drug testing and *court reviews* to make sure that the parent is also in compliance with their substance abuse-focused child welfare case plan.

Each parent has court-ordered weekly random drug testing. Most parents are also drug testing for another public agency, like probation, parole or the drug treatment program. Whenever possible we try to develop protocols to share test results. Another indicator of clean and sober living is when the parent is meeting their other commitments. Their attendance at 12-step meetings, their meetings with social workers, sponsors, other service providers and their visits with their children are all part of the clean and sober experience.

It is wonderful if we can prevent the use of drugs and alcohol. It is even more wonderful, however, if we can see that the parent is engaging in the process of **RECOVERY**. We all know that a person who is not invested in changing old behavior will go back to it when out of the spotlight. Some folks wait it out and "fake us out" and they are back again in front of our courts in short order. We can easily spot those people. What is more remarkable is when we can see the sparkle come back into someone's eyes and they begin to transform their lives right in front of us. When they are engaged in their own recovery, we see long-term changes.

We not only believe that it is crucial to monitor sobriety with frequent random testing, but we also believe it is crucial to review case compliance and changes in behavior.

Key Component #6: It is critical that the court team work together to develop a coordinated response to a parent's compliance with the case plan and the treatment mandates.

Parents who live in the Transitional Housing Units and the Residential Treatment facilities get a case conference which occurs outside the Family Drug Court setting. These are vital to the oversight and coordination of the parent/child case. Drug and alcohol treatment experts meet on a quarterly basis with the social workers and clients to make sure that the parent is on track in both domains: treatment and case plans. The goal is for the client who is living in the THU or residential program to reach milestones for transition and self-support within a six -to nine-month period of time. The social worker and the treatment experts confer on issues such as housing and job searches, educational opportunities, mental and medical health interventions, child care, and so on. The routine meetings also allows for the team to work together to ensure that the parent is in compliance with treatment and the case plan.

Similarly, each time the parent has a court appearance the team "staffs" the parent's case before the actual review occurs. At this "staffing" is the Drug Court Coordinator, the Social Worker or a representative of the social workers, the attorney for the social worker, FIRST 5 representative, the CalWorks Eligibility Worker, the Mental Health Specialist, the Domestic Violence Specialist, the Child Advocate's office, the parent's attorney, the minor's attorney, the judge, the Drug and Alcohol Specialist and the Resource Coordinator. Other people are present as necessary. This approach allows for up-to-the-minute information on drug testing results, case compliance and progress of the parent. The team develops a strategy to address issues that may be present or to simply praise the parent who is on track and doing well.

Key Component #7: Ongoing judicial interaction with each drug court participant is essential with a judge who is well trained on trauma informed treatment modalities and makes at least a three year commitment to stay in the Family Drug Court assignment.

Enough cannot be said about the training and commitment of the assigned treatment court judge. Studies confirm that the parents are often as traumatized as the child that has come before the court. This is not to minimize the negligent actions that have brought the case before the court, but to urge that a trauma-informed lens be adopted as the chief perspective of any judicial officer working with parents in the child welfare courts.

It is also imperative that the judge desires to be assigned to this special court and that the judge be willing to make a three- to five-year commitment. The average child welfare case is likely to be in the court for as long as three years. The continuity of the judge is part of the magic of the success of the child welfare drug treatment court.

Key Component #8: Monitoring and evaluation measures the achievement of program goals and tracks re-entry rates into foster care, reasons for reentry, if any, and commitment to problem-solving and self-correction of systems in order to reduce family instability.

Monitoring and evaluation is critical to make sure that the interventions are working. Drug courts work. We have plenty of data to show that given the opportunity, people do well in the drug court setting. What seems to be even more critical in the child welfare setting is looking at why a family may come back into the systems after they have successfully completed a drug court program. Again, because we are looking at family units vs. one person, we must be cognizant of the need to promote family stability and not just keep one person clean and sober. To that end, life skills, clean and sober parenting, housing, aftercare and building independence are critical parts of the family drug court equation.

Key Component #9: Continuing interdisciplinary education promotes effective drug court planning, implementation and operations and promotes team building for better services to the parent and child.

In the non-adversarial setting of the child welfare court, it is especially important that state-of-the-art interventions, research and evidence-based practices be shared and implemented. These teams need to hold themselves accountable by being vigilant about a variety of topics such as child development, trauma, mental health, domestic violence and addiction. Having annual educational retreats is recommended; however, quarterly presentations from community experts are also a way to keep informed and to educate the team on current issues and practices.

Regular team meetings with an agenda that seeks to solve systemic obstacles and educate one another on current topics are critical to the growing and changing system responses that are vital in the child welfare court setting.

Key Component #10: Forging partnerships with criminal drug courts, public agencies, and community-based organizations generates local, statewide and federal support which guarantees the sustainability of the collaboration, and leads to structural changes that improve systems and service delivery to child welfare court families.

The Criminal Courts have access to resources that can often be shared with parents in the child welfare courts, because we have found that there is up to a 50% overlap in the parent/defendant population. By partnering with your local criminal drug court you and the other judges can work together to streamline court dates, court orders and encourage agencies to share information and not duplicate efforts. Other public agencies such as Drug and Alcohol Services, Mental Health, Housing Agencies, Transportation agencies, Public Health and Medical Services will bring vital resources and organizational streamlining of services to families that each agency has in common. Community-based organizations will have a rich population of families in need to fulfill their grant and contract obligations, and will build a bridge to community services that can be utilized long after the court case has been dismissed. Governing bodies such as local policy makers, state and federal legislators will bring much-needed political support during these trying budget times, and may think twice before cutting services that impact programs that you educated them about that are benefiting hundreds of citizens and saving county dollars.

Summary

As you can see, the solution is to apply the criminal drug court model to all families in our court system that suffer from addiction complicated by mental health disorders. There is no mystery about the value and success of these models. What is necessary is the willingness to look anew at the issues of addiction, timelines, the developmental and emotional needs of children and community resources in order to resolve to implement these models. The cost savings is there, the human capital that can be saved is there, the common-sense and compassion is all readily available for any policy maker to be convinced that to do business otherwise is wasteful on many levels. Below are more stories of transformation and resurrection.

PART II
LIFE IN A NEW LIGHT: PERSONAL STORIES OF TRANSFORMATION

LIFE AFTER DEATH

By Rosemary Smith

My name is Rosemary Smith.

I was an empty shell of a woman when that officer arrested me.

I was living in a motor home with my boyfriend and my daughter, and I was high on methamphetamine almost all the time. My daughter was fed, clean, clothed and innocent. I had no idea how my life was about to change.

I was arrested two days before Mother's Day in May, 2009-a Friday night. They took my boyfriend to jail, my 2 ½ year old to the shelter, my ride/home to the car jail and I went to jail as well. I was let out the very next day and proceeded to freak out. My baby was with a stranger and I did that. There was nothing I could do; I was helpless, homeless and confused.

Two days later was Mother's Day and my 24-year old son called to wish me a happy one. What he got was a broken, scared little girl in tears and I didn't want to tell him his sister was taken away because of my drug use. I couldn't hide it. I told him and he said "aw **** mom" and hung up on me. He didn't speak to me for about 5 months. I lost everything, EVERYTHING in the space of a single weekend.

I was taken through a new court system called Family Wellness Court. They gave me a mentor mom who helped me through the process. I had no idea what I was going to do. I got into a Transitional Housing Unit and then started going to something I had never heard of called N.A. I was going to do every single thing these people said I needed to do so I could get my baby back. At 46 years old I needed a change and I got it.

I was signed up for a lottery pull on a new apartment that wasn't even built yet. I got it. I started to work for CalWorks. I was given an interview to get a full-time temporary position with a County of Santa Clara department that works closely with many departments including the Sheriff's Office. This was a rare opportunity. I worked there for *a little over a year*. When my position was up I decided to go back to school and I am still in school right now, going for my BA to become a Probation Officer. I have never had a felony, so I am able to do something completely different with my life. Since I know the dark side of that coin, I believe I am someone that can understand what those in the Probation system are going through.

To get to this point in my life was hard work and worth it all. I did everything: meetings every day, sometimes 2 and 3 times a day. I did it without a vehicle. I rode the bus, took trains, and got rides with friends. I got there by any means possible. I went to counselors, parenting classes, and whatever Family Wellness Court said to do. I did what I had to do to get my daughter back. I got her back in 6 months. It was in fact, Christmas Eve, 2009. I worked very hard for that to happen.

Now I own a car and I go to school full time with my now 4 year-old daughter. If you ask her where she goes to school she will tell you "SAN JOSE SILLY COLLEGE". I still have my apartment that I received in the lottery pull, and I also received Section 8 Housing from the Family Unification Program. I volunteer 1 day a week at the Fleet Management Division for the County of Santa Clara. I am a sponsor[37] and that gives me the satisfaction of giving back. I am in service and continue to attend all the functions I can (when I am not studying).

---

37 A sponsor is a recovered addict/alcoholic who is now working the steps and is working with others to show/help them to stay clean and sober.

I love who I am today. I can look into the mirror and look straight into my eyes and see a beautiful woman both inside and out. I depend on my Higher Power, whom I choose to call God, on a daily basis. I would not change the happiness and love I have for anything. Thank you and FWC for participating in what I believe to be my resurrection.

With Admiration – Rosemary Smith

My Monica

By Anonymous

I was raised Jehovah's Witness. My mom raised all of us that way, my older brother, three younger sisters, and me. It kept me out of trouble until I was 18. I didn't like being raised Jehovah's Witness. Bad idea, but there were some parts that were actually worthwhile, and some parts that weren't. I got to meet a couple of great people;, a few actually. It was kinda cool, but I felt stifled. It's hard to be gay and Jehovah's Witness. They don't coincide.

My mother raised us all to the best of her ability. Most of the highlights I remember from my childhood are of her. There are some good points of my dad. There were some great times with him; but not many that I care to remember. My mom, on the other hand; it's kind of hard to not accept four girls that are gay. We talked to her about it and said "no, it's not you, it's just me". She's not *unaccepting* of it, but it's our life and she doesn't have to see us every day so she's cool with that. I didn't come out right away to her. After I left home I told her, that way I had an escape route. I didn't know what her reaction was going to be. Growing up, she didn't know. If she did, she didn't tell us about it, but I pretty much kept everything from her as best I could, but she's a mom - she had to have known. She was pretty devastated, but she was mostly worried about how she felt and how it was going to affect her, but I'm not living at home with her anymore, so I don't think it really does affect her. It wasn't about her and she was ok with it; at least that's what I thought. Actually, she wasn't really ok with it at all, but what was she going to do? I was a kid. And she does love me for whatever reason. That's just it: because I'm her kid, she loves me. We get along great these days. There's no if, ands, or buts about it. There's nothing that she did wrong as far as I'm concerned. She always asks, "did I do anything wrong, did I say something"? "No, Mom, this is just how I am". It took her some time to actually accept it, especially after my third sister came out to her. The only person I really keep in touch with is Neline. Sarah hardly ever calls me. Melanie - God only knows where she's at. We don't really talk anymore. Lawrence is off doing missionary work somewhere out of the States with his wife. He's happy and that's all that matters, really. My Mom sometimes goes to visit him. I love my family; I just like them where they are.

In the beginning, what got me there was drugs and alcohol, to be honest. It started out when I was 18. I got really drunk one night and I couldn't go to sleep. I was living outside under a bridge and I wanted to get arrested so I could have at least three hot meals, which is kind of stupid, but that's the main reason why. You know, it's funny: when you *want* to get arrested, you can't. I was sitting out on the corner of Monterey and Southside Drive at the gas station there. I was sitting right out front with a 40 ounce bottle in my hand, and a cop drove right by me. I was singing and being annoying, and loud, and obnoxious, and I didn't get anything from the cops. It wasn't until I got up and turned to walk away because I was getting fed up that the cop stopped me. I sat out there for five hours. I was so angry that day. I got arrested for being drunk in public. I asked him if he could take me in and he wouldn't until I actually threw the bottle on the ground and then he got me on being drunk and intoxicated and he took me in. I was in the "drunk tank" for only four hours--after five hours of waiting to go to jail! It wasn't very fun, and I wasn't very happy, but I did get food and sleep. That was the first time I got in front of a Judge Pierce. I was in front of him for about five minutes. I didn't get a lawyer. He said you'll be back, and

I said, I probably will, but I won't be back for a year or two. And I didn't go back for another year or two. That's when I stole my best friend's car and took it for a joyride and borrowed it for a couple weeks. I was driving it and got into an accident, but I couldn't fix it, so I called her and told her where her car was. She went to go see my family and they took her side because she was right and I was wrong. I was in the wrong, and she pressed charges. I got arrested because I had a $10,000 warrant on me for not showing up to court. I didn't even know I had a court appearance to go to for the stolen vehicle—grand theft auto. She reported the vehicle was stolen, but I didn't even realize I had a court case. Nobody had served me with the papers, until after I got out of jail and I went home. Then I got served with the papers at my mom's house. I got the papers, got released after about two weeks, and that started my career as far as jail was concerned. I was only in there off and on for a little bit for stealing, being drunk in public, and all that. Then they put me on Prop 36[38], but I kept finding myself in jail.

That's when I met Judge Bondanno. I quit drugs at first, and I had like three years of sobriety without sobriety – if you know what I mean. I didn't really work the program at all. It wasn't until my roommate decided that she was going to sell the house that we were living in so I didn't really have any place to go, so I was couch surfing at all of my friends' houses, and stuff just started happening. It got stressful. I was still taking classes, but eventually it just got harder. The more stressed out I got, the more I wanted to use alcohol; so I did. I was still going to court. Not DDTC, but a different court - criminal drug court - because I was on probation.

After I had my son, Sam, I started to get my life together, but it didn't really hold. It never really held. Not until now, anyway. It's funny, because you can be surrounded by all these people that have been in recovery, but you will never know until you get into a room to find out exactly who is. Now, though--that's what matters--I have something to live for. I'm looking at it and I have family and friends and people that care. The struggles are different. The people, the places, are somewhat the same, but not exactly. My life is different

---

38 Criminal Drug Court in California

in a lot of ways. I'm grateful for what I have today. As far as I'm concerned, I believe I am slightly overpaid with my quality of life. It could change at any minute, but the quality is a lot better than it was. I don't have to worry about when anything's coming, or how long I have to stay here before it's time for me to leave. I'm pretty comfortable.

I would like for it to change in a lot of ways, but that comes with time. Patience is not one of my best qualities. Sam lives in San Mateo with my mother now. I still owe back child support for him. He enjoys my mom. He does want to come home, though; he wants to come back here. He wants to come and move back home with me, but I don't see that happening anytime soon. Monica* misses her brother. They're great kids together. She calls him sometimes at night. I try to visit him as often as I can, but it takes at least two hours by train and bus to get there, so it's hard.

Monica was actually an accident, but it is what it is. Both my children were products of rape, but I don't believe in abortion so I kept them. When Monica met her father, she said she didn't like him and she said she never wanted to see him again, and I agreed. Then she met her grandfather and she didn't like him either, so we never saw him again either. She told me she was going to find another dad. That's when she found Papa. Papa became her Papa. She rejected her old reality and inserted her own. But the day I found out that he died - that was a rough day. I still remember it like it was yesterday, but it's also very sad. Monica pretty much cried all the way home. We were at St. James Health Center that day. When I found out about it, I fell to my knees right then and there in the hospital. I couldn't tell Monica at first, so I waited until we left. We got in the car and I told her, "you know I love you, right"? And then I just told her that Papa died. She yelled, "who's going to give me candy corn"?, because Halloween was their favorite holiday together. She just cried, and cried, and then she fell asleep. It still affects her. Recently it was her birthday and she was expecting his phone call.

The case with Monica started in 2006. I was still couch surfing house to house and all that. Then I realized that I didn't really have a stable place for my kid to go. You know, it got hard. And I was still wanted by the judge because I was testing dirty all the time, so eventually I just turned myself in. Monica was already gone. What happened was, I dropped Monica off at a friend's house, and I had to go get some money to get a room - a motel room for the night. I wasn't going to go prostitute myself or anything like that. That's not what I do. I was going to go fix a computer for a friend and he was going to give me double the money that I was going to charge to fix it for him. And I did, but it winded up taking longer than I expected at the time. It took 24 hours, and my friend called because he couldn't keep watching Monica. He was like 70-something years old. So he called that authorities and they came to pick Monica up, and Monica was gone. After that, I just went on a mad drug run for about a month. I don't recall any of that month-- I don't remember any of it at all. I remember that I just got tired. That's what I do remember. I remember distinctly saying to myself, "I can't do this anymore. My daughter is counting on me. I have to get her back. I have no place for her to go". I have to go to court anyway, so I'm just going to go turn myself in - which is what I did. I went to court to turn myself in, and the judge looked at me - I remember this distinctly - I was up for like five days, and I was just tired - dead dog, rock bottom tired. I looked at the judge and the judge looked at me. His face was all smiling, saying "you're doing great in school, but you've got all this other stuff". It was Judge Bondanno. He was going to release me two weeks after I got in, and I said, "no, don't release me". And he asked "why"? And I said, "At least let me find a program that's inside and let me go get my kid". And it's been like that ever since.

I went to a THU, and then I went to DDTC, and I talked to Judge Lucero. She and I really didn't get along. She taught me some good lessons though. I was living in the THU and when I finally got Monica back, I was ecstatic. I have to admit that I couldn't have done it without the help of all of them. They helped find a sponsor. I found a place to live. I went to different programs. I got a place of my own after two years of sobriety, and Monica and I have been together since then. She's just an awesome kid. I can't believe how she's bounced back. We get along well. We're still in therapy together just to get through the reunification process right. I really didn't want to see a therapist. I didn't like them. But I've kept going, and I am still in school online at Colorado University. I'm working on getting my Bachelor's degree in Business Management.

I graduated from DDTC in 2007. I still have the certificate; I have it in a frame. I never threw it away. That's a portion of my life I care to keep, not something I care to lose. I never ever want to go back in that direction, and the certificate is definitely a reminder of what not to do. I am grateful to Judge Lucero, although I have always had an issue with anybody with a robe. She was the first judge that didn't remand me. For some reason, every time I saw a judge, I would get remanded. That was in my head, and I didn't talk to her eye to eye until about a year or so into it. I realized that, despite me, I'm actually going someplace. I think Judge Lucero is an awesome person and I'm grateful for everything she's done for me. If it weren't for DDTC, I wouldn't have gotten Monica back. I also believe that if it weren't for them, I never would have seen half the stuff about myself that was worthwhile. If it weren't for them showing it in one way or another, I never would have seen it.

I learned that if I didn't take care of myself, I could not take care of Monica. I learned that from Deborah Dohse herself. That was kind of cool. I love that woman. She is a totally awesome woman! The Family Night classes were awesome. I learned how to be a better parent because of them. I still use and apply some of the stuff they taught me. If it weren't for them, I never would have found out that Monica possibly had ADD or to know when she was have problems.

They helped me out with a lot of stuff I was going through. I still have struggles, but now I can worry about what normal people worry about. I would much rather live a sober life over using drugs. Back then, I wasn't living life, I was just looking for the next fix. It wasn't living; it was just surviving. I did methamphetamine, I smoked marijuana, and I drank alcohol. I just don't want to do it anymore. And they helped me out with that.

*Indicates that name has been changed

Testimony

By Jonelyn Rosete

My name is Jonelyn Rosete. I am 32 years old with two beautiful children, Kristopher and Kaelynn. I made some really bad decisions in the past and I had my children taken away from me. I was lost and I did not know what to do.

In 2008, God led me to the House of Grace and there I was found. While at House of Grace, I was involved with Family Wellness Court. During my stay at House of Grace, I was blessed to meet so many loving people. I had a lot of support from the staff and my fellow sisters who were in the program with me.

Thanks to Family Wellness Court, I was able to get my children back. They gave me a second chance to have custody of my children. It was truly a blessing from God.

On Christmas of 2010, House of Grace and CityTeam helped me get a car for easier transportation for my children and me. I can never thank them enough for their compassionate hearts. They gave me a chance to start my life all over and be the mother that I need to be for my children.

On December 28, 2010, my case was completely dismissed.

God still continues to guide me and my children day by day.

RECOVERY FOR ME

By Brandy D.

I remember as if it was yesterday how my journey with recovery began. I was 23 years old, and had just removed both my children from living with their father. It was sometime in April of 2002, and I was completely unprepared. At this time I was only smoking weed and drinking every now and then. I thought I had my life pretty well laid out. Man was I wrong!

June or July of 2002, I made a call to Eastfield Ming Quong's (EMQ) Crisis intervention team because I could not find therapy for my son, who at the time was only four and a half. The reason I needed therapy for him was because, since I had removed him from his father, he was physically abusing my daughter who was three and a half. Everywhere I had called looking for therapy had a waiting list and I felt in my heart that something needed to be done immediately. I could not have my son hurting his sister like this.

When EMQ came to my home to evaluate my son, I was told they were going to have him removed from my home because they felt it was not safe for my daughter. This is when CPS came into my life. They came to my home and placed my son in their care. I was told that someone would contact me within the next couple of days and explain everything in detail.

In the next couple of days, I had a home visit from the follow-up social worker, and she walked in my home with a drug test. That worried me because I had told the initial social worker I never did drugs and I rarely drank. When I asked her what would happen if someone came up dirty after they told them they were clean, and she told me that they would remove any further children from the home. I got scared; scared enough to tell her that I was not clean and that I was willing to do whatever I needed to make things right again.

They placed my son in foster care, and I was possibly going to lose my daughter. I was notified of my first court hearing where I was to go before a judge, which happened to be Judge Edwards. This is where I would first face my ex-husband, the reasons I had removed the children from his home, and the reasons why my son was removed from me. The court gave me a choice to join something they called DDTC, Dependency Drug Treatment Court. It was explained to me that they would monitor my recovery - I had to stay clean, go to meetings, live in a recovery home, do an outpatient program and do random drug testing. At this point, I felt overwhelmed.

I didn't know whether I was coming or going. The world that I thought was all together had come to a complete halt. I did not understand things at first; I thought that when they said I needed to stay clean that meant I was not to use any drugs. I didn't understand that it also meant no drinking. So I went out and celebrated a friend's birthday and had a few drinks. The next day I was due to go into my first random drug testing. When I was speaking with the person at the desk and told them about my night before, they had explained to me that I was not to be drinking also. That freaked me out! I thought, "oh no they are going to remove my daughter". So the very next Monday, I contacted the social worker assigned to my case and explained everything to them. I had to be honest.

During this time, I was living with other adults who still partied. The more I got involved with the system and did what was asked of me, the more I worried that if a social worker came to the home and saw everything that they would talk my daughter. So, at the next court hearing, I asked if the DDTC program was still available to me; which of course it was.

It was only days before I was placed in my first SLE (sober living environment) or THU (transitional housing unit) a place where you can stay with or without your children in a safe environment. It was right before Thanksgiving at this time. I was scared, I felt like I placed my daughter and myself in God only knows what. The only phone that I was allowed to use was a pay phone and I felt I was in the middle of nowhere land. What had happened, how did my life get turned upside down? How do I fix it?

I was determined to do what I needed to get my son home, and to get my children and myself out of this mess. I was only in that first home for a few weeks before I was moved to a home where I would have only two other mother roommates and their children, and a house parent. Yes, a house parent - someone that can random drug test you, and make sure you do your chores. Oh yes, it was like becoming a child again and having to learn things all over again. I even had a curfew. What did I get myself into? Could I really get through all this? I had no other choice; it was up to me to do the right things for my children, but not just for them - for me too.

By the beginning of the New Year I was drug testing, doing out patient, taking two different parenting classes, attending meetings every day, going to therapy, visiting my son in a place to be supervised and losing my mind. I felt so overwhelmed, yet something kept me going. I remember during the first months of this outpatient program I was going through that I would say "I had a blast out there! When I get my son home it will be on again!" Seriously, what was I thinking?

A year after my son was removed from my care, I had been through many social workers, my visits kept being changed, my outpatient program was coming to an end, and I was still going to court every two weeks and still doing everything else they had asked of me. At this time I made a choice; a big one to me, I felt. I had never received my high school diploma and I wanted it more than ever by this time. So, I chose to enter a program that would include me getting my high school diploma and give me some other certificates in computer programs that would help me look for a better job.

I remember the day I went into the courtroom, there was a new attorney for the state or CPS, whatever you call it and she was just filling in for the regular appointed one. I remember telling them that I was going back to school and this lady sitting across from me asked me how I was able to do it with everything the court had me doing. I had explained to her, I wasn't doing everything for the courts and that I wasn't even doing this for the courts. I was doing it for me and that is what mattered. I told her I didn't know who she was and this is the first time she had ever met me, so before she could tell me it was all too much more me, she needed to know me and not judge me. At that point I had done everything the courts asked me to do without fail in my eyes so why couldn't I do this? I was going to do this, no matter what they were going to tell me. I had my mind set.

For once in my life I started feeling like my world was on track. I was clean and sober, on my way to getting my high school diploma and getting ready to move out of my THU. I felt things were changing for the best. I got a live-in job with a nonprofit THU as a house manager for women in recovery. Yes, things were looking up. I was visiting with my son who was now living with my great aunt and uncle in another county. I felt good.

During my job as a house manager I graduated from high school and got my diploma in a cap and gown. I was 25 and feeling better, though there was still something missing in my world - my son. I knew that I was doing all this for me and making me a better mom for him to come home to, but I wanted him there to see it all. Today I know there were reasons for this.

I enjoyed my new job as a substance abuse counselor and was still dealing with the courts. Yes, I know it was hard to believe that by now I had been part of this program for over two years. At this point, I was no longer part of the Drug Treatment Court for children in the system, I was just doing regular court hearings on my progress and what I still needed to do in order for my son to return home. At this point all I needed was a stable home; one where he had his own room.

How was I going to do this, and was this possible with just my income? Even though I enjoyed my job as a trainer in Drug and Alcohol counseling I need more hours if I was to provide a suitable place for my son. At this point I was living in a small, one bedroom apartment with my mother and my daughter. A new job with more hours was the only way. So here we went again with another job switch.

I got a job at a startup company that transferred old movies and pictures on to DVD. I had a desk job where I got to work 40 hours a week, plus overtime. The money was better and I finally got my chance at my own place. With the help family to make the deposit I finally got it - my very first apartment. It had two bedrooms and one bathroom. I had made the choice to give both my children their own rooms and I would sleep on the couch.

I felt at this moment that they needed their own space. They had gone through a lot in their short life. Sure enough, with my own place and a stable job, I remember hearing in the courtroom that I could have my son move back home on Thanksgiving. Sure enough, that morning, I went and brought my son home. I was able to take some time off of work to do this. He was finally coming home.

I knew the courts were going to follow us for a while longer. Not too sure how long, just that they were. I was going through so many different feelings at this point. Scared that I was going to make a mistake. Worried that if I did make a mistake they would remove my son again.

I registered my son into an after school program that he and his sister would be attending while I was at work. This did not last long, as my son had numerous outbursts. I realized that my son needed me more than ever, and that he would not be able to be watched by anyone but me.

I am going to float backwards in this story to give you a little understanding of my children. When my son was about 6-7 years old he and his sister explained to me some horrible things that happened to them while in their father's care. This caused some mental and emotional damage to my son who has been diagnosed with PTSD, severe ADHD, mood disorders, anxiety and sexual abuse disorders.

Yes, this was a lot to take in, and I stayed clean and sober through it all. WOW, a lot to deal with: having to stop working because of his blowups and emotional breakdowns. I lost the apartment because without a source of income I could no longer afford it. Where was I to go, what was I to do? Am I going to give up? NO! I took both my children and ended up in a homeless shelter. After everything I had done to make myself a better mother and a better person and this is how things were ending up? It was not going to push me down; I would get through it like I have gotten through everything else.

In the middle of my stay at the shelter with my children, I met a great person, which gave me hope and encouragement to keep moving forward. This person I met through AA meetings and the fellowship. We became friends and he asked me to date him; I laughed. I thought, "are you crazy"? But he was serious.

About a month into our relationship while I still in the shelter, my son had a mental breakdown and a crisis intervention team from EMQ had to be brought in to determine if he was stable enough to remain at home or needed to seek mental health attention. WOW, these people again. What was the court going to think about me - that I couldn't keep my son under control? While I felt like my life falling apart, something inside of me said that everything would be ok; give these people a chance, they are honestly here to help.

My son was placed in a youth mental hospital for a few days and during those few days I left the shelter and went back to my mother's one bedroom apartment. The social worker I had during this time took me to bring my son home from the hospital and told me I was doing everything she felt I should to care for my children the best I could during these tough times. Two days after bring my son home; something was wrong with him physically. The hospital he went to had changed his medication and his body reacted to it negatively.

I took him to a regular hospital and they transferred him to a children's hospital where I stayed with him for a week. I watched my eight year-old little boy detox off of medication that his body was rejecting badly. My son got better, and came home once again. Through everything I had been through with my son I finally went to my final court date where they told me they were closing my case. I ended up with full custody of both my children. I did it! I was the person I was always meant to be.

That person I told you that wanted a relationship with me became my husband and we became a big family with his three daughters, my son and daughter and, just a few weeks after the case closed, a daughter together. I was finally happy and full.

Over my years in the program I have met many different people. I have watched people relapse and people die from drugs and drinking. I watched my younger sister find her father deceased from the use of drugs.

I know in my heart if there wasn't a program like DDTC (Drug Dependence Treatment Court) mothers or fathers like me that hope to reunite their families and strengthen them wouldn't be here. I walked in the courts a scared young mother of two children and walked out a strong mother willing to do anything for her family, in a positive manner, and stand beside my children and love them no matter what. I thank each and every one of them daily for their pushing me and telling me that I could do it.

To this day I still stay in touch with the social worker that had my case closed. When they ask me to speak somewhere for them I jump at it, because I want to help others and show them that even though things seem tough, it will get better and things can be better no matter how hard it gets.

I have been through a lot, I have lost a lot, I have hurt, cried and so much more and I have learned that nothing and no one can make me relapse but me. The life I have may never be perfect, but I know that I do not want my children to ever have to feel the loss my sister did or to grow up in the arms of the county or state. I am BRANDY D. and my RECOVERY birthday is August 4, 2002. I do my best to live the AA way and to practice all the principles in all my affairs. I know that if I can do it so can you.

I love you JJ, Rirah and LaLa. You three give me the strength and courage to know that I wouldn't want to be anywhere else but here being your mommy!

Veronica's Story

By Veronica Esparza

Seven years ago my life was a disaster. I had lost everything: my children, my home, my relationship, my self-esteem, my job and the hope of ever having a second chance to be a good mother. Despite everything that I have done that hurt them, I always loved my children and meant to give them the best. I know that maybe it doesn't make a lot of sense considering my record, but my children are my life. Losing them made me realize that without them I have nothing.

I was homeless. I lived temporarily in the homes of family and friends. I had been convicted of child endangerment, in addition, to the charge of "under the influence of illegal drugs". It was a felony, which, fortunately, was later dropped to a misdemeanor. I was devastated because as a felon my future goals about work, credit, and many other issues were destined to fail. At the time I didn't know that eventually the charge would be changed to a misdemeanor and consequently I served 180 days and attended a 52-week parenting program. There was also a peaceful restraining order put in place with strict rules regarding my visits with my youngest daughter, Arianna. My record was recently expunged in May, 2010. Students from San Jose State University with the Record Clearance Project helped me.

I realized from the onset that I had only myself to rely on, in order to rebuild what I had destroyed and to somehow find a way to reunify my family. With the support of my social worker, Diana, who was a blessing because without her and the services I received from the county and the Dependency Drug Treatment Court, I would have been lost. With their support and by the grace of God, I have found the way to a better and more productive life.

I had to be very resourceful. There was a long waiting list for the outpatient substance abuse program (PSAP), but I was determined to get a placement. I bugged them every day with telephone calls. I guess they got tired of hearing from me on a daily basis or maybe they just understood how much I wanted to be in recovery. Whatever the truth was, in three weeks I began the program. Although the program required classes twice a week, I chose to attend three times a week. Without my children I was lonely and I needed support to help me get through this terrible crisis in my life. I was depressed. I needed structure in my life. Two days weren't enough. PSAP gave me a feeling of hope, that all was not lost and that I could still change my life around. Hearing others' success stories helped me to realize that anything is possible and that it's all up to me. I started to feel empowered.

The county provided a 16-week domestic violence class. My instructor, Nancy, helped me to understand that I suffered from Post-Traumatic Stress Syndrome as a result of the abuse I was subjected to during my past relationships. I began to realize the impact of domestic violence on my children and vowed that in the future I would protect my children from further exposure to any verbal or physical violence in our home.

Although I was court-required to attend one parenting class, I graduated from many more parenting programs and have received certificates of achievement from all of them. I attended the mandatory 10-week county program which was very helpful as it gave me some tools on how to be a more effective parent to my children. I felt that I wanted to know more so I attended a 12-week court approved parenting class from PSAP and I became more skillful in communicating with my children. Then I went to the 15-week drug court Family Parenting night. All the families sit down to dinner together with their children, which promotes a feeling of family and community. This was an important step in re-bonding as a family. I also attended a 52-week Parenting Without Violence program. I really appreciate the county providing me the opportunity to attend the parenting classes and I fully benefited from all of them. I have five kids now. I have to say with all the parenting skills that I learned from the system. I learned to forgive myself and to become a better parent by providing positive feedback to my children. I also learned patience through my recovery and how to listen. Most importantly I learned to respect my kids.

I have attended individual counseling sessions with Jeannie L., MSW, LCSW. She has provided me with guidance, education and reinforcement of parenting techniques. These therapy sessions have enhanced my approach to handling my children through health communication and limit setting. I always felt that I could really trust Jeannie and was able to open up to her and express my true thoughts and feelings. After graduating from DDTC, I kept myself in family therapy and individual therapy after the case was dismissed ongoing from 2004 until 2009. I also attend a processing group once a month that is offered through DADS to keep ourselves healthy and to be able to vent to a licensed therapist.

I lived at Sobrato Living Center from 2005 to 2006. The SLC is a temporary family housing solution with a sober living environment. I attended Sobrato's workshops and 12-step meetings. My children were returned back to me and we moved into a new apartment. I was working as a waitress then. I then moved away to Morgan Hill to keep my kids away from any drug or gang affiliation.

My dream is to someday be financially independent and to be able to make it on my own. I am now enrolled in classes at San Jose City College in order to make my dream a reality. I am studying Administration of Justice and want to become an adult probation officer. I do know that my life has changed and keeps changing daily. I am also in a relationship where I can now say I put my kids first and not the relationship or drugs. I love who I am today and what I have grown into.

I was in drug court with Judge Edwards and successfully graduated from his court. I have been a mentor parent since February 2008 and work about 25-30 hours at the Dependency Advocacy Center's Mentor Parent Program. I have attended trainings throughout my three years that I have been in the Mentor Parent program. As a mentor parent, I support clients in court, and talk about where and how I came into the dependency court. I also give other parents resources such as recovery pieces on where to find a meeting, and how to obtain a sponsor. If they need housing, I have some applications that they can fill out at my office. I also sit in court with them as a support person. I help with organizing their schedule using a planner that is provided by the courts. I am available for the clients who graduate and keep in contact for at least three months after they graduate. Some I keep in contact with continuously for support, or when they need someone to talk to. I love to help people who struggle in recovery by being a positive role model, staying clean, fulfilling my goals, and being around positive people.

I have an 18 month old son, Elijah, and I have to say it is a blessing that I can be a positive role model to him as well to my other for children. Eli is 18 years old and lives with me. Devina, 17 years old, lives with my mother. She made me a grandmother on June 24, 2010. Love it! I have another daughter Adina, 13 years old, and Arianna, 8. We've come so far. This is my story. Maybe it's not a beautiful story and there's plenty I'm not proud of. But it's a true story and it's my own. Most of all, I intend to devote the next chapters of my life to finding a way to gain back my children's trust in me. One day at a time. By the Grace of God.

My Story

By Gloria Hassett

Hi, my name is Gloria and I would like to share my story.

First off, I am from Salinas, California. I came to Drug Treatment Court because I thought I was going to die. I was alone, scared, pregnant and using drugs. Due to being on PROP 36, I had the option of going into a recovery program or serve time in jail. I knew I needed a program to better my life for my children and my baby on the way, so I chose a recovery program. The courts decided to send me to Heritage House which is part of City Team Ministries in San Jose, CA.

I came to Heritage House on July 9, 2009. I was scared and feeling so many different emotions. There I accepted Jesus Christ into my heart and surrendered all my problems to him. My life started changing for the better. I was loved, and I started a support group with other women that were going through the same problems. Then I started building a stronger relationship with Jesus Christ. My life had nothing but blessings. My daughter, Veronica, was born on December 16, 2009 and that's when Family Wellness Court got involved. When Veronica turned 4 months old, I moved to the House of Grace and started to grow even more. It was the same type of program, just more structured. There I found a job and I was able to start getting my life back on track. I graduated from Family Wellness Court on February 11, 2011 and then graduated from House of Grace on September 17, 2011. After graduating from House of Grace, I was able to move into my own place. I still stay in contact with my fellow sisters at Heritage House and House of Grace. I believe that coming to this program and accepting Jesus Christ into my life was the best decision not only for me but for my children as well. I am finally living the life that I thought I could never have. Anything is possible when you have Jesus Christ in your life.

GRATITUDE

By Vince Sandoval

I have so many things to be grateful for. For one, having my son, who means everything to me; the other, having a place to call our own with the help of numerous people I came to know. In the past two years I lost my son, and it took my mistake to happen the way it did for me to fight to get him back.

Even though I have my ups and downs, Judge Lucero, Rosa, Elsie Moreno, and many others did not give up on me. It feels good that there are people in San Jose, CA that really care. I am grateful to have been given a chance to prove that I can take care of my son - even though he's a handful at times – and I would not have it any other way. I strongly believe that if it was not for the parenting classes I took, I would not have the knowledge that I have now to cope with my son at times.

Meeting and getting to know clean and sober people is a whole lot better than running around with people who only want one thing from me. There were times when I had to be reminded of appointments, and sometimes scolded from my favorite judge, Judge Lucero; but I needed it during those times. Thank you, Judge Lucero!

When I forged a meeting slip, everyone put me back on track. The essay that I had to write taught me that the meetings are necessary in order for me to stay clean. When I was tired of going to the meetings, my addiction would creep up. The 12-steps and the books are really effective. Anyone who is in recovery knows that having a sponsor, a good support group, and having clean and sober friends can save another human being's life. Seeing what I have today has made me realize that I am not willing to lose it all ever again. I have been able to maintain my sobriety and it is awesome, it is great, and it is rewarding.

When I was growing up in the 70's, I wished that Child Protective Services (CPS) was an option for me. When my step-dad came into me and my mom's life, I received a lot of attention from him. Until my half-brother was born - then things changed. I began to receive negative attention from my step-dad; both verbal and physical abuse. My mother and step-dad would leave me at night to fend for myself and to take care of my brother, Adam, and my youngest half-brother, Craig. Back then, and into the 80's, my step-dad worked two jobs, smoked marijuana, and drank alcohol. When he would come home from work, he would come straight into my room. Once he picked me up from the top of my bunk bed and threw me against the wall. Another time he tied me up to a chair and left me there overnight. He would always talk down to me, and this took place until I was 16 years old. My mother let him do whatever he wanted because she feared the man. Through the years, I swore to myself I was going to pay him back, but I didn't go through with it.

The very first time that I became a father, my life felt like it wasn't meant to be. My first son, Jeremiah, was taken by CPS in 1998. In 2001, my twins, Cheyenne and Leilani were born and they were also taken by CPS. At the time, I really didn't care so much about my life. Then my son, Tyler, was born in 2002, while Tyler's mom and I were staying in a shelter. A social worker came to the shelter the next day to visit us and I immediately became defensive and thought the social worker was going to take Tyler. But that wasn't the case. We passed the probation date and Tyler was able to stay with us to raise. Ever since that day, Tyler has been my reason for living. When Tyler was a baby, I had sworn that I wouldn't do to him what was done to me.

Within the two years in Drug Court, I've experienced a lot and learned a lot. I've learned how to listen to Tyler, to have patience with him, to give him the love that he seeks, to be a nurturing father to him, to have allow him to have his opinions on decisions, to take time out when I'm upset with him, and to have quality, one-on-one time with him.

One day, Tyler turned around and began saying negative things about himself. After he calmed down, I approached him and told him that he wasn't any of the things he called himself. I explained to him that he can do anything he puts his mind to from now to the time he becomes an adult.

I am so grateful for everything that has come my way and for the people that I've encountered.

Vince Sandoval

P.S. Mrs. Deborah, you are one big-hearted lady and it has been a privilege to know you and everyone in the courtroom. I will be missing all of you. You all have been a big part of my recovery. I'm smiling now but I know later I will have tears due to my departure from all of you. Thank you!

BLESSINGS IN DISGUISE

By The Chavoya Family

Rosalio "Big Leo" Chavoya
(Parent, Partner, Father)

September 2006

Driving along in my White Jeep Cherokee and approaching my exit off Interstate 680 onto King Road in San Jose, I received a call from the individual I was on my way to meet. "Where you at, homie"? I explained to him where I was, to which he said "I'm kinda stuck in traffic. I'll be there in 5minutes". I'm thinking, no problem, I'll just park in this taqueria lot and wait for him maybe get a Horchata to pass time...Right? Wrong! What happened next puts an exclamation mark on my last run-in with "The Law"!

It was approximately 5 p.m. that day, blue skies; nice and warm. I was bumping to a local Bay Area rap artist's CD. The parking lot was full except for one space. As I backed into the space, and just as I placed my vehicle in "Park", aggressively blocking me head-on was an unmarked Tahoe with red and blue lights flashing! I knew then that I was set up and there was nowhere to run! I was busted!

I see the undercover officer leap out of his vehicle from his passenger side, gun drawn and yelling "Hands up, Hands up!" Now, my street instinct tells me first to run and get rid of all the evidence! The problem with that was the only thing running was my car. I didn't have a chance to turn off the ignition, plus I still had my seatbelt on. So I grabbed the dope I had on my lap and tossed it out the window; only to have it land on the hood of the vehicle parked next to me 2 feet away! I put both arms in the air and both eyes on the officer circling the front of my vehicle to my open passenger side window, still shouting "Hands up, Hands up"! But suddenly, he shouts "He has a gun!" and shoots...!

Before I give you the conclusion to this portion of my story, allow me first to explain my wrongdoings at the time and what led up to that day.

September 2005

I had been off parole from my 2nd C.D.C (California Department of Corrections) number for about 12months, and had decided I was going to make a run at being legit. Our 3rd daughter Julissa had been born. Vero (my love) and I stayed clean and I was searching for a job applying at sites, visiting employment agencies, while riding our local transits. I was also in the process of acquiring my driver's license. An employment agency called me and I was lined up with a couple of jobs. One became steady at a local meat packing company for about 90 days.

Within those 90 days my family and I received a housing opportunity for our own apartment. I was able to receive my license after three tries. I was able to buy us a White Jeep Cherokee. Things were looking really good for our family of six.

Also within those 90 days, I bumped into one of my homies who happened to live in the same apartment complex as us. He had heard we were doing great and he was happy for us. But he expressed also that he was struggling, living with his pregnant girlfriend, still getting high and selling dope. I thought, man I'm happy that's not me!

A few weeks later, after I had gotten paid, my loving girlfriend and mother of all my children announces that she feels like getting high! Now, up to this point, my response was always a firm "NO". But this time, there was a pause in my response, and we proceeded to work out where we could get it, because it would only be "this one time". We couldn't get it from just anyone because then the word would get out that we were getting high again! So we decided to get a twenty ($20 worth of meth) from my homie that I had just bumped into; especially since he lived in the same apartment complex as us. Once, became twice, and after that it was a 40 sack! Suddenly, we were fully engaged again in our methamphetamine addiction.

Allow me to clarify that, silently, I truly wanted this to happen because I did not want her to seek elsewhere, and I thought I'd be able to control it!

Then my job hours and title changed to sanitation working graveyard shift! This made me really sink deep into my addiction because now I really need help staying up through the night! So, I needed to do more dope! SO MY SICKNESS SAID!

Something else occurred during this time. I was working at a meat packing place- it's very cold; refrigerator cold. I had just established a Primary Care Physician (assigned doctor) for my rheumatoid arthritis (at 30yrs old!). One night, I was working with the water hose cleaning the place. It was cold, I was wet, and I was high – a destructive combination for somebody with rheumatoid arthritis! My body could no longer function due to the arthritis, cold and wet. I became a liability to them and was no longer able to work with the company. What made it worse is that they were considering hiring me full time!

Now I have no job; but I have a White Jeep Cherokee, a license, and insurance. But I needed money, plus we are deep into our addiction...What to do? It seemed like the only option for me was make a couple of calls and score some dope; enough that I could sell, make some money, with enough left to get high for both my love and me.

You're probably asking, "What about the kids"? The kids were fine (our state of mind suggested), occupied in their rooms, watching DVDs. They had a roof over their heads, clothes on their backs and food! In between getting high, we would take turns tending to the children's needs. Most of the time that meant putting in a new Dora the Explorer DVD to babysit our children: our oldest daughter, Sirena, had just turned 11years old. Our son, Rosalio, was 7 years old. Our next daughter, Liana, was 2 years old and our youngest daughter, Julissa, was 11 months old. To give you an idea how sick we were, we would actually argue over whose turn it was to leave the room! Neither one of us wanted to leave the dope!

At midday around the last day of August 2006, I was getting ready to go and meet up with a friend to get some dope. Before that, though, I needed to go see my father-in-law.

As I cruised along Alum Rock Ave. heading west, then making a right onto East Gate Drive I noticed a cop car facing west directly in front of me, parked with an officer looking my direction! As I approached the stop sign I'm thinking, "Act normal"! But in reality, what is normal? Especially when I'm high and have dope in my lap! At the stop sign one either has to make a left or right. I get to a complete stop with my right blinker on; I look left, then right, I catch eyes with the cop and give him a respectful nod, look left again and proceed with my right turn. But, as I'm doing so the officer proceeds to make a U-Turn right behind me with his pullover lights on! DAMN IT! Right away, my street instincts kick in: FLEE! GET RID OF THE DOPE!

Now, I'm in a residential area and I accelerated, zooming past my in-laws house with the family outside, watching! As I zoomed by, I tossed my black leather fanny pack (which included my paraphernalia and dope) out the window directly behind a parked vehicle. When I next looked in my rearview mirror, I noticed the cop car was at a standstill! That's when I remembered that officers can no longer go on hot pursuits within residential areas! Woo hoo! I'd gotten rid of the dope and got away...well, kind of!

I purchased my Jeep Grand Cherokee from a family that lives two houses from my in-laws! Right away, law enforcement starts tracking me. They started with the family I bought the vehicle from. They informed the police that they sold the vehicle to the family two houses down. Later the police found their way to my love. They told her to tell me to call the sergeant!

My first thought was "Yeah right, I am not calling the Sergeant and telling on myself!" But they already knew it was me. Plus, I was thinking if the police are contacting my in-laws and my family then obviously I'm not the only one being affected! So I decided I would call the Sergeant.

The Sergeant gets on the phone and I relay to him who I am and that I am willing to face the consequences for my actions. He acknowledged he knew who I was and proceeded to scold and lecture me about what a real careless and stupid decision I made to flee! I had put a lot of people at risk, including myself. We agreed to meet the next morning at a Starbucks on the East Side.

The next day arrived with me high as a kite. I made it to our designated meeting place. When I approached I noticed he was not alone. There were 4-6 other police cars there! Naturally, my instinct was to run, but I decided to go ahead with the meet. I parked 6 parking slots from him, got out and approached him. We made eye contact he gave me a smile and said, "Boy, you've got guts showing up". So we spoke while his officers were searching my vehicle. Actually I was being interrogated by him and 2 other officers. They believed I had a lot of dope or guns. So it went on and on…But at the end I was ticketed for misdemeanor reckless driving and evading! (What a blessing!) It was very easily a felony, but he told me since I showed up and kept my promise to meet him it was dropped to a misdemeanor. He sent me on my way and wished me luck. Oh, and the reason he was attempting to pull me over? Because I had NO FRONT LICENSE PLATE!

This all happened exactly one week before where my story began.

Back to the taqueria ....

I have both hands up, maintaining eye contact with the officer circling the front of my vehicle with his gun drawn yelling, "Hands up, Hands up". As he gets to my open passenger side window he yells, "He has a gun", and shoots! The next thing I remember is a bunch of shuffling and hands grabbing me! I hear one of the officers say, "Just take his seatbelt off". As soon as the seatbelt was released I was yanked from my driver's seat through my passenger side door! I remember the black-topped pavement quickly approaching my face, and my arms being yanked this way and that, all the while being punched on the right side of my face with the left side of my face slamming on the pavement! I'm also hearing, "Stop resisting, stop resisting"!

Suddenly, I'm cuffed, turned over and my clothing is being cut off of me! That's when I realized I was shot all right - with 4 Tasers! I had to be taken by ambulance to the hospital and the Tasers were removed. The left side of my face looked like ground beef and the right side extremely swollen. I was charged with possession for sale, transporting and resisting arrest. It took about a half day to get me situated and housed in the county jail's 4th floor lockdown unit.

The next few days are sketchy, but, apparently I received a visit from my love, telling me she was going to bail me out. She found the rest of my dope, sold it and bailed me out within two or three days. Now I'm out with two different cases that I caught one week apart. I had no vehicle and no license. My plan was to stretch these cases out as long I could, and eventually combining the cases to do one stretch of time if it came to that. This would go on from September 2006 thru July 2007.

The day I got out on bail I got high, doing what I felt I had to do to get money. But one time in particular, around Christmas Eve 2006, my love and I were pregnant. But she started having pains and spotting. She was in the hospital for a day or two. When I had left earlier in the day to change and get high, the doctors told me she would be released later on that night. When I returned to pick her up I noticed three or four police cars lined up near the entrance of the hospital emergency room. My love was being interrogated by the police concerning a bruise that she had around her back area. She insisted to the police that it was not domestic violence. So, due to her "lack of compliance" our children were removed, and placed in my in-laws' care. An informal case was opened. My love had to engage in a case plan to get our kids back. She got clean and proceeded to do all she was required to do in her case plan. All the while, I continued doing what I did best - getting high and selling dope!

After 6 months, she completed her case plan, graduated from her programs and reunified us with our kids. About 2 months after that, I ended up consolidating the cases with no probation and two years in state prison with parole. I was about one hour late to my sentencing, trying to get as high as I could on meth for the last time. But I did make it to the courthouse, was sentenced, remanded into custody and taken away to do my time.

Three weeks later, I received a legal document with Old English writing stamped saying "Superior Court-Juvenile Dependency"! Did something catch up to me from when I was a juvenile? Was my son now in Juvenile Hall? I was hesitant to open it.

So I took a deep breath and opened it. I began to read what was on the pink ditto paper. Then I read it again. Then I understood it to say that my children were removed from their mother's care! The children were in a children's shelter, while my love was taken into custody! I had no other details and I was in shock. I felt my heart being squished – picturing my babies being removed and placed in an unfamiliar place! I began to cry. With tears in my eyes and a lump in my throat I began processing this information with my bunkie whose name was Laughter.

Suddenly my name was called, and I was told to start packing my stuff because I'm being transferred to Trans-Pack! This meant I would be transferring to another prison's mainline. I wasn't told immediately where I was going, but, as a State inmate, you can be sent anywhere there is room in California. Your only hope is that it's close to home. I found out that I was being transferred to the mainline at San Quentin State Prison.

There are a couple of things I need to point out. First, is the unfortunate news that my family had been broken up on the outside. Second was the news that I was going to a mainline which had a lot more "privileges" and "freedom" within an institution. It turned out to be a blessing. The odd thing is it is very rare that one gets shipped out after only two weeks of being in a Reception Center (another blessing). Even more rare is the opportunity to stay local (another blessing). Although I thought I was just getting away with something at the time, I recognize and acknowledge that I was being blessed with a golden opportunity. After I read the news of my children being placed in a shelter, it really weighed heavy on me! For one I wasn't there! I had made no effort to stop the dope when I was out. Instead I left it all to my love to bear! So it was my fault!

When I got a chance to call home and speak to my love, I heard in her voice she was really distressed! Right away she began apologizing. I quickly expressed my love to her and owned my part in all that had transpired. She told me she was going to do everything she had to get the kids back. I was relieved and I was confident that she would do it.

For the next 7 months, I did my very best to balance prison with learning to create a better me. I was assigned a job in San Quentin's Print Shop (another blessing). I enjoyed my assignment at the Print Shop. I eventually was granted a pay number receiving $13 a month (another blessing). The yard I was housed in, which was a Level 1 and 2 minimum security yard, began a pilot program that gives prisoners the chance to develop the tools and learn to be better persons, citizens and parents. By this time I knew what I would have to do when I got out: take parenting classes, work substance abuse programs, and attend Domestic Violence Batterer's classes.

Within those seven months I remained busy learning and working. I became a father for the 5th time in January, 2008 to our son Victor. Even though I wasn't there, I vowed to be there, present, for my family from the time I got out onward.

In March of 2008, my prison history caught up to me. After seven months of enjoying "freedom" within prison walls, it all came to an end. Although I had done nothing wrong, my presence was a threat to the safety and security of the institution. My history had caught up to me. I would have to do the duration of my time (5 months) in "The Hole".

Before I ended up in the Hole I had to come up with a parole plan. I had burned a lot of bridges with my careless character and attitude. So I knew there was only one option. I wrote a letter to my loving Tio Tony and Tia Lupe asking for an opportunity to be allowed to live with them on parole. I truly needed to prove I was done with my past lifestyle, and I needed to let them know I understood if they couldn't accommodate me. I received a letter back from my Tio and Tia informing me that they were happy to help me out! Besides being family, they have played key roles my family's life. I admire my Tio and Tia for so many things, and I love them dearly. They have never once looked down on me (yet another blessing).

On August 25th, 2008, my parole officer was at the Institution to pick me up and take me home. He had hair as long as "Cheech and Chong" and very pale skin. By this time all the children were back in my love's care. I had to have supervised visits with my all of my children except the baby. Fortunately, the visits were supervised by my love or my in-laws.

Now, I had a little over 5 months left to prove to the courts that I was willing to change. I remember what Judge Lucero once said about me doing those programs while in custody. She said, "It doesn't matter that those programs in custody don't count towards your case plan. It matters that you had a choice to take them or not and you chose to take them". That was very motivational and encouraging to me.

When I got out, my lifetime partner started schooling me about DDTC (Dependency Drug Treatment Court), encouraging me to join. I accompanied her to her Drug Court reviews. I started seeing how it was in the waiting rooms and lobby. It was a whole bunch of moms, and maybe one or two fathers. I was introduced to my love's Mentor Mom, Kimberly. Kimberly allowed me a few weeks to think about signing up for DDTC. I told myself I would stay open-minded and just do everything I was asked or expected to do. The bottom line was that everything I would have to do for DDTC were things that I would be required to do for my own case plan. The only difference is I would be receiving expert advice and assistance on completing my case plan. Still I was leery all the way up to the day Kimberly called me to complete the application. We did it, then I called my attorney and left a message that I was on board for DDTC.

My first Drug Court review came in October 2008. Now here I am thinking, "What Have I Done"? I am very nervous, but why? I'm clean and sober. I've done nothing wrong and have nothing to worry about. Well it took me a few times sitting in front of the Judge, who wanted to talk to me, and hear how I'm doing before I realized that all this nervousness was because everything about this court is different. I'm almost uncomfortable because everybody's saying nice things about me, pointing out the good things I'm accomplishing. Awkward! But, after I left, and got past that initial hearing I thought, "Well, that wasn't that bad".

I flashed back to when I was transferred from San Quentin to the county jail for my six month review. I was visited by the assigned social worker who was very considerate - she came in primarily just to meet me. At this visit, we really just chatted and engaged each other; at times getting very emotional. She expressed no authority and simply engaged me as a person; never once making me feel "less than". I truly believe that visit played a key role in allowing me a sneak peak of what to anticipate when I got out.

When I got out, we were assigned a DDTC social worker, who continued that same level of respect and understanding in her own way. Honestly, when somebody usually speaks about a social worker, it's generally negative! Social workers are considered Enemy #1 to the Dependency Court population, based on the fact that they are there to take your kids and will be there to keep them until they say the kids can go home! It doesn't matter that in most cases we were neglecting our children or placing them in harm's way. Or, that in most cases, we're high and can use/need the help to get off the dope!

I began therapy sessions per my case plan. Initially I thought of therapy as for somebody who has problems-not me! But, in my current state of mind, I thought what "Why not maintain an open mind, satisfy my case plan and learn something along the way"? Every time I showed up for my sessions I thought I wouldn't have anything to talk about. Still, each time I went we spoke for all ninety minutes! One of my biggest issues that I worked on with my therapist was the DDTC judge communicating with me directly. No negative reflection on Judge Lucero. It's just that I was never accustomed to a judge talking to me, or wanting to hear how I'm doing or what my concerns were. Another issue was dealing with my daughter - it turned out I just had to go with the flow and that it was a phase she was going through. So, time with a therapist really was useful for me. I was truly fascinated by how I could go in with nothing to talk about, but talked for ninety minutes - intriguing!

From day one of my release I began attending N/A (Narcotics Anonymous) meetings. Those were hard for me; nonetheless, I always tried to put the blinders on and just listen to the speakers. I was required to connect with a sponsor, which was also difficult for me. Eventually I did find a sponsor by the latter part of my case plan.

Among my other classes, I began a 16 week "Parenting Without Violence" course. I learned that within these treatment courses you get out what you put in. If everybody is quiet and doesn't participate with any scenarios or feedback then we really don't learn anything. In this course, we were all fathers with different backgrounds and experiences. Aside from the great communication we had, what really stuck with me is the last lesson assignment. It's called the "Empty Chair"! You would write a good-bye letter without saying I'm sorry to your children and read it in front of the class to an empty chair! It was very touching and emotional.

My outpatient drug treatment was happening as well. I really enjoyed my counselor's personality and sense of humor. Especially when he would ask "How are you going to handle it when life shows up"? What he really meant was how was I going to stay clean and sober when dealing with my real life problems.

Once I was able to receive unsupervised visits and spend as much time with my family as I wanted. I truly looked forward to taking two of my daughters to preschool and picking them up. This school was named "Happy Hands" and was a preschool for children ages 3-4 whose parents still had an open dependency case. The teachers were always caring and the children loved them. It was a very sad day when those doors had to close due to funding cuts. We are still very thankful for those times and teachers.

I was also participating in what was called "Family Night". Here we would learn parenting skills and activities. We would either meet our children there (brought by the social worker) or bring them ourselves. We would participate in playing games and activities with our children. We would eat with our children and we would sit down and read to our own children. Here is where I read to my children for the first time. Even now, when we pass by where the classes were held, my children always mention Family Night.

Allow me now to mention that I had to do all those things while taking local transit. I would have to leave two hours in advance to arrive on time. Missing a bus time was inconceivable because being five minutes late would be counted as an absence. The reason I'm mentioning this is to send out major respect to the parents who have to do this case plan, by themselves, on the bus, pregnant, with children and a stroller, in the heat or the rain, having to leave perhaps three or four hours in advance, understanding if they miss one bus - be it the bus arrived early or late - then it's considered an absence. Those parents truly deserve our respect for showing their dedication to right their wrongs and bring their children home.

In all, my case plan was five months and two weeks long. I totally hit the ground running upon my release, and was able to satisfy all the requirements with the time I had left on the case. On paper it appeared nearly impossible. I'm sure that was secretly the belief of some people. But that didn't matter - I was ready to face it all and succeed, to the best of my abilities. I participated/graduated from all the necessary programs, except for my Domestic Violence class. This class was in my case plan because I never addressed it since I got Domestic Violence criminal charge in 1999. But I was encouraged and welcomed to complete it by the facilitators.

Once Feb. 9th 2009 came around our case was dismissed after 18 months. I received a letter of participation from Dependency Drug Treatment Court approximately three weeks after the case closed and I was able to finish "Family Night". The day our case was officially dismissed, I was approached by the Program Manager of the Mentor Parent Program. She introduced herself to me and asked if I was interested in joining their team of Mentors assisting parents in their journey of the Dependency Courts!?

Can you believe that? I definitely couldn't and I didn't. My response to her was "Okay, I'll think about it". But what I was really thinking was, "Yeah Right"! and "They want me to work among Social Workers, Sheriffs, District Attorney's, Judges, ..." She told me she would call me in a few weeks to see if I was interested. Sure enough, she called me to set up an interview. I still couldn't and didn't believe it. But I was a "go with the flow, see what happens kinda guy". I went along with it and, sure enough, she really is offering me a position to help the fathers in Dependency Court. I had a couple of concerns that I had to mention to make sure she understood me. My first was making sure she knew I'm on parole. Yes, she is aware, no problem. Next, making sure she knows I don't have any money to buy new clothing. Yes, she is aware, no problem. In other words, I'm being accepted the way I am, and as I am. All that's required is that I maintain my recovery. No problem-I was truly done with that lifestyle anyhow.

Between then and now, I have taken part in many trainings and workshops both as a participant and as a presenter regarding fatherhood engagement. I was able to create my own digital story along with six other fathers in different counties with the help of Bay

Area Academy Personnel and Students. I was awarded The 2010 Bay Area High-Promise Father of The Year award. Most importantly, I have been able to be mentally and physically present in each one of my children's lives. I am able to help fathers like myself; going through a Dependency Court struggle to regain parental stability. My presence and story tells them they are not alone and that nobody is perfect!

April 20, 2011

Today I'm 38 and have 45 months (3years, 9months and 6 days) free of drugs that ruled my life since the age of 13. Although I'm heavier than I'd like to be, I welcome my weight. I've been working as a Mentor Parent since March 3, 2009. Life has been so much more relaxed and easier since I've come to the realization that I have majority control of how my life pans out. "Negative Measures Generate Negative Outcomes" and "Positive Steps Generate Positive Results" - that's what my bottom lines are. If you go out seeking trouble, trying to hurt people or yourself using drugs and trying to get away with things, guess what happens? Negativity... If you stay positive in all you do bearing in mind others' well-being, not hurting yourself or others within your means, guess what happens? Positivity... Straight Ahead Moving Forward...

My Clean Date is 7/14/2007

Special Thank You To:

My Love Veronica

My In-Laws Victor, Julia and Sonia

My Loving Tia Lupe (R.I.P.)

My Appreciated Tio Tony

My Mom, My Dad, My Sister, and My Brother

All Five of My Children

All the DDTC Team, Mentor Parent Program, Dependency Advocacy Center

Especially my Grandparents on both sides of my family:

My Grandma Lopez for being extremely strong and firm in her own style and putting up with all of our negative, "crazy" lifestyles. I apologize for my part and I Love You, Grandma.

Grandma and Grandpa Chavoya, I apologize for all that you had to experience through me.

You've always expressed that there is a better way...I Love You Grandma and Grandpa.

I UNDERSTAND NOW. I BELIEVE I HAVE FOUND A BETTER WAY.

Veronica
(Loving Mother, Parent, Partner, Daughter, Sister)

On August 9th 2007, my life changed completely. I was at home with three of my kids-my oldest was visiting one of my sisters. Another sister of mine was visiting me. There was a knock on the door. My son looks through the window and tells me its security so I take a look and it's the police! I'm under the influence, so I'm thinking if I don't answer the door they'll leave. Well, that didn't happen. They went and got the manager to open the door!

So I'm like, "May I help you with something"? They said, "We got a phone call saying your kids were home alone", so they were doing a welfare check. I said, "Well I'm here, so you can leave now". By that time they had already run my name and all my priors came up, so they knew I was a drug addict. They knew I was high and they're asking me where all the drugs are. I'm telling them there are no drugs here! They start looking through everything, and they didn't find anything. So they tell me they're taking me to jail for being under the influence and child endangerment. They don't let me call my parents so they can pick up my kids. He goes (I can still picture this moment like it was yesterday), "No I'm taking your kids to the shelter". I was like, "No! My family will pick them up". And he goes, "I'm going to teach you a lesson. It seems like you haven't learned your lesson from all the times you've been arrested".

At that moment I couldn't believe what was happening. I really did it this time! All I could think about were my poor babies! This isn't their fault! It broke my heart, seeing my kids have to watch me get handcuffed and taken away. I've been in jails, prisons and programs and I've always done it without worrying about my kids.

The day after I jailed, a social worker came to see me. She told me my kids were in Child Protective Services, and since I have a long history of drug use that they are going to remain there even though my parents were trying to get them! My dad was arrested for a DUI like 20 years ago, so he had to get it expunged from his record before the kids could go home with them. I asked her if my kids were together, and she said the two big ones were in the shelter and the two little ones were in a satellite home. She explained to me that because they were under two or three they couldn't stay in the shelter.

After being in jail for five days, I was bailed out. When I went to my parents' house, I thought my kids were going to be there and found out that they were still in the shelter. They were preparing the house for the kids. My dad was looking at me with this disgusted look on his face, and it was breaking my heart. I knew I didn't deserve anything but that. He had found out I was pregnant. He didn't understand how I was having another child when I couldn't even take care of the ones I have. He told me straight up that the kids are going to be coming home soon, and when they come I was not welcome because they were not going to jeopardize the kids being here for me. It hurt when he told me that because that meant that I couldn't have contact with my kids. Everything had to be supervised. I already knew I couldn't be there, but to hear it really hurt.

So now I'm alone, and I couldn't depend on the people that have always been there for me. My partner is in prison at this time. I was really scared because I knew he was going to flip when he found out! He was in custody for less than a month when all this happened.

I started going to court and they start to bring everything up. They were making it seem like I couldn't change because of the number of times I've been in jail, and the recovery programs that I've been in that didn't succeed. To them, nothing had worked so what's going to be different this time? I remember thinking of just giving up; that they probably were right and that my kids were better off without me. I have always been a strong believer that everything happens for a reason. God doesn't put us through things we cannot handle.

I changed my way of thinking. I stopped blaming everyone else and accepted the fact that it was me and my actions that had my kids removed from my care. I kept telling myself "I can do this; it's not going to be easy but these are my kids". I was going to do whatever they told me to do, because there was no other option.

I was at court one day and I met Kim, a Mentor Mom for Dependency Drug Treatment Court. As she was telling me about Dependency Drug Treatment Court, I liked what I heard because I know me; and I needed something like this. I put in the application and waited to see if I would get accepted.

At this time, I'm 5 or 6 months pregnant. I was going through a lot during this period - I had to move from where I was living because the apartment complex had a policy that if you have Police contact for drugs you have to move or they will evict you; so I put in a 30-day notice. I couldn't go to my parent's house, so my Aunt (Tia Lupe) and Uncle (Tio Tony) said I could go stay with them. I was so grateful to them because they were willing to help me even though I had really made a mess of my life.

By now, I'm already doing my case plan and my plate was full. Let me break it down: I had all-day outpatient sessions four times a week. In the evenings, I had classes in different locations. I had to attend four Narcotics Anonymous meetings a week. I also had to random drug test in two different places. I'm also looking for a place to live because you have 60 days to find a place or they terminate your housing. I also had criminal court because, when I was arrested, I was charged with Felony Child Endangerment and Under the Influence. I'm pregnant and I'm doing all of this by bus.

It was very humbling to me because for the first time in my 17 years of using drugs, I couldn't count on my family to be there for me. Even in my addiction, when I was running the streets, when I was in county, even when I went to prison they were always there sending me mail, money, stamps, and boxes. I never went without. When I went to Mother Infant, a mothers prison program, they would come to visit and bring my daughter, Sirena. I have always been blessed to have my family there for me. I always took my family for granted.

On January 17, 2008, I gave birth to my 5th child, Victor Lukas He's named after my Dad (Victor), and I told my Tio Tony he could pick his middle name - and he picked Lukas.

I was doing everything I was told to do, so I was able to keep Victor. There would be an open case for 6 months, but then it would be closed. I was able to get my kids back in six months but, because I had picked up those charges when the kids were removed, I had a 90-day jail sentence. Instead of them putting me in jail they let me go to a Residential Program through drug court and I was able to take Victor with me. After being there for a month, they let me have weekends with my kids at home so we could get used to being a family again. After my 9-month review, I got physical custody of my kids. Since it was almost the end of the school year, we agreed to let my kids stay with my parents until the last day of school. When my kids came home for good, I was so happy. Before going into drug court, I was told by the courts that I couldn't do it. I strongly believe if someone wants to change, and they are given the opportunity, it's possible.

When my year review came up I requested my case to stay open another six months because I didn't want Leo, the father of my kids to lose his parental rights. It didn't bother me to do that because I wasn't doing anything wrong. So when Leo got out in August 25, 2008, I was telling him that I wanted him to get into drug court and that it would benefit him. He was like "No! Why am I going to set myself up for failure"? I kept trying to explain to him that it wasn't like that, so, the next time we had court he signed the application. I honestly thought he was going to get denied, but to my surprise they accepted him. I was so happy because they gave him a chance, and he too did everything they asked. On Feb 9, 2009, our case was closed.

I hate that I put my kids through all of this because they didn't deserve any of it. I know now this is what I needed to happen in order to change my life.

My Clean Date Is 8/27/2007

I want to say thank you to the Drug Court Team

for believing in me and giving me a chance to be the person I am today....

To Sirena, Leo, Liana, Julissa, Victor and my family,

I just want to say that I love you and thank you for not giving up on me

Sirena
(Daughter, Sister)

I just remember getting a phone call from my Aunt Sonia saying, "Sirena get ready". I thought, "Okay we're going somewhere". People came in that I didn't recognize, telling me, "Sirena we're going to take you"! But I thought they couldn't, because I was with my Aunt Martha. But, when I had arrived at my Grandma's, somebody did come and take me! I had only three pairs of pants and maybe five shirts!

When I was sitting in the car I didn't know what to think. I was scared, thinking I wasn't going to be able to see my brother and sisters again! When they told me what my Mom did, I was very upset with her! All I could think was, "Why would she do that? Did she not care? Was this more important to her"? When they said I could go with my original dad, I just said "no" because I couldn't think of having to live in the same house with him because he wasn't a good father. We hardly knew each other. I only knew he was someone whose name was on my birth certificate. But just because he was known as my father, he sure didn't act like one. So I chose to stay at the shelter. I didn't think I was going to see my Mom again.

When I saw her with my social worker, I just wanted to cry, but I didn't want my Mom to feel bad, because it already seemed like she was going through too much. Deep down, I really love my Mom. But I was very upset with her.

Since then, she's been doing better and I'm glad everything is better now. Yes, I am happy - for now. I was only 12 years old and in my Middle School years having to deal with this.

My name is Sirena. I'm 15 years old, and I am a freshman in High School.

Rosalio Jesus
"Double 'L' Cool J"
(Son, Brother)

All I remember is on August 9th, 2007, I was watching television in my room. After my favorite show was over I heard the doorbell ring. I told my mother (Veronica) that the doorbell was ringing. She said, "Who's at the door"? I said, "I don't know who it is".

She opened the door and it was the police! She said, "Can I help you sir"?

The Officer said, "We are taking your children to the children's shelter"! My mom told me, "Go tell your sisters that you guys are going with this nice Police Officer". So I got the thing that was my prized possession - my toy car that I got at a San Francisco Giants game.

We were riding in a police car and we asked the Officer, "Where are we going"?

He said, "We are going to take you to a shelter".

When I got there I saw my older sister. The next day, my younger sisters were taken to a house with another family! I was crying that night because I missed my sisters and my parents. But the next day, I was picked up with all my siblings. My Grandpa bailed my mom out of jail.

As far as I know my family is doing well now. I now have a new baby brother.

My name is Little Leo "Double 'L' Cool J". I was 8 ½ years old in Elementary School when this all happened.

Now I'm 12 years old and in 7th grade Junior High.

Through These Eyes

Written by Christine V.
(Former Foster Youth Whose Mom was in DDTC)

My day was bright.

It was my birthday.

My life changed.

It's not the same.

They came and took but really never gave back.

There were tears but they did their job.

My parents were shaken but I was numb.

I was left alone and strangers were among.

My parents needed help and I needed my siblings.

We were apart for the longest time.

I grew up and matured on my own I did.

I was raised to be strong but wasn't prepared for abandonment.

There were social workers and court.

My largest annoyance:

I missed my family but those people kept us separated.

I was a bad child; misunderstood is the word.

They thought a 10 year-old was old enough.

So, never nurtured.

Visitations were the best but going back home was a nightmare.

I dreamed of being reunited but brainwashing was a daily thing.

They filled my head with nonsense.

But I believed in positive and never gave up.

Visitations increased an hours were longer.

My baby brother was older and lil' sis was tall.

Almost the worst feeling of all,

I was there for them and it hurt to be apart

But at the time was for the best.

I never understood it but my head was a mess.

The day finally came.

The moment of relief, I was <u>home </u>with my parents

But a piece was still missing.

My other half never returned

But came while she could as you can see through my writing;

I'm still not quite healed.

PART III
REFLECTIONS

By Judge Katherine Lucero

As you can see from the book, the work is transformative for the families and for the professionals. We are all changed by the opportunity to intervene in a positive way in the lives of others. We are transformed by an opportunity to save a family. This is why most of us came into the work. We came so that we could make a difference in the lives of children everywhere.

The therapeutic court model is good for society and it is good for the courts. Judges who work in therapeutic court settings report enjoying their work more than in other settings. Child Welfare workers develop relationships with their clients that they may not have ever had the opportunity to develop with the more traditional court models. Parents report feeling like their social workers care about them and that they want to see their families heal instead of just ripping their families apart. It saves money[39]. It saves families.

Family Drug Court has demonstrated that the individualized treatment clients receive is better than the ordinary Dependency Court process. One goal will be to transform the Dependency Court process into a more individualized rehabilitative process through the Family Drug Court. If we want to make changes in society that are fiscally and socially responsible, then we advocate for more Family Drug Courts across the nation.

---

39   Appendix V: Sacramento Cost Benefit Analysis

I want to thank my team for helping me put this book together. We will continue to do the work here in Santa Clara County, one day at a time, believing in people, even when they do not believe in themselves.

Appendix I

Timeline of Major Federal Legislation Concerned With Child Protection, Child Welfare, and Adoption

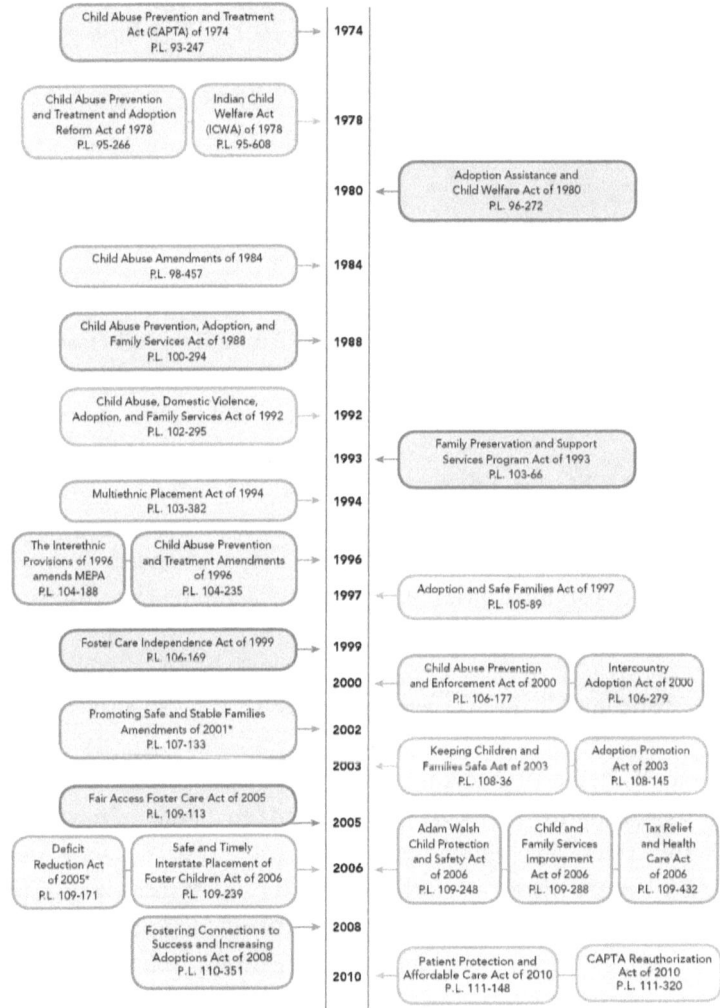

Child Abuse Prevention and Treatment Act (CAPTA) of 1974 P.L. 93-247	1974	
Child Abuse Prevention and Treatment and Adoption Reform Act of 1978 P.L. 95-266 / Indian Child Welfare Act (ICWA) of 1978 P.L. 95-608	1978	
	1980	Adoption Assistance and Child Welfare Act of 1980 P.L. 96-272
Child Abuse Amendments of 1984 P.L. 98-457	1984	
Child Abuse Prevention, Adoption, and Family Services Act of 1988 P.L. 100-294	1988	
Child Abuse, Domestic Violence, Adoption, and Family Services Act of 1992 P.L. 102-295	1992	
	1993	Family Preservation and Support Services Program Act of 1993 P.L. 103-66
Multiethnic Placement Act of 1994 P.L. 103-382	1994	
The Interethnic Provisions of 1996 amends MEPA P.L. 104-188 / Child Abuse Prevention and Treatment Amendments of 1996 P.L. 104-235	1996	
	1997	Adoption and Safe Families Act of 1997 P.L. 105-89
Foster Care Independence Act of 1999 P.L. 106-169	1999	
	2000	Child Abuse Prevention and Enforcement Act of 2000 P.L. 106-177 / Intercountry Adoption Act of 2000 P.L. 106-279
Promoting Safe and Stable Families Amendments of 2001* P.L. 107-133	2002	
	2003	Keeping Children and Families Safe Act of 2003 P.L. 108-36 / Adoption Promotion Act of 2003 P.L. 108-145
Fair Access Foster Care Act of 2005 P.L. 109-113	2005	
Deficit Reduction Act of 2005* P.L. 109-171 / Safe and Timely Interstate Placement of Foster Children Act of 2006 P.L. 109-239	2006	Adam Walsh Child Protection and Safety Act of 2006 P.L. 109-248 / Child and Family Services Improvement Act of 2006 P.L. 109-288 / Tax Relief and Health Care Act of 2006 P.L. 109-432
Fostering Connections to Success and Increasing Adoptions Act of 2008 P.L. 110-351	2008	
	2010	Patient Protection and Affordable Care Act of 2010 P.L. 111-148 / CAPTA Reauthorization Act of 2010 P.L. 111-320

*Some acts were enacted the year following their introduction in Congress.

Image courtesy of Child Welfare Information Gateway
Available online at www.childwelfare.gov/pubs/otherpubs/majorfedlegis.cfm

205

Appendix II

Child Abuse and Neglect Institute
Permanency Planning for Children Department
National Council of Juvenile and Family Court Judges

Timeline of Key Child Protection, Child Welfare, and Adoption Federal Legislation

1974 Original Child Abuse Prevention and Treatment Act (CAPTA), P.L. 93-247

Established the National Center on Child Abuse and Neglect; authorized funding for fiscal years 1974-77 for demonstration projects on the prevention, identification, and treatment of child abuse and neglect.

1978 CAPTA Amended, P.L. 95-266

Reauthorized through fiscal year 1981 and amended; funded the Adoption Opportunities program to facilitate the adoption of children with special needs.

1978 Indian Child Welfare Act (ICWA), P.L. 95-608

Established standards for the placement of Native American children in foster or adoptive homes. All child welfare court proceedings involving Native American children were to be heard in tribal courts if possible, and tribes had the right to intervene in state court proceedings. Created exclusive tribal jurisdiction over all Native American child custody proceedings when requested by tribe, parent, or Indian custodian.

Granted preference to Native American family environments in adoptive or foster care placement. Required State and Federal courts to give full faith and credit to tribal court decrees. Set a "beyond a reasonable doubt" standard of proof for terminating Native American parents' parental rights.

1980 Adoption Assistance and Child Welfare Act, P.L. 96-272

Authorized appropriations for adoption and foster care assistance to States. Required States to provide adoption assistance to parents who adopt a child who is AFDC-eligible and is a child with special needs. For foster care assistance, States are required to make reasonable efforts to prevent placement or to reunify children with their families.

1984 CAPTA Amended, P.L. 98-457

Reauthorized through fiscal year 1987; required States to have procedures in place to report medical neglect, including instances of withholding medically indicated treatment from disabled infants with life threatening conditions; required State-level programs to facilitate adoption opportunities for disabled infants with life-threatening conditions; provided for Federal adoption and foster care data-gathering and analysis system.

1988 CAPTA Amended, P.L. 100-294

Reauthorized through fiscal year 1991; established the Inter-Agency Task Force on Child Abuse and Neglect; broadened scope of research to include investigative and judicial procedures applicable to child abuse and neglect cases; established a national data collection system; expanded Adoption Opportunities Program.

1992 CAPTA Amended, P.L. 102-295

Reauthorized through fiscal year 1995 and amended CAPTA; revised provisions for research and assistance activities to include cultural considerations; provided assistance to States through community-based child abuse and neglect prevention grants; required HHS to operate a National Resource Center for Special Needs Adoption.

1993 Court Improvement Program, Omnibus Budget Reconciliation Act of 1993, P.L. 103-66

Provided grants to state courts to assess and improve the handling of proceedings relating to foster care and adoption. Initially authorized for four years, Congress has since extended authorization through fiscal year 2011, and in 2006 added two new grant programs (to improve data collection to ensure that the safety, permanency and well-being needs of children are met in a timely and complete manner and to conduct training of judges, attorneys and other legal personnel in child welfare cases, including cross-training with the child welfare agency).

1993 Family Preservation and Family Support Services Program established as part of the Omnibus Reconciliation Act, P.L. 103-66

Title XIII, Chapter 2, Subchapter C, Part I authorized funding for the family preservation and support services program through fiscal year 1998. Encouraged States to use funds to create a continuum of family focused services for "at risk" children and families. Required a comprehensive planning process to develop more responsive family support and preservation strategies.

1994 Multiethnic Placement Act (MEPA), P.L. 103-382

Prohibited State agencies, and others receiving federal funding who are involved in foster care or adoption placements, from delaying, denying, or otherwise discriminating when making a foster care or adoption placement decision on the basis of the parent or child's race, color or national origin. Required States to develop plans for recruitment of foster and adoptive families that reflect the ethnic and racial diversity of children in the State for whom families are needed. Allowed an agency to consider the cultural, ethnic, or racial background of a child and the capacity of an adoptive or foster parent to meet the needs of a child with that background when making a placement.

1996 Multiethnic Placement Act-Interethnic Placement Provision. Amends MEPA, P.L. 104-188

Strengthened MEPA's diligent recruitment requirement by making it a Title IV-B State Plan requirement. States and other entities receive graduated financial penalties if they do not comply with the Title IV-E State Plan requirement established under this law. Repealed language in MEPA that allowed States and other entities to consider the "cultural, ethnic or racial background" of a child, as well as the "capacity" of the prospective parent to meet the needs of such a child. Amended Civil Rights laws to prohibit persons and governments involved in adoption or foster care from denying to any individual the opportunity to become an adoptive or foster parent on the basis of race, color, or national origin of the individual or of the child; or delaying or denying the placement of a child for adoption or into foster care on the basis of the race, color, or national origin of the adoptive or foster parent, or the child.

1996 CAPTA Amended, P.L. 104-235

Reauthorized and amended, adding new requirements to address false reports of abuse and neglect, delays in TPR, and lack of public oversight of child protection. Required expedited TPR process for abandoned infants or when the parent is responsible for the death or serious bodily injury of a child. Minimum definition of child abuse to include death, serious physical or emotional injury, sexual abuse or imminent risk of harm. Recognized the right of parental exercise of religious beliefs concerning medical care.

1997 Adoption and Safe Families Act (ASFA), P.L. 105-89

Legislation sought to promote the safety, permanency and well-being of children in foster care; accelerate the permanent placement of children in care (including by providing adoption incentives to states); and increase the accountability of the child welfare system. Reauthorized the Family Preservation and Support Services Program, renaming it the Safe and Stable Families Program, and extended categories of services to include time-limited reunification services and adoption promotion and support services.

Key provisions include:

Clarified the intent of the "reasonable efforts" requirement stressing that **the child's health and safety shall be the paramount concern** in determining what is reasonable, and consistent with the plan for timely, permanent placement of a child. The "reasonable efforts" requirement can be waived entirely in certain circumstances, such as if the parent had committed a felony assault causing serious bodily injury to the child or sibling; committed or attempted murder or voluntary manslaughter of a sibling; aggravated circumstances including abandonment, torture, chronic abuse or sexual abuse; or if the parental rights to a sibling had been terminated involuntarily.

Emphasized that the **safety of children in foster care must be considered in case plans and case reviews. Concurrent planning is allowed.** That is, reasonable efforts may be made to reunify the child with his family concurrently with efforts to place a child in an adoptive family or with a legal guardian. **Criminal records checks** must be conducted for prospective foster and adoptive parents before they are approved for placement of a child who qualifies them to receive maintenance or adoption assistance payments, unless a State opts out.

Shortens time frames for permanent placement. Services to reunify families funded under Title IV-B should not extend beyond 15 months. A **petition to terminate parental rights** shall be filed for parents whose child has been in foster care for 15 of the last 22 months; if a court has determined a child is an abandoned infant; or in the circumstances described under "reasonable efforts" above. **Permanency planning hearings** must be held within 12 months of a child's placement. When reasonable efforts are not required to reunify a child with his parents, a permanency planning hearing must be held within 30 days of such determination.

Foster parents, relative caregivers or pre-adoptive parents to receive notice of, and the opportunity to be heard at, any review or hearing concerning the child. The provision does not intend that these individuals should be made parties to the review or hearing.

1999 Foster Care Independence (Chafee) Act, P.L. 106-169

Amended Title IV-E of the Social Security Act to provide States with more funding and greater flexibility in carrying out programs designed to help children make the transition from foster care to self-sufficiency.

Requires that a portion of funds provided to States for independent living program programs be used to assist youth aged 18 to 21 who exit foster care.

2000 Child Abuse Prevention and Enforcement Act, P.L. 106-177

Authorized Federal funds for States to improve their criminal justice systems to provide history record information to child welfare agencies.

2000 Strengthening Abuse and Neglect Courts Act, P.L. 106-314

Legislation to improve the administrative efficiency and effectiveness of the Nation's abuse and neglect courts and for other purposes consistent with the Adoption and Safe Families Act of 1997.

2000 Intercountry Adoption Act, P.L. 106-279

To provide for implementation by the United States of the Hague Convention on Protection of Children and Cooperation in Respect of Intercountry Adoption.

2001 Promoting Safe and Stable Families Amendments, P.L. 107-133

Authorized vouchers for the Chafee Foster Care Independence Program. Created a matching grant program to support mentoring networks for children of prisoners. Made amendments to Title IV-B of the Social Security Act. Added findings to illustrate the need for programs addressing families at risk for abuse and neglect and those adopting children from foster care, the definition of family preservation services to include infant safe haven programs, and the strengthening parental relationships and promoting healthy marriages to list of allowable activities.

2001 No Child Left Behind Act, P.L. 107-110

Designed to improve academic achievement of disadvantaged children through accountability, flexibility, and school choice. Requires schools, local educational agencies, and states to be held accountable for improving the academic achievement of all students, and identifying and improving low-performing schools.

2001 McKinney-Vento Homeless Education Assistance Improvements Act, (in No Child Left Behind Act), P.L. 107-110

Requires each state to ensure that homeless children have access to the same public education as other children and youth, including public preschool programs. Provides child's guardian the right to choose where the child should attend school, including the child's school of origin. Also, requires schools to immediately enroll a homeless child in the selected school, even if the child is unable to provide records normally required for school enrollment. Has been interpreted by some as applicable to children and youth in foster care.

2003 Keeping Children and Families Safe Act, P.L. 108-36

Reauthorized CAPTA through fiscal year 2008, including Adoption Opportunities, Abandoned Infants Assistance, and Family Violence Prevention and Services Acts. Mandated changes to State Plan eligibility requirements (e.g., policies and procedures to address the needs of infants born and identified as being affected by prenatal drug exposure) and implemented programs to increase the number of older children placed in adoptive families.

2003 Adoption Promotion Act, P.L. 108-145

Reauthorized the adoption incentive program under Title IV-E; provides additional incentives for adoption of older children (age 9 and older) from foster care.

2004 Individuals with Disabilities Education Improvement Act (IDEA), P.L. 108-446

Provides federal funds to assist state and local education agencies in meeting needs of disabled children. Public schools must identify children with disabilities (including homeless youth and wards of the state) who may need specialized education and provide them with individualized education programs and related services, including those designed to prepare them for employment and independent living. Requires referral to Part C Early Intervention Services for children aged 0-3 involved in substantiated child abuse and neglect cases. Requirements also promote links between child welfare and mental health agencies for evaluation and treatment.

2005 Fair Access Foster Care Act, P.L. 109-113

Amends Title IV-E of the Social Security Act to make foster care maintenance payments available to private for-profit agencies.

2005 Deficit Reduction Act of 2005, P.L. 109-171

Title VII, Subtitle D provides new court improvement grants for improved data collection and training for judges, attorneys, and other legal personnel in child welfare cases. Also requires collaboration between courts and agencies; and revises eligibility for foster care maintenance payments and adoption assistance, among other provisions.

2006 Safe and Timely Interstate Placement of Foster Children Act, P.L. 109-239

Amends Titles IV-B and IV-E of the Social Security Act to improve the orderly and timely interstate placement of children; complete home studies requested by another State within a specified period; and accept home studies received from another State. Requires that the court determine at permanency hearings whether a child's out-of-home placement continues to be appropriate and in the children's best interest. Provisions include: State must provide for a child's health and education records to be provided to the child at no cost when leaving foster care by reason of having obtained the age of majority; and in order to receive federal Court Improvement Project funds, the highest court in the state must have a rule that foster parents, pre-adoptive parents, and relative caregivers are notified of proceedings.

2008-2009 Fostering Connections to Success and Increasing Adoptions Act: H.R. 6893 / P.L 110-351

On October 7th, 2008, H.R. 6893 Fostering Connections to Success and Increasing Adoptions Act, received the President's signature and became Public Law No: 110-351. The bill is designed to connect and support relative caregivers, improve outcomes for children in foster care, provide for tribal foster care and adoption access, and improve incentives for adoption. H.R. 6893 will provide state options for subsidized guardianship payments for relatives, incentives for adoption, adoption assistance, kinship navigator programs, new family connection grants, and federal support for youth to age 21

Appendix III

Conference Of Chief Justices Conference Of State Court Administrators

CCJ Resolution 22
COSCA Resolution IV

In Support of Problem-Solving Courts

WHEREAS, the Conference of Chief Justices and the Conference of State Court Administrators appointed a Joint Task Force to consider the policy and administrative implications of the courts and special calendars that utilize the principles of therapeutic jurisprudence and to advance strategies, policies and recommendations on the future of these courts; and

WHEREAS, these courts and special calendars have been referred to by various names, including problem-solving, accountability, behavioral justice, therapeutic, problem oriented, collaborative justice, outcome oriented and constructive intervention courts; and WHEREAS, the findings of the Joint Task Force include the following:

- The public and other branches of government are looking to courts to address certain complex social issues and problems, such as recidivism, that they feel are not most effectively addressed by the traditional legal process;

- A set of procedures and processes are required to address these issues and problems that are distinct from traditional civil and criminal adjudication;

- A focus on remedies is required to address these issues and problems in addition to the determination of fact and issues of law;

- The unique nature of the procedures and processes encourages the establishment of dedicated court calendars;

- There has been a rapid proliferation of drug courts and calendars throughout most of the various states;

- There is now evidence of broad community and political support and increasing state and local government funding for these initiatives;

- There are principles and methods grounded in therapeutic jurisprudence, including integration of treatment services with judicial case processing, ongoing judicial intervention, close monitoring of and immediate response to behavior, multidisciplinary involvement, and collaboration with community-based and government organizations. These principles and methods are now being employed in these newly arising courts and calendars, and they advance the application of the trial court performance standards and the public trust and confidence initiative; and

- Well-functioning drug courts represent the best practice of these principles and methods;

NOW, THEREFORE, BE IT RESOLVED that the Conference of Chief Justices and the Conference of State Court Administrators hereby agree to:

1. Call these new courts and calendars "Problem-Solving Courts," recognizing that courts have always been involved in attempting to resolve disputes and problems in society, but understanding that the collaborative nature of these new efforts deserves recognition.

2. Take steps, nationally and locally, to expand and better integrate the principles and methods of well-functioning drug courts into ongoing court operations.

3. Advance the careful study and evaluation of the principles and methods employed in problem-solving courts and their application to other significant issues facing state courts.

4. Encourage, where appropriate, the broad integration over the next decade of the principles and methods employed in the problem-solving courts into the administration of justice to improve court processes and outcomes while preserving the rule of law, enhancing judicial effectiveness, and meeting the needs and expectations of litigants, victims and the community.

5. Support national and local education and training on the principles and methods employed in problem-solving courts and on collaboration with other community and government agencies and organizations.

6. Advocate for the resources necessary to advance and apply the principles and methods of problem-solving courts in the general court systems of the various states.

7. Establish a National Agenda consistent with this resolution that includes the following actions:

   a. Request that the CCJ/COSCA Government Affairs Committee work with the Department of Health and Human Services to direct treatment funds to the state courts.

   b. Request that the National Center for State Courts initiate with other organizations and associations a collaborative process to develop principles and methods for other types of courts and calendars similar to the *10 Key Drug Court Components*, published by the Drug Courts Program Office, which define effective drug courts.

c. Encourage the National Center for State Courts Best Practices Institute to examine the principles and methods of these problem-solving courts.

d. Convene a national conference or regional conferences to educate the Conference of Chief Justices and Conference of State Court Administrators and, if appropriate, other policy leaders on the issues raised by the growing problem-solving court movement.

e. Continue a Task Force to oversee and advise on the implementation of this resolution, suggest action steps, and model the collaborative process by including other associations and interested groups.

Adopted as Proposed by the Task Force on Therapeutic Justice of the Conference of Chief Justices in Rapid City, South Dakota at the 52nd Annual Meeting on August 3, 2000.

Appendix IV

Santa Clara County Dependency Drug Court Outcomes from Final Report by NPC

Research March 2007-Selected Outcomes

Santa Clara Substance Use Characteristics

Characteristic	Drug Court Sample	Comparison Sample
	% (n)	% (n)
Primary drug of choice	N=85	N=335
Methamphetamine	54% (54)	57% (190)
Cocaine	8% (7)	7% (23)
Marijuana	9% (8)	8% (28)
Alcohol	14% (12)	20% (66)
Other	5% (4)	8% (28)
Mothers with at least one prior treatment episode	N=100 19% (19)	N=553 14% (96)
Age at first use	N=71	N=316
Mean	18	19

Relationship Between Time to FTDC Entry and Outcomes

Relationship Between Time to FTDC Entry and:	Statistically Significant?	Nature of Relationship
Likelihood of treatment entry	YES	Mothers entering FTDC more quickly were more likely to enter treatment.
Time to treatment entry	YES	Mothers entering FTDC more quickly also entered treatment more quickly.
Time spent in treatment	NO	No relationship
Treatment graduation	NO	No relationship
Likelihood of reunification	NO	No relationship

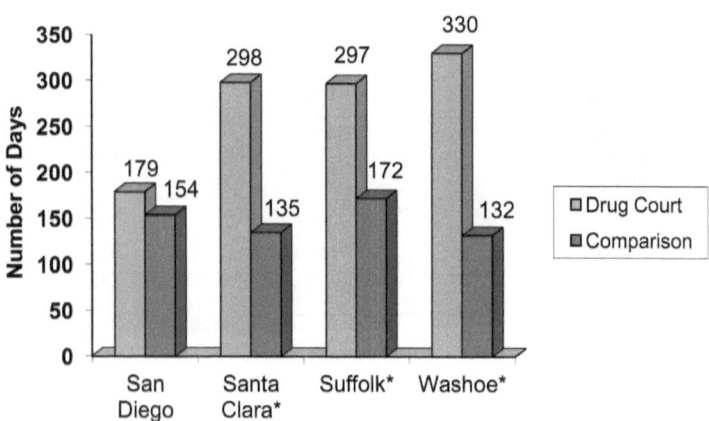

Days Spent in Treatment

* Statistically significant at p<.001.

Percent of Mothers with at Least One Treatment Entry

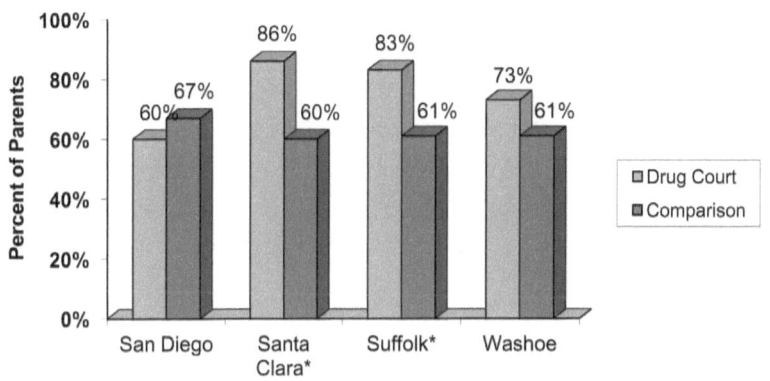

* Statistically significant at p<.001.

Santa Clara Permanency Decisions

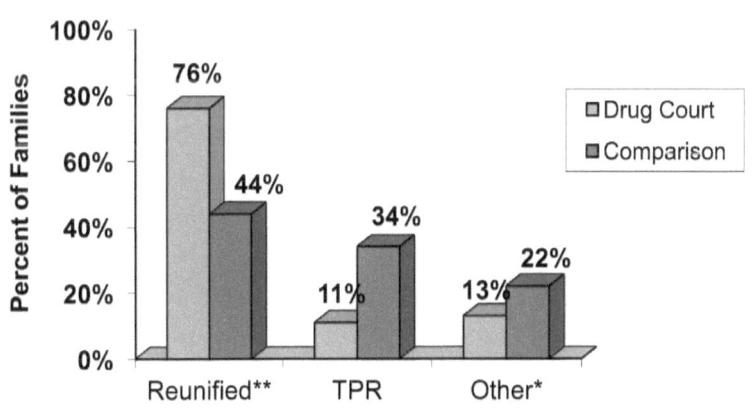

*Statistically significant at p<.05. **Statistically significant at p<.001.

New Drug-Exposed Babies

Site	FTDC	Comparison
San Diego	12 out of 70 (17%)	5 out of 29 (18%)
Santa Clara*	**1 out of 16 (6%)**	**23 out of 76 (30%)**
Suffolk	3 out of 6 (50%)	2 out of 7 (29%)
Washoe	1 out of 14 (7%)	7 out of 19 (35%)

* Statistically significant at $p < .01$.

Appendix V

Sacramento County Dependency Drug Court Year Eight Outcome and Process Evaluation Findings

Authored by Sharon Boles, Ph.D. and Nancy K. Young, Ph.D. July 2011

COST ESTIMATES

12 Month Estimates

Impacts of Costs Related to Increased Reunification Rates (see Table 25). Since its inception, it is estimated that the DDC has saved $28,074,460 due to the higher 12 month reunification rate of DDC children relative to the comparison group. This is an average savings of over $3.5 million per year. Cost estimates are available for the comparison group and first eight court-ordered cohorts (n=4,566).

The 12 month reunification rate for the comparison group was 19.1%. The 12 month reunification rate for the court-ordered group was 39.8%, which accounted for 1,819 children. If we assumed a reunification rate of only 19.1% for the court-ordered group, then 947 fewer children would have reunified. By deducting the time to reunification for the DDC group (6.3 months) from the average length of out-of-home care for the comparison group (22.8 months), we find a 16.5 month difference. The savings due to the estimated additional 947 children who reunified through the DDC program totals $28,074,460 (947 children multiplied by 16.5 months multiplied by $1,796.72 monthly out-of-home care costs).

Table 25: 12 Month Cost Savings Due to Increased Reunification Rates

Number of children	Reunify rates	Children reunified	Assuming 19.1% reunification rate	Difference in children	Time to reunification	Time of out-of-home care	Time difference	Cost/month	Savings
Comparison Group									
173	19.1%	33				22.8 months			
Court-Ordered Group									
4566	39.7%	1819	4566*19.1% =872	1819-872=947	6.3 months		22.8-6.3 =16.5 months	$1796.72	$1,796.72* 16.5*947 =$28,074,648

18 Month Estimates

Impacts of Costs Related to Increased Reunification Rates at 18 months (see Table 26). At 18 months, the DDC has saved $38,489,407 due to increased DDC reunifications relative to the comparison group. This means that each of the first seven court-ordered cohorts saved $5.5 million per year due to increased reunifications through 18 months. 18 month cost estimates are only available for the comparison group and first seven court-ordered cohorts (n=3,911).

The 18 month reunification rate for the comparison group was 24.9%. The 18 month reunification rate for the court-ordered group was 49.8%, which accounted for 1,947 children. If we assumed a reunification rate of 24.9% for the DDC group, then 973 fewer children would have reunified. By deducting the time to reunification for the DDC group (8.3 months) from the average length of out-of-home care for the comparison group (30.9 months), we find a 22.6 month difference. The savings due to the estimated additional 973 children who reunified through the DDC program totals $38,489,407 (973 children multiplied by 22.6 months multiplied by $1,750.33 monthly out-of-home care costs).

Table 26: 18 Month Cost Savings Due to Increased Reunification Rates

	Reunify rates	Children reunified	Assuming 24.9% reunification rate	Difference in reunification children	Time to reunification	Time of out-of-home care	Time difference	Cost/ month	Savings
Number of children									
Comparison Group									
173	24.9%	43				30.9 months			
Court-Ordered Group									
3911	49.8%	1947	3911*24.9% =974	1947- 974=973	8.3 months		30.9-8.3 =22.6 months	$1750.33	$1750.33* 22.6*973 =$38,489,407

24 Month Estimates

Impacts of Costs Related to Increased Reunification Rates at 24 months (see Table 27). Over the 24 month time period, the increased reunification rate of the DDC children led to a savings of $38,960,524. This means that each of the first seven DDC cohorts saved $5.6 million per year due to increased reunifications through 24 months. Cost estimates are only available for the comparison group and first seven court-ordered cohorts (n=3,911).

The 24 month reunification rate for the comparison group was 27.2%. The 24 month reunification rate for the DDC group was 50.0%, which accounted for 1,955 children. If we assumed a reunification rate of only 27.2% for the court-ordered group, then 891 fewer children would have reunified. By deducting the time to reunification for the DDC group (8.9 months) from the average length of out-of-home care for the comparison group (33.1 months), we find a 24.2 month difference. The savings due to the estimated additional 891 children who reunified through the DDC program totals $38,960,524 (891 children multiplied by 24.2 months multiplied by $1,806.89 monthly out-of-home care costs).

Table 27: 24 Month Cost Savings Due to Increased Reunification Rates

Number of children	Reunify rates	Children reunified	Assuming 27.2% reunification rate	Difference in children	Time to reunification	Time of out-of-home care	Time difference	Cost/ month	Savings
Comparison Group									
173	27.2%	47							
Court-Ordered Group						33.1 months			
3911	50.0%	1955	3911*27.2% =1064	1955-1064=891	8.9 months		33.1-8.9 =24.2 months	$1806.89	$1,806.89* 24.2*891 =$38,960,524

228

60 Month Estimates

Impacts of Costs Related to Increased Reunification Rates at 60 months (see Table 28). For the first time, cost estimates based on 60 month reunification rates and time to reunification were examined. Over the 60 month time period, the increased reunification rate of the DDC children led to a savings of $17,638,560. This means that each of the first four DDC cohorts saved $4.4 million per year due to increased reunifications through 60 months. Cost estimates are only available for the comparison group and first four court-ordered cohorts (n=2,086).

The 60 month reunification rate for the comparison group was 27.2%. The 60 month reunification rate for the DDC group was 44.9%, which accounted for 936 children. If we assumed a reunification rate of only 27.2% for the DDC group, then 369 fewer children would have reunified. By deducting the time to reunification for the DDC group (11.71 months) from the average length of out-of-home care for the comparison group (38.22 months), we find a 26.51 month difference. The savings due to the estimated additional 369 children who reunified through the DDC program totals $17,638,560 (369 children multiplied by 26.51 months multiplied by $1,803.13 monthly out-of-home care costs).

Table 28: 24 Month Cost Savings Due to Increased Reunification Rates

Number of children	Reunify rates	Children reunified	Assuming 27.2% reunification rate	Difference in children	Time to reunification	Time of out-of-home care	Time difference	Cost/ month	Savings
Comparison Group									
173	27.2%	47				38.22 months			
Court-Ordered Group									
2086	44.9%	936	2086*27.2% =567	936-567=369	11.71 months		33.22-11.71 =26.51 months	$1803.13	$1,803.13* 26.51*369 =$17,638,560

Overall, the increased reunification rates for the DDC group led to substantial foster care savings. These costs associated with the program in this analysis do not include other administrative costs such as court, social workers, attorneys, and clerical staff time. Nor does it account for potential Dependency Court cost.

The analyses presented here do not account for the costs of implementing the DDC, nor have we attempted to estimate the savings to society or the economic productivity that result from higher family reunification rates. Based on past, standard estimates of court and administrative costs, it is clear that the savings generated from reduced foster care costs alone are sufficient to justify the cost of the Dependency Drug Court to the County and the State.

Appendix VI

Santa Clara County Dependency Drug

Court Stakeholder Values Statement

Value Category[40]	Values
Collaboration	No single agency has the resources and expertise to respond adequately to the parent who is addicted and is involved in the child welfare system (CWS). Collaboration is an essential element to effectively achieve joint outcomes. All collaborating partners have a shared role in achieving safety, permanency and well-being outcomes for children and families.[41] Collaboration requires a commitment to effective communication, a willingness to be non-judgmental and an understanding of how other systems work. As appropriate, a family's substance use disorder shall be addressed when working with related agencies such as health care providers, housing, employment, education, domestic violence advocacy, and mental health services; and when working with the family involved in other courts such as domestic violence, criminal and delinquency. When services are being defined and funding priorities are being set, family and community input shall be part of the process.
Systemic Change	
	All collaborating partners shall be willing to consider changes to agency policies, procedures and methods of service delivery to ensure systemic change; vs. business as usual[42]

40 Modified and adapted from the NACSACW document "Synthesis of Cross System Values and Principles" and Sacramento and Cuyahoga values statements.

41 The definition of family extends beyond parents and siblings to include extended family members and others who are important in the child's life.

42 Note: Discussion on attempting waiver for Federal child welfare timelines

Joint Accountability And Shared Outcomes	
	Effectively addressing substance use and related problems among families involved in CWS and the dependency court system will contribute to better results for children and their families.

Value Category	Values
	All collaborating partners have accepted their shared role in achieving safety, permanency, and well-being outcomes for children and families. Outcome data across all partners shall be used to inform policy leaders and communities to develop, fund, and prioritize services that are known to be effective in improving outcomes.
Principles of Daily Practice	
	Appropriate alcohol and drug treatment shall be available and accessible for children and families who suffer from a substance use disorder. Treatment shall be outcome-informed
	There is no wrong door for accessing services and creating opportunities for children and families to receive court, agency, and community-based services within their local service systems.
	Children and their families shall be provided with access to the timeliest, most appropriate, and most effective treatment/prevention services and supports in the least intrusive environment possible. Assessments and services shall be provided as early as possible in the process. Assessments will include child and family needs and these needs shall be identified at the beginning of the assessment process.
	A family team approach shall be utilized to work cooperatively, together with the parents and children, to develop and implement treatment/ case plans to meet each family members individual needs.
	The family shall be part of the process at each level of planning, service delivery and evaluation.
	A continuum of prevention, intervention, treatment and recovery supports shall be incorporated into the daily practice of all collaborating partners.
	Given the complexity of serving children and families, it is crucial to have a comprehensive array of services.
	A cross-systems multidisciplinary approach shall be used to treat children and families in need of services. Services will be coordinated across systems and provided seamlessly.

Value Category	Values
	Field practice and service delivery should be:
	Child-focused
	Family centered
	Culturally/linguistically appropriate
	Strength-based
	Age and developmentally appropriate
	Community-centered
	Evidence based/data driven
	Trauma informed
	Recovery oriented
	Respect based
Child-Focused	The best place for a child is at home, with clean and sober parents, free of abuse and neglect. If a child is removed, ensuring children and families remain closely connected is essential. Child well-being shall be the first priority. Assuring the well-being of the child is critical for the success of the family's plan. Well-being includes ensuring child safety and "developmental needs" are met
Working with the Community	
	When services are being designed and funding priorities are being set, family and community input shall be part of the process.

---

43 Need to further define both developmental needs and well-being.

Value Category	Values
	The family shall be part of the process at each level of planning, service delivery and evaluation. As appropriate, a family's substance use disorder shall be addressed when working with related agencies such as health care providers, housing, employment, education, domestic violence advocacy, and mental health services; and when working with the family involved in other courts such as domestic violence, criminal and delinquency.
Information and Data Sharing	
	Collaborating partners shall constructively share good quality data and information to assure delivery of effective services to clients. Providers and caregivers from all collaborating partners shall develop common knowledge and shared values about child protection and substance use disorders to assist children and families to achieve positive outcomes.
Training and Staff Development	Services and supports for families affected by substance use disorders in the child welfare system shall be provided by knowledgeable, skilled providers who understand and address the cultural diversity of the families and communities they serve. Policies shall support culturally competent service delivery in procedures, outreach, advocacy, and training throughout the service delivery system, and incorporate knowledge of the Indian Child Welfare Act and tribal governments. Competencies-Federal and state confidentiality laws and HIPAA privacy provisions shall guide and direct the client information sharing process between all collaborating partners. Community colleges, universities, graduate and law schools shall develop and offer classes that satisfy professional accreditation requirements. Professionals in these fields shall participate in cross and joint training opportunities. All staff should develop a basic understanding of other agency systems, services, policies, processes and methods of working collaboratively to provide integrated services to families.

Value Category	Values
Budgeting and Sustainability	
	Services and funding streams shall be coordinated across all systems to maximize the use of limited resources and to ensure ongoing funding for the target population. Building a sustainability plan is an essential component to ensure future success.

Appendix VII

Excerpts from Santa Clara County Report to Congress-
November 2011, prepared by the
Santa Clara County Social Services Agency

How Family Wellness Court has changed the lives of children, families and systems is first summarized, then accomplishments over the last six months are highlighted

Children and families have a dramatically different experience in the child welfare and partner systems as a result of the systemic changes that have taken place. This section is specific to the changes in systems and service delivery that directly impact families. Changes within the last six months are highlighted in the Project Goals section. In addition, a number of these improvements have been expanded to include other families in the child welfare system.

How the System has Changed for Children

Prior to the implementation of Family Wellness Court, assessments and services to address developmental and behavioral needs were very limited, as was focus on such critical issues as attachment and bonding. The following describes the current process and service array for children. These services are expanding beyond FWC into the broader child welfare system.

All children from one month to 5.5 years receive immediate developmental and social-emotional screening, utilizing the Ages and Stages (ASQ) and Ages and Stages-Social Emotional questionnaires as well as bio-psycho-social assessment from a Public Health Nurse.

Children are then referred on to the FIRST 5 STARTS (Screening to Assessment, Referral and Treatment) System). This is a critical component of the FIRST 5 System of Care services offered to children and families in Family Wellness Court. It is a consistent and coordinated community screening, assessment, referral and treatment system for children birth through five years of age with special needs – especially those with serious social/emotional and behavioral concerns.

Kid Connections provides this multidisciplinary team approach by leveraging Medi-Cal's Early Periodic Screening, Diagnosis, and Treatment (EPSDT) Program revenue, and through blended funding provided jointly by the Department of Mental Health and FIRST 5.

There are two levels of assessments available; Level 1 (Assessment/Screening for Intervention) which is conducted by mental health and developmental specialists, and Level 2 (Targeted Diagnostic Assessments) which is conducted by a multidisciplinary team that may include a developmental pediatrician, psychiatrist, mental health specialist, speech pathologist and occupational therapist. Both assessments include the parents and the child (see attached for details). The assessments also include referral to the San Andreas Regional Center's Early Start Program (http://www.sarc. org/earlystart.html) when appropriate.

Based on the recommendations from the assessment team the child and family are referred to appropriate home visitation and or therapeutic services.

Home Visitors (utilizing the evidence-based PITC model (http://www.wested.org/cs/we/view/serv/98) engage parents/ caregivers, provide information on ages and stages of early child development, and coach and mentor to foster a positive parent/caregiver and child relationship that will contribute to the child's healthy development. Home visitors provide the services in the child's natural environment.

Therapeutic services span a continuum that includes: promotion of wellness, prevention of mental health disturbances and intervention and treatment of mental health problems that may interfere with the healthy development of children prenatal through age 5. Therapeutic services are provided as part of a coordinated care team within the FIRST 5 System of Care. Therapeutic service providers utilize developmentally appropriate evidence-based practices for service delivery along with the integration of substance abuse treatment and medication management.

Children between the ages of birth and 1 year old are referred to our Infant Neurodevelopment (IND) Clinic. The IND Clinic serves as the essential first phase in providing neuro-developmental assessments, identifying and coordinating services, and educating parents. The IND Clinic serves newborns and infants who are born between 32 to 36 weeks gestation, have birth weight over 1500 grams, and who do not qualify for California Children Services–High Risk Infant Follow-Up Clinic.

Children have access to Public Health Nurses. Utilizing the Public Health Nursing Home Visitation Model, Public Health Nurses engage parents/caregivers and provide information on ages and stages of early child development; educate and refer parents/caregivers to pregnancy planning, prevention and/or prenatal care; coach and mentor to foster a positive parent/caregiver and child relationship that contribute to the child's healthy development.

Children and parents also have access to FIRST 5 Family Resource Centers located throughout the county. The Family Resource Centers provide a continuum of programs, services and activities from prevention to early intervention services. Some of the services include but are not limited to the following:

- Early literacy and oral language development activities

- Art enrichment and creative expression activities

- Triple P Positive Parenting Program

- Information and referral services

- Oral health information, resources, and screening

- Transition to kindergarten support and information

- School readiness information and activities

- Children's Health Insurance information, enrollment assistance, and resources

In addition, as a child-focused court, FWC's physical environment is configured for the child's comfort in the courtroom. A First 5 family specialist is a key member of the court team and regularly shares insights about each child's developmental needs with the parents during FWC review hearings. Parents receive support from home visitors and public health nurses as well as mental health therapists, the latter through the form of dyadic therapy, parent child interactive therapy and other modalities. Unlike traditional criminal drug courts, where the focal point for discussion is the parent's recovery, FWC also includes regular discussions about the child—all to reinforce the parent-child relationship and to use that relationship to motivate the parent in his or her recovery work.

Even where the parents fail to reunify, 100% of FWC's children benefit from the child-focused approach because of early screening, assessments and interventions!

How the System has Changed for Men
with a Positive Impact on Children

Men were not included in the initial FWC model. It became very clear at the early stages of FWC that a family-focused approach was warranted. With respect to family composition, currently 47% of families involved in FWC involve both parents and seven percent of families have a father only engaged. Male engagement was limited in the child welfare system and men did not consider themselves to have an equal opportunity for reunification. As a result of FWC, more men are not only more fully engaged, but are reunifying with and regaining custody of their children, even when the mother has not been successful in doing so.

Men now have male mentors and there is a Transitional Housing Unit that was developed specifically for the purpose of giving fathers an opportunity to have close, daily contact and bond with their children. Gender specific treatment for men was promoted with the assignment of male treatment counselors with training and expertise in the dependency system. A men's services expert was retained to observe interactions with men and provide the court team feedback. FWC providers were trained on the impact of trauma on men.

Male mentors have been utilized to educate social workers on male engagement and retention and have expanded this educational opportunity to other professionals, both locally, nationally and federally. The Department of Family and Children's Services has implemented a male involvement initiative.

How the System has Changed for All Parents with Positive Impact on Children

Drug and Alcohol Services

At the time the FWC grant was written, it was estimated that parents waited up to four months to access drug and alcohol treatment on average. While challenges remain in improving time to treatment, the data in the program evaluation section of this report demonstrates that substantial positive change has taken place. In addition, there is now a dedicated counselor in one of the women's treatment facilities who has direct interface with the court. Other drug treatment professionals who contract with the Department are engaged and are active participants in FWC planning and assessment.

Ninety-percent utilization of a formerly underutilized residential treatment center for women and children has been achieved, three beds have been added utilizing CalWorks dollars and FWC has partnered with a faith-based organization with residential treatment and a THU to increase the capacity for women to achieve earlier access to residential treatment and have additional THU access. A male THU was implemented and, with the grant funding received from the recently acquired BJA/SAMHSA grant, continuing care will be provided in the very near future.

In addition, children are now screened for safety and trauma and domestic violence related questions have been added to assessments to ensure more comprehensive support for those in drug and alcohol treatment is provided.

Mental Health Services

Parental access to mental health services was very limited prior to FWC and access has expanded in multiple ways that are highlighted in the table referenced to above and include dedicated counseling services and the addition of a mental health adult therapist on the court team who serves as linkage to a coordinator for mental health services. Families are now able to obtain access to these services in an expedited fashion and have access to services through the Federally Qualified Health Clinics (FQHC's).

A children's mental health and development specialist is now funded as in-kind position and is a member of the FWC Court Team. In addition, Mental Health provided FWC graduates with access to dual diagnosis groups for aftercare and has funded a parent mentor position.

Child Welfare Services

Trauma and male engagement initiatives have been implemented. Family Team Meetings that include service providers, family, relatives and friends have been implemented to enable a very comprehensive perspective and family voice into the initial child welfare case plan. While there is no formal measure to track the impact of the FTM on disposition, it is believed that children may be more likely to remain at home because of the number of providers who regularly engage with the family and the additional support and services.

As mentioned under self-sufficiency, an eligibility worker sits on the court team and is also available to other child welfare families at court. This has greatly expanded access to benefits and has enabled stretching of mental health and substance treatment resources, via CalWorks funding.

Self-Sufficiency

Due to the placement of a dedicated Eligibility Worker from DFCS in the courts and as a member of the FWC Court Team, families that were eligible who were not accessing the benefits for which they qualified have been granted that access. 100 child welfare families, a high proportion from FWC were provided vouchers for long-term housing.

Linkages and partnerships with housing providers have enabled families to access a multitude of housing resources that were not previously available to them. Job trainings and union partnerships, along with a multitude of financial and other workshops assist families in obtaining employment. Support for basic needs on a limited basis also ensures that families are able to more fully focus on the activities in their case plans.

Trauma Related Services

FWC has partnered with trauma experts Vivian Brown, Stephanie Covington and Chandra Ghosh-Ippen with trauma training, consultation and systemic transformation since August 2008.

Trauma Specific Services are provided by DADS, who require utilization of Seeking Safety for AOD treatment providers. Mental Health treatment options for children include Trauma-focused cognitive behavioral therapy (TF CBT) and Trauma-Focused Play Therapy. Child Parent Psychotherapy is also being implemented.

Trauma Informed Services were identified as a core value prior to the inception of FWC and substantial efforts have been made. The FWC Project Director is member of the local Trauma-Informed Coalition. Numerous general trauma trainings for FWC service providers and staff from partner agencies have been provided including workshops on gender-responsive and trauma informed services, trauma-Informed interventions for women, how Service Providers Can Address Intersecting Issues of Substance Abuse, Mental Health, and trauma and trauma triggers and de-escalation strategies. Of particular significance was the first ever trauma training held for court personnel, with Sheriff's deputies in attendance!

Targeted trauma trainings have included training specific to impact of trauma on early child development and mental health and men and trauma. The men and trauma training has had an astounding impact and has resulted in male service providers recognizing both the presence and impact of trauma in their own lives. Workshops on creating trauma-informed systems from both an administrative and service delivery perspective provided structure to enable partners to implement strategies in their own systems as have discussions on creating trauma informed services at the FWC Oversight Committee, Systems, Implementation and Court Team levels.

Trauma expert Vivian Brown observed FWC in action with a trauma lens. She had very few suggestions and thought we had the most trauma informed court she had ever seen. Ms. Brown developed a trauma assessment tool and an assessment was performed by the FWC Systems team, who identified mitigation strategies and created a trauma mitigation plan. Several FWC partners performed trauma assessments of their own systems. Tips on trauma-informed practice were distributed to all FWC service providers.

Vivian Brown was engaged to create child specific trauma activities to enable children to recognize and make sense of their own trauma and training was offered to all partners. She was also contracted with to create trauma-specific parenting training modules with a goal of assisting parents to recognize their own trauma, impacts on parenting and to identify and assist their children to cope with trauma. Training was held for parenting trainers and consultation hours were added to the contract to help support implementation.

The Department of Family and Children's Services has implemented a trauma initiative, with utilization of Implementation Science to ensure institutionalization into practice.

SSA and Mental Health partnered to submit an application for a grant focused on utilizing evidence-based, trauma specific services and transforming the child welfare system into a trauma informed system.

Summary Of *Primary* Systemic Changes In Service Delivery

While there have been numerous other systemic changes that positively impact sustainability and other components of partners work, the following table highlights just the primary systemic changes in service delivery.

Children's Services

- A comprehensive system of care that ensures the developmental and behavioral needs of children in the child welfare system are being met is in place. A detailed description is provided in the xx section, above.

- Common assessment tools now being used for children's behavioral and developmental assessments

- Bonding and attachment are emphasized, supported and enhanced

- All clinicians and home visitors have been trained and all will be accredited in Triple P levels 4 and 5 by the end of September 2011

- FIRST 5 is piloting utilization of an evidence-based home visitation model, SafeCare with their home visitors.

- A mental health expert for children who attends FWC staffings, etc. was funded

- A universal, evidenced-based, cross-systems method for promoting parent-child attachment (Touchpoints) was implemented.

■ Eligible children in the child welfare system began to be routinely enrolled in Head Start to ensure that they were provided with the cognitive, social and health benefits unique to this program.

■ PHN services for children and families in FWC will expand in December 2011 to serve all children under the age of 6 and their families in DFCS and feedback the information to the social workers

■ Highlights of the PHN services include:

■ All children under the age of 6 will receive developmental screens as well as standard nursing assessments

■ Mothers will be screened for maternal depression and referred for appropriate services

■ PHN's will ensure that are children are immunized and are connected to and utilizing a medical home

■ PHN's will case manage all children under the age of 1, including medically fragile infants and ensure that when appropriate they will be connected with the Infant Neurodevelopmental Clinic

Department of Alcohol and Drug Services (DADS)

■ Access to residential treatment beds was granted to DADS assessors. The assessment procedure for House on the Hill (HOH) was modified so that court-based DADS assessors could recommend residential treatment and access beds. (Prior to implementation of FWC, only the HOH assessors were able to do so).

■ Residential treatment access was improved. The number of beds at HOH was increased by three, utilizing CalWorks dollars

- Residential treatment bed and THU capacity was further increased by partnering with faith based organizations such as CityTeam Ministries.

- 90% utilization of HOH was achieved. Previously this resource was underutilized.

- The waiting time for DADS assessments was eliminated. The additional assessor funded by FWC reduced the backlog of cases.

- DADS created a male Transitional Housing Unit in which men could stay with their children.

- DADS is performing safety assessments for FWC children.

- DADS licensed staff has increased their capacity to provide services for Dual Diagnosed clients

- Trauma and DV based questions were added to DADS assessments.

- A continuing care model will be implemented via a grant secured by FWC partners

Mental Health Services

- An adult mental health provider was added to the Court Team.

- FWC coordinator receives and processes referrals for mental health services. Individualized consideration is given to the parent's mental health needs, housing status, location, transportation issues, recovery status, benefits status, cultural and language needs, etc. Additional funding resources such as Victim Witness are also explored

■ The connection to a provider has been reduced to 2-4 weeks, on average as estimated by the FWC adult mental health therapist

■ A Dependency Drug Treatment Court therapist position funded by DADS was shared, a therapist and part-time psychiatrist for medication management was funded by Mental Health. Mental Health developed a mechanism to refer FWC families to access private mental health resources (not tracked).

■ FWC parents were granted access to the primary care and mental health services of the East Valley FQHC[44], regardless of Medi-Cal status in

■ The mental health provider network for FWC parents has been expanded to include all county clinics, mental health dept. contract providers, and other community resources.

■ Coordination between the FWC coordinator, social services, and providers for parents and children has increased allowing for closer monitoring and collaboration.

■ FWC coordinator attends Family Team Meetings (FTM) at social services, which allows for a better understanding of the parents' needs, a connection to the parent(s) and collaboration with the social worker at an earlier stage in the case.

■ Access to aftercare services was provided via the development of weekly WRAP groups for FWC parents

■ For those who don't qualify for the FQHC, efforts to link to a VMC Primary Care Physician assignment and obtain a Medi-Cal card prior to case dismissal were implemented.

---

44   Federally Qualified Health Center

- Mental Health counseling by Drug and Alcohol Services was accepted as qualifying by the Department of Family and Children's Services.

Parent Mentor Program

- All parents have gender specific mentors who serve as role models, examples of success, assist them in navigating the child welfare system and provide critical support in recovery. These mentors and their dedication to parents are essential to family reunification.

- The parent's voice is included in all levels of FWC planning, with mentor representation on all FWC teams

- Mentor fathers have played a critical role in increasing the number of fathers who engage and are retained in FWC and ultimately, the number of fathers who reunify with their children.

- Mentor parents have drawn attention to the unique needs of Spanish speaking families and mentor mothers have supported those families by educating FWC providers on how to better understand and engage the Spanish speaking population and how to break down barriers to engagement.

- Mentors have trained service providers and team members to improve service delivery in general.

- Mentors have successfully recruited parents for participation in focus groups and other FWC assessments and events. This is significant systemically because, since mentors are known, trusted and have additional means to reach parents, participation in this events has been greatly enhanced.

- Mentor aftercare support and alumni groups will be available via a grant secured by FWC partners.

■ Male mentors have been utilized to educate social workers on male engagement and retention and have expanded this educational opportunity to other professionals, both locally, nationally and nationally.

Courts

■ A Board of Supervisors resolution which was championed by the court to prioritize the child welfare population, as well as a Year of the Child agenda for 2011 by the Board President

■ A therapeutic court environment in which the focus is problem solving and parent support was established. Movement from a single vision of reunification towards a wraparound court model that addresses all the major domains of the families and children was implemented.

■ A specialized 0-3 courtroom was created.

■ Court staff was engaged in trauma trainings and awareness.

■ The Courts established a non-profit in order to be able to accept donations on behalf of FWC families.

■ A FIRST 5 Family Advocate for each child 0-5 in the Dependency System was added for court referral and court meetings with families.

■ A child friendly courtroom with child scaled play areas was created.

■ A mental health medication assessment on site was implemented by partnering with Prop 36 court.

■ SSI evaluations were implemented by partnering with Prop 36 Court to promote self-sufficiency.

- Expungement, Financial and Budgeting workshops were added at the Courthouse to promote self-sufficiency.

- Relationships with workforce community partners who take court referrals such as CET and Work to Future were developed to promote self-sufficiency.

- Planned Parenthood workshops are now held across the street from the Courthouse.

- A partnership was formed with the local Dental Association to enable parents to receive dental services free of charge. This is particularly significant because dental pain can be a trigger for relapse.

- Efforts began to coordinate criminal and dependency court issues and to assist parents in clearing up warrants before they are arrested via grant funding for a crossover case manager.

- Seven bulletin boards are posted in the court that list current resources for medical, dental, housing, drug treatment, tattoo removal, mental health, food and clothing.

- Protocols were developed for easy calendaring and access to other court services like the Self- Help center and turning court fines into community service.

- Regular stakeholder meetings which act as a self-correcting vessel to best serve families and children at every level were implemented.

Department of Family and Children's Services (DFCS)

- Family Team meetings to enable FWC service providers, parents and family members to engage in developing the initial case plan were implemented.

■ DFCS became involved in the direct provision of housing to drug court clients and parenting youth via grant funding for a Family Unification Voucher program. One hundred vouchers were secured for DFCS families; families were assisted in becoming housing ready and provided with stable, long term places to live.

■ An Eligibility Worker position was added to the FWC court team. This support was extended to all DFCS families by the co-location of the EW at court three days per week. (No data on the number of parents served. Quarterly reports are generated, but have duplicate counts).

■ Cross departmental efforts to improve parent self-sufficiency/improve access to benefits and to fully utilize TANF funds to support mental health and drug and alcohol services were implemented. A joint DFCS and Department of Employment and Benefits Services workgroup was formed to improve access.

■ DFCS implemented trauma and male engagement initiatives.

■ The Implementation Team was trained by DFCS to ensure full utilization of Family and Children's Services client support streams and to ensure maximum access of stimulus funds for parents.

Court Appointed Special Advocates Program (Unfunded Partner)

■ Provided advocates for an expanded number of FWC children.

■ Are represented on court team, thus bringing the child's voice into the courtroom.

Changed their model to include support for biological parents.

Family Wellness Court will continue to be operational once grant funding ends in September 2012. Positions sustained after grant end will include all currently funded and in-kind positions, with funding still being sought for the mentor program and court resource coordinator positions. FIRST 5 will continue to provide children's services in-kind and has expanded services to other children in the dependency system. Funding has been obtained to continue assessor and dedicated treatment counselor positions for two years beyond grant end, the Project Director position is now integrated into DFCS operations and we are working with Administrative Office of the Courts to fund the Court Resource Coordinator. As previously mentioned, a formal mentor program evaluation was implemented to make the case for sustaining mentor services, the child development and mental health position will be continued to be provided in-kind and it is highly probable that support for the adult mental health coordinator will be provided after grant ends.

Appendix VIII

Mentor Program

Dependency Advocacy Center

The mentor parents are former dependency court clients who due to a drug/alcohol addiction had their children removed from their care. Due to their successful completion of the existing dependency drug court they have since reunited with their children and had their case dismissed.

Role of the Mentors

- Provide a strong support system that gives encouragement, hope and motivation for clients involved in the current Dependency/Drug Court and the Family Wellness Court.

- Empower clients to believe there are compassionate, clean, and positive role models accessible to them during this process.

- Contact clients frequently for the first 30 days, once a case is identified as Family Wellness Court, and a minimum of once a week thereafter.

- Facilitate, along with legal counsel, the process of attaining the necessary tools, community resources and path to address treatment and successful completion of the case plan.

- Address areas that include but are not limited to-- drug assessment, NA/AA Meetings, securing a sponsor, drug testing, parenting or domestic violence classes, transportation, housing and employment.

- Focus on barriers that limit client's growth and progress to reunification and providing insight how to identify negative setbacks and flourish in personal strength.

Protocols

Mentors are part-time employees of Dependency Advocacy Center, a law firm that represent parents in Santa Clara County Dependency Court. The following are protocols related to their roles:

- **All communications between clients and mentors are communications protected under attorney-client privilege.**

- Mentors cannot relay information shared by a client to anyone other than the client's attorney, except if the client gives explicit permission to do so.

- Service providers for Family Wellness Court and Dependency Drug Treatment Court can speak to the mentors about any concerns they have with a client; however, the mentor cannot reveal any information about the client without the client's permission.

- Any release of information that includes Dependency Advocacy Center (Family Legal Advocates and Office of Dependency Counsel), by extension, includes the mentors as employees of the law firm.

www.ingramcontent.com/pod-product-compliance
Lightning Source LLC
Chambersburg PA
CBHW030253290526
45785CB00001B/76